818.309
B 39n

84760

DATE DUE			

NATHANIEL PARKER WILLIS

S. Lawrence. 1837.

Illman & Sons.

NATHANIEL PARKER WILLIS.

BY

HENRY A. BEERS

AMS PRESS
NEW YORK

Reprinted from the edition of 1885, Boston
First AMS EDITION published 1969
Manufactured in the United States of America

Library of Congress Catalogue Card Number: 70-89458

AMS PRESS, INC.
New York, N.Y. 10003

PREFACE.

THE materials for a life of Willis are rich enough to be embarrassing. Most of his writings are, in a greater or less degree, autobiographical; and it would be possible to make a very tolerable life of him, by arranging passages from these in the right order, and linking them together with a few paragraphs of cold facts. Then, he lived very much in the world's eye, and was constantly talked and written about, so that there is abundant mention of him in newspaper files, and in volumes of "Recollections," etc., by his contemporaries. In addition to these printed sources, I have been furnished, by the kindness of Mrs. N. P. Willis, Miss Julia Willis, and Mrs. Imogen Willis Eddy, with private letters, journals, and other MS. memoranda by Willis, which extend from his school days at Andover down to a few weeks before his death — of course not without *lacunæ*. Although I have not quoted very freely from these letters, they have been of the greatest service, by supplying facts which I have incorporated with the body of the narrative, and by correcting or verifying data otherwise obtained. A biography of Willis could have been written without them, but this particular biography could not; and I take occasion hereby to acknowledge my debt to the ladies whose courtesy gave me access to this material.

There are many others who have helped my undertaking in various ways — too many for me to thank them all by name. But I cannot withhold mention of my obligations to Mr. Richard S. Willis and to Mr. Morris Phillips, the editor of the "Home Journal."

HENRY A. BEERS.

CONTENTS.

———◆———

CHAPTER I.

CHAPTER VIII.

NATHANIEL PARKER WILLIS.

CHAPTER I.

1806–1823.

ANCESTRY AND EARLY YEARS.

WILLIS was born January 20, 1806, in the little old seaport city of Portland, Maine, celebrated by the "Autocrat" for its great square mansions, the homes of retired sea-captains. The town had already made some noise in literature, as the residence of that wild genius, John Neal; and on February 27, 1807, little more than a year after the date with which this biography begins, it witnessed the birth of its most illustrious citizen, Henry Wadsworth Longfellow.

A comparison at once suggests itself between the subsequent fortunes in the republic of letters of these two infant poets, fellow townsmen for some five years. Willis was the earlier in the field. In 1832, when Longfellow, then a young professor at Bowdoin College, began to contribute scholarly articles to the "North American Review," the former had been five years before the public, and was already well known as a poet, a magazine editor, and a foreign correspondent. When "Outre-Mer" was issued in 1835, Willis had won a reputation as a prose writer on both sides of the Atlantic by his "Pencillings" in the "New York Mirror;" and by 1839, when Longfellow published his first volume of original poetry, "Voices of the Night," his senior by a year had printed five books of verse. But there is no question as to which has proved the better continuer. Longfellow is still the favorite poet of two peoples; a singer dearer, perhaps, to the general heart than any other who has sung in the English tongue. His brilliant contemporary, after being for about fifteen years the most popular magazinist in America, has sunk into comparative oblivion.[1] This is the

---

[1] This statement needs, however, some qualification. Mr. Clark, of Clark & Maynard, who publish Willis's poems, tells me that there is a steady sale for these of about two hundred copies annually. Fifty years after date this is not bad. How many copies of *Something and Other Poems*, issued in 1884, will be asked for at the booksellers' in the year of grace 1934 ? The copyright of most of Willis's poems having lately expired, a cheap reprint of them has just been put forth, bearing date 1884 and forming No. 352 of "Lovell's Library." This seems to point to a continued popular demand. His prose writings are at present out of print. The fourth volume of *Stories by American Authors* contains his " Two Buck-

fate of all fashionable literature. Every generation begins by imitating the literary fashions of the last, and ends with a reaction against them. At present " realism " has the floor, sentiment is at a discount, and Willis's glittering, high-colored pictures of society, with their easy optimism and their unlikeness to hard fact, have little to say to the readers of Zola and Henry James.

Without presuming any native equality between Willis and the Cambridge poet, it is fair to add that the former never found opportunity to deepen and ripen such gift as was in him. His life was passed not "in the quiet and still air of delightful studies," but in the rush of the gay world and the daily drudgery of the pen; in the toil of journalism, that most exhausting of mental occupations, which is forever giving forth and never bringing in. His best work — all of his work which claims remembrance — was done before he was forty. His earlier writings are not only his freshest, but his strongest and most carefully executed.

Willis is a glaring instance of inherited tendencies, being the third journalist in succession in his line of descent. The founder of the family in this country, and the progenitor of our

ets in a Well," and it is understood that the publishers of that series have in mind the publication of a volume of selections from Willis's prose.

subject in the seventh generation, was a certain George Willis, born in England in 1602, who arrived in New England probably about 1630. He was a brickmaker and builder by trade, and is described as " a Puritan of considerable distinction," who resided in Cambridge, Massachusetts, some sixty years, having been admitted to the Freeman's Oath in 1638 and elected a deputy to the General Court. Probably the most noteworthy of the poet's forbears, at least upon the father's side, was the Rev. John Bailey, his ancestor in the fifth generation, a non-conforming Independent minister in Lancashire, who, having been silenced and afterwards imprisoned, escaped to Massachusetts in 1684, and was settled, first as minister over the church in Watertown, and later as associate minister over the First Church in Boston, where he died in 1697. Increase Mather preached his funeral sermon. His tomb is in the Granary Burying Ground, adjoining Park Street Church, and his portrait in the cabinet of the Massachusetts Historical Society. What more could a man ask for in an ancestor? No New England pedigree which respects itself is without one or more fine old Puritan divines of this kind. Accordingly, when Willis began to take that mild, retrospective interest in his own genealogy which foretokens the oncoming of age, — when new twigs upon the family tree give an unthought-of importance to the roots, — he bestowed the name of this particular forefather upon his youngest boy, Bailey Willis.

The poet's great-grandmother Willis, born Abigail Belknap, was granddaughter to this Rev. John Bailey, and had some traits which cropped out in her posterity. At the time of the destruction of the tea in Boston harbor, she cannily saved a little for private use. She used to say, "I have got some Belknap pride in me yet;" and among her favorite maxims were, "Never go into the back door when you can go into the front," and "Never eat brown bread when you can get white." The husband of this lady was Charles Willis, a sail-maker and patriot, who was present on the occasion when tar and feathers and hot tea were administered to his Majesty's tax-collector in Boston. His position and action in the affair were represented in an ancient engraving, bought long afterwards by his grandson, Deacon Nathaniel Willis, our Willis's father. A copy of the same is now in possession of the Massachusetts Historical Society. The son of Charles and Abigail Willis was Nathaniel, the third, though by no means the last, Willis with that baptismal name; the first literary man in the family, and the poet's grandfather. He conducted in Boston, during the Revolutionary

War, the "Independent Chronicle," a Whig newspaper, published from the same building in which Franklin had worked as a printer. This Nathaniel senior, as we may call him, was an active man. He was a fine horseman, took part in the Boston tea-party, and was adjutant of the Boston regiment sent on an expedition to Rhode Island under General Sullivan. In 1784 he sold his interest in the "Independent Chronicle," and became one of the pioneer journalists of the unsettled West. He removed first to Winchester, Virginia, where he published a paper for a short time; then to Shepardstown, where he also published a paper; and thence in 1790 to Martinsburg, Virginia, where he founded the "Potomac Guardian" and edited it till 1796. In that year he went to Chillicothe, Ohio, and established the "Scioto Gazette," the first newspaper in what was then known as the Northwestern Territory. He was printer to the government of the territory, and afterwards held an agency in the Post Office Department. He bought and cultivated a farm near Chillicothe, on which he ended his days April 1, 1831. His wife was Lucy Douglas, of New London, Connecticut.

His son and the poet's father, Nathaniel Willis, Junior, — the fourth Nathaniel in the family, — was born at Boston in 1780, and remained

there until 1787, when he joined his father at
Winchester and was employed in his newspaper
office, and subsequently at Martinsburg on the
" Potomac Guardian." In the infancy of American journalism, the editor and publisher of a
paper was usually a practical printer. Young
Nathaniel was put to work at once in folding
papers and setting types. At Martinsburg he
used to ride post, with tin horn and saddle-bags,
delivering papers to scattered subscribers in the
thinly settled country. N. P. Willis himself
served a year's apprenticeship at his father's
press in Boston, in an interval of his schooling;
and in his letters home from England alluded
triumphantly to his having once been destined
by his parents to the trade of a printer. His
particular duty was to ink the types. " We remember *balling* an edition of ' Watts's Psalms
and Hymns,' and there are lines in that good
book that, to this day, go to the tune we played
with the ink-balls, while conning them over."
A sketch of the old office of the " Potomac
Guardian," made by " Porte Crayon," is in the
possession of Mr. Richard Storrs Willis of De-
troit.

At the age of fifteen young Nathaniel returned
to Boston and entered the office of his father's
old paper, the " Independent Chronicle," working in the same press-room in Court Street

where his father had once worked, and the great
Franklin before him. He also found time, while
in Boston, to drill with the "Fusiliers." In
1803, invited by a Maine congressman and
other gentlemen of the Republican party, he
went to Portland and established the "Eastern
Argus" in opposition to the Federalists. Here
the subject of this biography was born three
years later. "Well do I remember that day,"
his father wrote to him fifty-seven years after
the event, "and the driving snow-storm in which
I had to go, in an open sleigh, to bring in the
nurse from the country. Francis Douglas
boarded with us at that time. He was a very
pleasant young man, and had a half promise (if
it was a boy) it should be called *Francis*. But
your mother soon overruled that, and decided
that you should have both of our names, for fear
she should never have another son! You was a
fine fat baby, with a face as round as an apple."

Party spirit ran high at this time, and political articles were acrimonious. Libel suits were
brought against the publisher of the "Argus,"
which involved him in trouble and expense; and
six years after its establishment it was sold for
four thousand dollars to the same Francis Douglas who had come so near imposing his Christian name on the infant Willis. At Portland
Nathaniel Willis came under the ministrations

and influence of the Rev. Edward Payson, D. D.,
— on whose death, many years after, his son
composed some rather perfunctory verses, — and
began henceforth to devote himself to the cause
of religion. From 1810 to 1812 he sought to
establish a religious newspaper in Portland, but
met with no substantial encouragement. At the
latter date he returned to Boston, where, after
years of effort, during which he supported himself by publishing tracts and devotional books,
he started, in January, 1816, the "Boston Recorder," which he asserted to be the first religious newspaper in the world. It was in this
periodical that the earliest lispings of Willis's
muse reached the ear of the public. The "Recorder" was conducted by his father down to
1844, in which year it was sold to the Rev.
Martin Moore. It still lives as the "Congre-
gationalist and Boston Recorder."

Nathaniel Willis also originated the idea of
a religious paper for children. "The Youth's
Companion," which he commenced in 1827 and
edited for about thirty years, was the first, and
remains one of the best, publications of the kind
in existence. In a letter to his son he gave the
following account of its inception: "He was in
the habit of teaching his children, statedly, the
Assembly's Catechism, and to encourage them to
commit to memory the answers, he rewarded

them by telling them stories from Scripture history without giving names. The result was that the Catechism was all committed to memory by the children, and the idea occurred of a children's department in the 'Recorder.' This department being much sought for by children, it suggested the experiment of having a paper exclusively for children." Around the fireplace where Mr. Willis sat with his children were some old-fashioned Dutch tiles, representing scenes from the New Testament, and it was in answer to their questions about these that he began his narrations. One sees in this little domestic picture the beginnings of the young Nathaniel's literary training and the germ of his "Scripture Sketches." Years after, a college lad, when shaping into smooth blank verse the story of the widow of Nain or the healing of Jairus's daughter, his memory must have gone back to their rude figures about his father's hearth, seeming to move and stir in the flickering light of the wood fire; and the recollection of his father's voice and the listening group of brothers and sisters gave tenderness to the strain.

He was only six when the family removed from Portland to Boston, and he appears to have kept little remembrance of his birthplace. The noble harbor, with its islands, which were the Hesperides of Longfellow's boyish dreams, the old fort on the hill, the mystery of the ships, the Spanish sailors with bearded lips, the noise of the sea fight far away, and the faces of the dead captains as they lay in their coffins, did not enter into Willis's experience. Indeed, the period of childhood, which has been to many poets so fruitful in precious memories, seems to have left few deep traces on his mind, if we except its religious impressions. The life of his father's household, though rich in domestic affections, was probably not stimulating to the imagination. It was the life of a Puritan home, of what is called in England a "serious family," — that life which oppresses Matthew Arnold with its *ennui;* its interests divided between "business and Bethels;" its round of long family devotions, strict Sabbath observances, catechisms, and visiting missionaries. Dancing, card-playing, and theatre-going were, of course, forbidden pleasures. The elder Willis, though a thoroughly good man and good father, was a rather wooden person. His youth and early manhood had been full of hardship; his education was scanty, and he had the formal and narrow piety of the new evangelicals of that day, revolting against the latitudinarianism of the Boston churches. He was for twenty years deacon of Park Street Church, profanely nicknamed by the Unitarians "Brimstone Corner."

"My recollection of a particular occasion," says an old member of that society, "when, at a conference meeting in the church, he, as presider, was expounding John xv., is that I regarded it as a memorable illustration of a man's attempting to expound without ideas. I hear him saying, — more than fifty years ago, — 'v. 4. Abide in me. Abide is to dwell,' in a most monotonous tone, and the rest in the same manner of appreciation." His rigidity was, perhaps, more in his principles than in his character, and his austerity was tempered by two qualities which have not seldom been found to consist with the diaconate, namely, a sense of humor — "dry," of course, to the correct degree — and an admiration for pretty women, or, in the dialect of that day, for "female loveliness." These tastes he bequeathed to his son, as also a certain tenacity of will, which, latent throughout the latter's career, came to the surface in an astonishing way during the trials of his last years. This trait is amusingly illustrated in the senior Willis's correspondence with his son by his allusions to an interminable litigation that he was carrying on in his eighty-fourth year. "I should have written you sooner," he says, "but that Irishman, Garbrey, has sued me the *fourth* time about that old drain which he dug up before my front door, in Atkinson Street, that we never knew before was there. He has lost his case in three different courts, and now sends to the Supreme Court a 'Bill of Exceptions,' which all my friends think he cannot recover. It has been a great trouble and expense to me. But I have carried the case in prayer to God, constantly, and He has three times defeated the extortioner." Willis always retained a cordial affection and respect for his father, but between two such different natures and divergent lives there could be little genial sympathy or real intellectual intimacy. The tough old deacon outlived the inheritor of his name and calling by some three years, and died May 26, 1870, at the age of ninety.

For his mother Willis cherished, as boy and man, a devotion that may well be called passionate, and which found utterance in many of his most heartfelt poems, such as his "Birth-Day Verses," " Lines on Leaving Europe," and " To my Mother from the Apennines." Her maiden name was Hannah Parker. She was born at Holliston, Massachusetts, and was two years younger than her husband. She was a woman whose strong character and fervent piety were mingled with a playful affectionateness which made her to her children the object of that perfect love which casteth out fear. Like many another poet's mother, — like Goethe's, for example, — she supplied to her son those elements of gayety and softness which were wanting in the stiffer composition of the father: —

"Von Mutterchen die Fröhnatur,
Die Lust zu fabuliren."

He inherited from her the emotional, impulsive part of his nature as well as his physical constitution, his light complexion, full face, and tendency, in youth, to a plethoric habit. "My veins," he wrote, "are teeming with the quicksilver spirit which my mother gave me. Whatever I accomplish must be gained by ardor, and not by patience." She was his confidant, his sympathizer, his elder sister. The testimony to her worth and her sweetness is universal. The Rev. Dr. Storrs of Braintree, in an obituary notice written on her death, in 1844, at the age of sixty-two, spoke of her as "the light and joy of every circle in which she moved; the idol of her family; the faithful companion, the tender mother, the affectionate sister, the fast and assiduous friend."

Willis was the second in a family of nine children, all of whom reached maturity, and two of whom, besides himself, achieved literary reputation. These were Sarah Payson Willis, afterwards famous, under the *nom de plume* of "Fanny Fern," as a prolific and successful writer for children, and Richard Storrs Willis, his youngest brother, formerly editor of the

" Musical World," the author of " Our Church Music," and known both as a musical composer and a poet. Julia Willis, his favorite sister and constant correspondent, was also a woman of remarkable talent, with a gift of tongues and a sounder scholarship than her more showy brother. She wrote many of the book reviews in the " Home Journal," but always declined to renounce her anonymity.

Such were the influences which surrounded Willis's early years. And if, at the first touch of the world, the youthful members of the household flew off like the dry seeds of the *Impatiens*, it need not therefore be hastily concluded that the home training, though perhaps too repressive and severe, was without lasting effect for good. Among the children and grandchildren of Nathaniel Willis are Catholics, Episcopalians, Unitarians, and representatives of other shades of belief and unbelief. But this is the history of many a New England Puritan family, and such are the disintegrating forces of American life. In the case of the eldest brother, it may be affirmed that, from a career which was certainly worldly, and in some of its aspects by no means edifying, the light that shone from his mother's face uplifted in prayer for him never altogether faded away.

Willis began school life under the tuition of

the Rev. Dr. McFarland, of Concord, New Hampshire. " I have forgotten every circumstance," he wrote long after, " of a year or two that I was at school at Concord, New Hampshire, when a boy, except the natural scenery of the place. The faces of my teacher and my playmates have long ago faded from my memory, while I remember the rocks and eddies of the Merrimac, the forms of the trees on the meadow opposite the town, and every bend of the river's current." Later he was brought home and sent to the Boston Latin School, then under "its well-remembered Pythagoras, Ben Gould." A few reminiscences of his slate-and-satchel days are scattered here and there through his writings. Thus he vaguely recalled Ralph Waldo Emerson as " one of the boys whose fathers were Unitarians," and he was greatly impressed by Edward Everett, then a young Harvard professor, whose stylishly dressed figure used to appear occasionally in Atkinson Street, at No. 31, in which thoroughfare the Willises dwelt. He remembered " the rousings before daylight," on May-day, " to go to Dorchester Heights, and the shivering search after never found green leaves and flowers; the buttoning up of boy-jacket to keep out the cold wind, and pulling out of penknife to cut off the bare stems of the sweet-brier in search of the hidden odor of the belated bud." In "The Pharisee and the Barber," one of the two or three stories of Willis whose scenes are laid in Boston, the description of Sheafe Lane is evidently from the life. The Pharisee of that tale, Mr. Flint, an " active member of a church famed for its zeal," who " dressed in black, as all religious men must (in Boston)," was doubtless a sketch from memory of some pious familiar of his father's house, whose black eyes and formal talk left upon the lad a mixed impression of awe and distrust.

Harvard was the natural destination of a Boston Latin School boy intending college. But the line between the Orthodox and the Unitarians was drawn more sharply in 1820 than in 1884. Even now stray youths from Boston are found at other colleges than Harvard, attracted elsewhere by family ties or theological affinities. But at that time the cleavage made by the schism in Eastern Massachusetts was still raw, and Deacon Willis would almost as soon have sent his boy into the jaws of hell as into such a hot-bed of Unitarianism as the Cambridge college.

"Larry's father," wrote Willis in "The Lunatic's Skate," "was a disciple of the great Channing, and mine a Trinitarian of uncommon zeal; and the two institutions of Yale and Harvard were in the hands of

2

most eminent men of either persuasion, and few are
the minds that could resist a four years' ordeal in
either. A student was as certain to come forth a
Unitarian from one as a Calvinist from the other;
and in the New England States these two sects are
bitterly hostile. So to the glittering atmosphere of
Channing and Everett went poor Larry, lonely and
dispirited; and I was committed to the sincere zeal-
ots of Connecticut, some two hundred miles off, to
learn Latin and Greek, if it pleased Heaven, but the
mysteries of ' election and free grace,' whether or no."

Of the two great fitting-schools founded by
Samuel and John Phillips respectively at Andover and at Exeter, the latter had been cap-
tured by the Unitarians. But the Andover
academy, under the sheltering wing of the
famed theological seminary in the same town,
though barely thirty miles from Boston, remained an insoluble lump of Calvinism, a
wedge of defiant Orthodoxy *in partibus infide-
lium*. To Andover, accordingly, young Willis
was sent, after a course in the Latin School, to
complete his preparation for Yale. The academy was then under the headship of that sound
classical master, John Adams, who was principal from 1810 to 1833. It gave an excellent
fit in the classics, insomuch that Willis, though
the reverse of diligent in college, was carried
along a good way, with little study, by the im-

petus acquired at Andover. At Andover, too, he began to give signs of literary tastes and in particular to scribble verses, which had already given him the reputation of a poet among his fellows before he came up to college. A letter dated July 3, 1823, and addressed to his elder sister Lucy, about a fortnight before her marriage, incloses a copy of verses which is perhaps the earliest poem of Willis now extant. It has no merit, but as containing hints of his later manner and the unformed germs of that smooth, diffuse blank verse in which his "Scripture Sketches" were written, the opening lines may be not without interest : —

> " There was a bride, and she was beautiful
> And fond, affectionate ; her soul did love.
> 'T was not the transient feeling of an hour,
> That loves and hates, and loves and hates again, —
> Oh, no ; it was a purer, kindlier feeling, —
> A something rooted, grafted on the soul,
> That cannot help but live and bud and blossom."

He also began to wreak thought upon expression in that common vent to the *cacoethes scribendi*, of young writers, — keeping a diary, " a red morocco volume, of very ornate slenderness and thinness, in which I recorded my raptures at spring mornings and blue sashes, my unappreciated sensibilities, my mysterious emotions by moonlight, and the charms of the incognita whom I ran against at the corner. This pre-

cious record shared in the final and glorious con-
flagration of Latin themes, grammars, graduses,
and old shirts, on leaving academy for college."

"The Lunatic's Skate" opens with some reminiscences of school life at Andover : —

"In the days when I carried a satchel on the
banks of the Shawsheen (a river whose half-lovely,
half-wild scenery is tied like a silver thread about my
heart), Larry Wynn and myself were the farthest
boarders from school, in a solitary farmhouse on the
edge of a lake of some miles square, called by the undignified title of Pomp's Pond. An old negro, who
was believed by the boys to have come over with
Christopher Columbus, was the only other human being within anything like a neighborhood of the lake
(it took its name from him), and the only approaches
to its waters, girded in as it was by an almost impen-
etrable forest, were the path through old Pomp's
clearing and that by our own door. Out of school
Larry and I were inseparable. We built wigwams
together in the woods, had our tomahawks made in
the same fashion, united our property in fox-traps,
and played Indians with perfect contentment in each
other's approbation."

One of his school-fellows here was Isaac Mc-
Lellan, who afterwards became a contributor to
Willis's "American Monthly." He published
a long poem, "The Fall of the Indian," which
Willis reviewed in the same periodical, referring

to the poet as "the very boy that has tracked the woods with us, and called us by our nickname over a hedge, and cracked nuts with us by the fire in the winter evenings. Which of us dreamed, as we read in our blotted classic, 'Quam sit magnum dare aliquid in manus hominum,' that he should ever be guilty of a book? How it would have swelled our idle veins, as we lay half asleep, bobbing our lines over the bank of the Shawsheen on those long Saturday afternoons, that we should ever play for each other the gentle office of critic!"

In after years the rice fields of Georgia, with their embankments and green surfaces, reminded Willis of "the gooseberry pies which formed part of my early education at Andover, and which are among the warmest of my recollections of that classic academy." "We have fine times picking berries here," he wrote to his sister Julia. "Every kind grows in profusion in Andover, — raspberries, black, blue, thimble, and whortle berries. The woods are crowded with them. After tea we generally start, and after we have eat enough go and bathe in the Shawsheen, our Andover river."

This Indian Ilyssus was the scene of an adventure recorded in certain "Tête-à-tête Confessions" in the "American Monthly," doubtless with some exaggerations for literary effect and with a *dénoûment* suspiciously dramatic. The passage may be given, however, for what it is worth : —

"Cytherean Venus! How I did love Miss Polly D. Low, the pride of the factory on the romantic Shawsheen! I saw her first in the tenderest twilight of a Saturday evening, washing her feet in the river. I was a lad of some impudence, and I sat down on a stone beside her, and by the time it was dark we were the best friends possible. She was beautiful. I think so *now.* She was about eighteen, and, though four years older than I, my education had more than equalized us. At least, if not the wiser of the two, I was the most skilled in the subtlety of love, and practiced with great success *les petites ruses.* She was a tall brunette, and I sometimes fancied, when her eye exhibited more than ordinary feeling, that there was Indian blood under that dark and glowing skin. The valley of the Shawsheen, just below the village where I was at school, is a gem of solitary and rich scenery, and the overhanging woods and long meadows afforded the most picturesque and desirable haunts for ramblers who did not care to be met. There on Sunday afternoons, when she was released from her shuttle and I from my Schrevelius, did we meet and stroll till the nine o'clock bell of the factory summoned her unwillingly home. I could go without my supper in those days, though I doubt if I would now on such slight occasion. By the time vacation came, I found myself seriously in love, declared my passion, and left her with my heart half broken. We were gone four weeks, and when I returned the butcher's boy was engaged to Miss Low, and I was warned to avoid the factory at the peril of a flogging."

In his last year at Andover Willis experienced religion and joined the church. Any one who has witnessed one of those spiritual epidemics, called "revivals," in some school or college needs no description of the kind of pressure brought to bear on the thoughtless but easily excited young consciences there assembled. At the first rumor of an unwonted "seriousness" abroad, occasioned perhaps by the death of a fellow-student, by a general sickness, or the depression of gloomy weather in a winter term, the machinery is set in motion. Daily prayer-meetings are held, in which the elders play part, — the movement at Andover was taken in hand by the " Seminarians," that is, the students of the Divinity School ; — the unregenerate are visited in their rooms by classmates who are already church members, and are prayed with and urged to attend the meetings and submit themselves to the outpourings of the Spirit. Under this kind of stimulus there follows a great awakening. Many are " under conviction," the air becomes electric, and there is a strange spiritual tension which is felt even by the resisting. Momentous

choices are made in an instant and under the
stress of contagious emotions. The awful issues
of eternity are set before a roomful of boys in
the midst of prayers and sobs and eloquent
words, exhorting the sinner not to let pass this
opportunity of salvation, — perhaps his last.
And then the movement subsides, leaving an impression which endures with some, and with others quickly wears off. Those who believe that
the Christian character and the Christian life
are the result of nurture and slow endeavor look
with distrust upon these sudden conversions.
The hardened sinner may need some such violent call to repentance, but there is a sort of in-
decency in this premature forcing open of the
simple and healthful heart of a boy, substituting
morbid self-questionings, exaggerated remorse,
and the terrors of perdition for his natural brave
outlook on a world of hope and enjoyment. The
story of Willis's conversion is fully told in his
letters home, and it reads like a chapter of
" Doctor Johns."

In 1821, being then fifteen years of age, he
had written to his father : —

"I can plainly see an answer to prayer in the delay of my admission to the church. I prayed that
God would, if I was in danger of making a hasty
step, by some means or other prevent it. I doubted,
till it became almost a certainty, whether it was

proper. I doubted myself, my pretensions to a change of heart; and my very heart seemed to sink under me every time I thought of the solemn engagement. I was unhappy, extremely unhappy, when in Boston, and have been, I might say, miserable ever since."

And again in 1822 : —

" As to becoming a Christian, it is morally *beyond my power.* I have not an objection against it that would weigh a feather, and yet I feel no more solicitude than I ever did about my eternal welfare."

In a letter of the same year to his mother, who had his conversion much at heart, he says : —

" I do have times when the tears of regret flow, and I make the resolution of attending to the subject of religion. But my light head and still lighter heart dismisses the subject as soon as another object arrests my attention, and my resolutions and regrets are soon lost in the mazes of pleasure and folly."

It is curious to reflect that these " mazes of pleasure and folly " meant nothing more than innocent school-boy diversions, such as black-berrying and swimming parties, or at worst a juvenile flirtation with some rural belle. The oldness and gravity of the phrase, in contrast with the boyish tone of other parts of his letters, illustrate well that moral precocity — precocity of the conscience as distinguished from the mind

— developed in New England boys of the last generation by the Puritan training.

In January, 1823, the great revival which had been in progress at Boston struck the Andover academy. Mr. Willis made his son a visit, and urged him to join the church. After his return to Boston he received the following letter : —

ANDOVER, MASS., *January* 12, 1823.
Sunday afternoon.

DEAR FATHER, — I received your package last evening, with my Testament, etc., inclosed. As the word of God I prize it, and as the gift of my affectionate father I love it, and shall always look upon it as a remembrance of an era in my feelings which I hope I shall always be thankful for. You cannot imagine how much your visit and advice strengthened me in my resolutions, and spurred me forward in the good work I had begun. I hope I have now the assurance of being an heir of life and a recipient of the protection which the wings of a Saviour's mercy must afford to those who are gathered under them. My hope is sometimes shaken when I find my thoughts wandering to other subjects while the ordinances of God are administering before my eyes. But the moment that I get upon my knees and pray for strength I feel my assurance renewed, and rise happier and happier from every renewal of my supplications. . . . Saturday evening I attended our usual meeting in the academy for the *first time* since I have been in Andover. It is conducted by the pious scholars of the academy in succession, and is very interesting. This evening Dr. Shedd preached the lecture, and after meeting there is to be another at Mr. Adams's house. So you see, pa, we are engaged here, and have reason to hope that *many* will be inquiring the way to the foot of the cross. . . . — *Nine o'clock.* I have been to meeting at the chapel, and after that attended a prayer-meeting at Mr. Adams's. They were both very solemn. Louis Dwight led the last. — *Monday evening, 12 o'clock.* I have truly spent an evening of happiness, and I thought I must open my letter and tell you. At half-past six William Adams and I had appointed a meeting, to be conducted wholly by ourselves. We had invited only a few, but when we got there it was so crowded that I could scarcely make my way through the room to the Bible-stand. I believe nearly all our unconverted brethren were there. . . . After it was dismissed, many seemed to linger, as if they did not want to go, and we conversed with some of them. I then went into Cutler's room, and Allen and I stayed there till almost eleven o'clock. There were several of the Seminarians there, and we prayed and sung, *prayed and sung*, till it seemed a little heaven on earth. The seriousness increases ; many more are deeply impressed, and the academy presents solemn countenances generally. It is late, and my eyes smart badly.

Your affectionate son,
N. P. WILLIS.

The William Adams here mentioned was a son

of the principal of the academy, and was afterwards Willis's classmate at Yale. Louis Dwight was a theological student, who a year later was married to Willis's second sister, Louisa. The subsequent progress of the revival is related in the following letter, written two or three days later: —

ANDOVER, MASS., January 15.
Wednesday evening, 12 o'clock.

MY DEAR FATHER, — My heart is so overflowing with joy and gratitude and happiness that I could not rest till I hád sat down and told you *all*. We have had a meeting in Allen's room to-night. Mr. Styles was there, and talked so that I thought I could almost see a halo round his head, and expected him to turn into St. Paul come down again from heaven. After meeting Mr. S. told them the meeting was closed, but if any wished to converse with him or the other professors of religion in the room, they might tarry. The room was crowded, body and all, so that you could not have got through, but no one stirred. Sobbing and weeping was heard all round the room. William Adams, Allen, Styles, and I then went round and conversed with them. They all burst into tears immediately, and listened with the greatest eagerness, and when I got up to go to the next one, they held on to me as though salvation depended on my talking with them. *Isaac Stuart* sobbed aloud the whole meeting time. *Joseph Jenkins was in tears*, and came down to my room after meeting and asked me to pray for and with him. He said he *could not* pray

himself; he *dared* not. I gave him the best advice
I could and prayed with him, and he is now in his
room, as I *hope praying for himself.* I talked with
little Joshua Huntingdon, and told him about his
father. He wept, and promised to go home and pray.
J. C. Alvord, a member of my class and a *fine fellow*,
was in the greatest misery. He could not sit upon
his chair, and took me out of the meeting to go to my
room and pray with him. Jno. Tappan of Boston
was very deeply affected. I conversed with Darrach
of Philadelphia, Carter of Virginia, King of Convers,
and several others. They all seemed to feel very
deeply, and all begged me earnestly to pray for them.
We could not get them away. They stood round
weeping and looking for some one to say something
to them. Oh, my dear father, what *can* we render to
God for all his mercies! Allen has been down in my
room several times to pray for some *particular one.*
There were so many to pray for that we have been
on our knees from seven o'clock till now almost all
the time. Kennett, my room-mate, is very much affected. He fears to delay repentance, but says his
father won't like it when he goes back to Russia, and
that there are no Christians in Russia. . . . Prayer as-
cends continually, sinners are repenting, and I am as
proud as Lucifer. I feel as if I was going to do all
myself; as if I could convert a thousand without God,
if I only told them the truth. Oh, pray that I may
have humility! It is and must be the burden of my
supplications."

Of the names mentioned in this letter, that of Isaac Stuart is not unknown to fame. Joseph Jenkins afterwards became Willis's brother-in-law, marrying his sister Mary in 1831. He was from Boston, and was graduated at Yale the year after Willis.

CHAPTER II.

1823–1827.

COLLEGE LIFE.

In the fall of 1823, Willis entered Yale.
Commencement was then held in September
and first term opened late in October. College
life left a more enduring impress upon Willis
than upon almost any other American writer.
It furnished him with a fund of literary material. It brought him into the sunshine, and
changed the homely school-boy chrysalis into a
butterfly of uncommon splendor and spread of
wing. During freshman year he lodged in the
family of Mr. Townsend, opposite South College, with other members of the Andover contingent. One of these was Henry Durant, who
was Willis's chum all through the four years
of the course. He was a serious-minded lad,
a hard student, who took high rank in the appointment list, and his influence over his less
steady room-mate was always for good. He
became in time the founder and first president of the University of California, and a man

of wide influence in educational and religious
matters on the Pacific coast.   Among Willis's
other intimates in his own class were Joseph
H. Towne, also a Boston boy, and afterwards a
doctor of divinity; and "Bob" Richards, of
New York, who took him home with him in
vacations, and introduced him to the gayeties
of the metropolis.   Class lines were not drawn
very sharply then, and one of his best friends
in college was George J. Pumpelly of Owego,
New York.   Their friendship was continued
or resumed in later life, when Willis bought
from Pumpelly the little domain of Glenmary;
and settled in his neighborhood on Owego
Creek.

Next after Willis himself, the most distinguished member of the class of 1827 was Horace Bushnell.   In senior year the two roomed
in the same hall — the north entry of North
College; and in 1848, on the occasion of Bushnell's preaching a sermon at Boston to the Unitarians, which excited much public comment,
Willis gave some reminiscences of his quondam
classmate in the "Home Journal," telling, among
other things, how Bushnell once came into his
room and taught him how to hone a razor.   He
described him as a "black-haired, earnest-eyed,
sturdy, carelessly dressed, athletic, and independent good fellow, popular in spite of being both

blunt and exemplary." Bushnell was a leader
in his class; Willis decidedly not. They belonged to different sets, and there was little in
common between the elegant young poet and
ladies' man and the rough, strong farmer lad
from the Litchfield hills. They met once more
in after years, — in 1845, on the Rhine, both in
pursuit of health.

Henry Wikoff of Philadelphia — afterwards,
with the titular embellishment of "Chevalier,"
a familiar, not to say flamboyant, figure in several European capitals, and the winner of fame
at home as the importer of Fanny Elssler and
founder of the "New York Republic" — happened to be in New Haven during the summer
of 1827. He was preparing to enter college,
which he did with the class of '31, but was
prematurely graduated by reason of sundry
irregularities. In his amusing "Reminiscences
of an Idler," published in 1880, he gave the following description of two undergraduates with
whom he was subsequently more nearly associated : —

"I also remember two men who graduated in the
class of 1827, that were frequently pointed out to
me as its most conspicuous members. One was the
son of a very prominent statesman, which, in fact, explained the notice he attracted; but there was enough
of individuality about John Van Buren to command

3

attention.   He had already revealed the traits which
distinguished him in after life, — easy and careless
in manner, bold in character, and of an aggressive
turn of mind.   His rival in notoriety had no hereditary claims to support him, but he was gifted with
a rare poetical talent that had already secured him
distinction both in and out of college.   His tone and
bearing were aristocratic, not unmixed with *hauteur*,
and though admired for his abilities he never commanded the sympathies of his comrades.   Such was
N. P. Willis, and such he remained to the end of his
life.   Neither of these graduates, if I remember,
bore off ' honors; ' but Willis was requested by his
class, with the approval of the faculty, to deliver a
poem at the Commencement of 1827.   I was too
young to approach these Titans, as I regarded them,
and was content to gaze on them with deference as
they swept by me in the street.   In after years I
became intimate with them both."

The genial chevalier's memory misled him
slightly in placing " Prince John," as he was
called, in the same class with Willis.   He was
a member of '28, which he joined in junior
year, and like Willis was a great wit and a
great beau.   These three contemporaries, senior, junior, and sub-freshman, were strangely
juggled together again by Time, the conjurer.
They met in the famous Forrest trial, where
Van Buren figured as the defendant's counsel,
and Willis as a *particeps criminis* and witness

for the plaintiff. Wikoff, who had known Forrest intimately before and after his marriage, and had traveled extensively with him in Russia and elsewhere, was at first made a party in the actor's charges against his wife, but his name was withdrawn from the case before it came to trial.

Yale was then under the mild government of President Day. Silliman, Knight, Kingsley, Fitch, and Goodrich were among the professors, and among the tutors were Theodore Woolsey and Edward Beecher. The last afterwards sustained another relation to Willis, as pastor of Park Street Church. Student life in the twenties was a much simpler existence than it is in the eighties. That network of interests which makes the college world of to-day such a stirring microcosm, — with its athletic and social clubs, its regattas, promenade concerts, and class-day gayeties, its undergraduate newspapers and magazines, and its lavish expenditure upon society halls, boat-houses, ball-grounds, etc., — was all undreamed of. Far from owning a yacht or a dog-cart, the Yalensian of those days seldom owned a carpet or a paper-hanging. When those unwonted luxuries were introduced into his room by Freshman Wikoff, the rumor of this offense against the unwritten sumptuary laws of the college reached the ear of Professor

Silliman. He visited the apartment, and after inspecting it gravely said, with a frown, to its abashed occupant, " All this love of externals, young man, argues indifference to the more necessary furniture of the brain, which is your spiritual business here." The time - honored paragraph in the catalogue on " necessary ex-penses " gave the annual maximum as two hun-dred dollars. That paragraph has always been oversanguine, but probably four or five hun-dred a year was the average cost of a college education in 1825. During each of his last two years Willis spent about six hundred. Life in college was not only plain, but decidedly rough. It was the era of " Bully Clubs," town and gown rows, " Bread and Butter Rebel-lions," etc. It was the thing to paint the president's horse red, white, and blue, and to put a cow in the belfry. In 1824 a mob threat-ened the Medical School because a body had been dug up by resurrectionists. The South-erners, then a large element at Yale, were par-ticularly wild and turbulent. Christmas, which the Puritan college refused to make a holiday of, was their recognized Saturnalia.

" The day," wrote Willis in a freshman letter to his father, " is the greatest of the year at the South, and our Southern students seem disposed to be rest-less under the restriction of a lesson on playday.

There were many of them drunk last evening, and still more to-day. Christmas has always been, ever since the establishment of the college, emphatically a *day of tricks :* windows broken, bell-rope cut, freshmen squirted, and every imaginable scene of dissipation acted out in full. Last night they barred the entry doors of the South College, to exclude the government, and then illuminated the building. This morning the recitation-room doors were locked and the key stolen, and we were obliged to knock down the doors to get in; and then we were not much better off, for the lamps were full of water and the wicks gone. However, we procured others, and went on with the lesson."

Wikoff tells of a fight in a college room, in which a dirk was used, between a South Carolina student named Albert Smith and another Southerner, which resulted in the expulsion of both. Smith, who stood at the head of his class, afterwards changed his name to Rhett, and became a member of his state's legislature, but died prematurely.

New Haven in 1823–27 was not the considerable manufacturing city of to-day, but a rural town with a population of about nine thousand. West of the college yard only two streets were laid out. Beyond these, along the Derby turnpike, stretched a level of sandy pastures, alive with grasshoppers, where the young orators, practicing for debates in " Linonia " or " Broth-

ers," or for declamations before the Professor
of Rhetoric, used to go to "explode the elements." Down by the bay, in a region now
occupied by great factories, stood the old "Pavilion," a famous seaside hotel much resorted
to by Southern families. The first railroad
from New Haven was laid in 1839. As yet
even the Farmington Canal was only projected.
Willis and the Boston contingent used to come
all the way by stage-coach, passing through
Framingham, Worcester, and Hartford, — in
which last he had acquaintances, with whom he
sometimes spent a day *en route*. Anthracite
coal was not in use in New Haven before 1827.
Citizens and students alike depended on wood,
the latter buying theirs at the regular wood-
stand near South College, and having it *cut* in
the yard behind the colleges, wood-saws not
being in general vogue. The habits of the collegians, from a hygienic point of view, were
usually bad. They sat up late drinking strong
coffee in their rooms, rose very early perforce,
prayed and recited on an empty stomach, and
took little regular exercise. Dyspepsia was naturally rife.

But *en revanche* New Haven was a beautiful
little city, with a homogeneous population and a
charming society, and better fitted in some respects for the seat of a university than it is

to-day. It was already, thanks to the public
spirit of Governor Hillhouse, the City of Elms;
and it is hard to walk through Temple Street of
a moonlight evening without a regretful recollection of Willis's "Rosa Matilda description," in
"Edith Linsey," of a place that must have
been all Temple Streets, — a dream-city of
shaded squares and white - piazzaed mansions
shining among cool green gardens. In "The
Cherokee's Threat" he has recorded his first
eager impressions of the new community that
he was entering, as he stood and looked about
him in the side aisle of the old chapel on the
opening day of the term: "It was the only
republic I have ever known, — that class of
freshmen. It was a fair arena. . . . Of the
feelings that stir the heart in our youth, — of
the few, the *very* few, that have no recoil and
leave no repentance, — this leaping from the
starting post of mind, this first spread of the
encouraged wing in the free heaven of thought
and knowledge, is recorded in my own slender
experience as the most joyous and the most un-
mingled."

This was in the retrospect. He did not employ such fine language in 1823. His first letters from college are like those of any other
freshman, simple in style, filled with affectionate
messages to the folks at home, thanks for bun-

dles, etc., received, requests to mother touching
shirts and suspenders, and details of his daily
routine. They describe the prayers at early
candlelight and the meals in Commons Hall,
with its twenty long tables, its big dumb-waiter,
and its too abstemious tutor, who, from the van-
tage-ground of a raised platform, returns thanks
when the dinner is only half done. "You may
sit down afterwards *if you wish*, but it is not
generally the case. There is an old woman who
has been in the college kitchen twenty years,
and in all this time done nothing but make pies.
We have them Sundays, Wednesdays, and Fri-
days; the worst of it is we can only get one
piece. I have fared rather better than the rest
generally, for Durant seldom eats pie, and most
always sends me his piece." Then there was the
round of study and recitation: Livy in the morning, mathematics at eleven, and Roman antiquities at four. "At recitation I have one of the
descendants of the Dutch settlers in New York
on each side of me. Their ancestors are mentioned by Knickerbocker in his history of New
York." These were doubtless Cortlandt Van
Rensselaer of Albany, and Washington Van
Zandt from Long Island. Between study hours
there is foot-ball on the green in front of the
colleges, "which game is not generally very edifying to the shins of the freshmen." These last

have subscribed twenty-five cents apiece "to support the lamps in the entry," — a venerable trick of the sophomores, who "collected in this way five or six dollars, and had a scrape upon it, and the conclusion of the matter was their getting so intoxicated as to be unable to reach home." The freshmen have likewise had their windows broken, and Willis's chum has been smoked out, during the former's absence from his room, by cigars inserted in the keyhole. A somewhat distant and impersonal form of the persecution this will seem to modern freshmen. But Sophomore Kneeland, from Georgia, having been collared by Tutor Stoddard, red-handed, in the act of breaking windows, and having knocked down the tutor and run, has been publicly expelled, the president reading out his mittimus in chapel to the whole college. Willis has joined the Linonian Society, — "Calhoun, the candidate for the presidency, was once a member of it" (an ancient "campaign" argument); also a freshman debating club, the officers of which "are almost all professors of religion," and in which he has been chosen, in his absence, "critic on composition and speaking." He has drunk tea at Miss Dunning's. He has called upon Mrs. Daggett and Mrs. T. Dwight, finding the former of these two ladies to be "a very pious woman, and a woman of uncommon understanding," and the latter "a woman of noble mind, though plain in person." He has taken a walk to the Cave of the Regicides on West Rock, — time out of mind the goal of the freshman's first pilgrimage. He has been appointed one of the committee to solicit subscriptions in his own class for the Greeks, and is also one of the managers of the Bible Society, and active at the Friday evening prayer-meetings, there being just at present considerable "engagedness" among "professors" in the several classes. Meanwhile Tutor Twining has been hissed and scraped at while conducting services in chapel. The government " are growing more and more rigorous. Almost every member of the freshman class is called up and questioned. Many are dismissed, and an examination is made of everything, from the stealing of a sugar-bowl out of the hall to the prostration of a tutor. Tutor Woolsey was smoked the other evening by two fellows who were too drunk to make their escape, and were caught without any difficulty. They did it at twelve o'clock at night, wrapped in sheets, and are both dismissed." The disturbances between the sophomores and freshmen culminated for Willis in a short suspension in the winter of 1823–24 for honorably refusing to disclose the names of sophomores by whom he had been smoked and squirted, or the names of persons in whose rooms he had seen a squirt, — an instrument of torture whose possession involved expulsion. The letter in which he announced his suspension is very long and filled with heroic sentiments.

" All my friends have been to see me, and justify me in my conduct. There are two professors of religion in the sophomore class who have done exactly so, and will be treated accordingly. And though it is a matter of policy with the government to pursue this course, it is said, and justly, that they despise an informer. My meeting with this squirt was entirely unavoidable, not originating (as perhaps you may suppose) from being in company where I ought not to be."

Willis suffered frequently from homesickness and low spirits during the winter of his freshman year. He had the poetic temperament, and was subject to his moods, easily elated and easily depressed. His chum was away somewhere teaching, and Willis, in his loneliness, had recourse to his pen.

" I find but few among the students," he wrote to his father, " whom I should choose as companions. Most of them are profane and dissipated, and their highest ambition seems to be to show off as a high fellow, and one who can overreach the government and laugh at its officers. The pious students in my class are mostly *men*, without any refinement either of manners or feeling, — fresh from the country, — whose piety renders them respectable, and who without it would be but boors. But there are a few students who have both piety and refinement, and some who, though not professors of religion, respect it, and who are moral in their outward conduct, whatever be the state of their hearts. These I can generally associate with, but when they are *all* out of the way, and I am in need of something to brighten my feelings, I can find in the flow of fancy a forgetfulness of the darker side. I have written a great deal in this way since my college life commenced, and my writing will *always* depend on the thermometer of my feelings."

As the youthful scribe gained readier power of expression his home correspondence became fuller and more effusive. He wrote with much minuteness a narrative of an evening spent at a country parsonage in West Haven, of a walk to the light-house, a visit to the cave of the hermit of East Rock, and of a trip by steamboat to New York. He dwelt at length upon all the impressions which the varying seasons and his daily experiences made upon his mind. There is, of course, no literary art in most of these juvenile confidences. The language is apt to be sophomorical, and the letters, as a whole, will seldom repay quotation, but an extract may be given here and there as a specimen of his epistolary style. The following is from a letter of

July 11, 1824, to his sister Julia, with whom
he was always particularly unreserved : —

" I wish you were here to walk with me these
beautiful moonlight evenings. I have seldom gone
to bed and left the mild Queen of the Night riding
in the heavens, for it seems a waste of noble feelings.
When I am walking on such evenings as we have
had this week past, and amidst such scenery as New
Haven presents, chastened and softened in its beauty
by the pure and quiet light of the moon, I have an
elevation of thought and sentiment which I cannot
drown in sleep without reluctance. I really think we
had better lay it down as a rule never to go to sleep
while the moon is shining. In fact, Julia, I suspect
(for I find no one who sympathizes with me in this
feeling) that I am something of a lunatic, — affected
by the rays of that beautiful planet with a kind of
happiness which is the result of a heated imagination,
and which is not felt by the generality of the common-
sense people of the world. Last Friday evening, you
know, was beautiful. I attended a meeting of the
professors of religion, statedly held on that evening
in the theological chamber, and when it was out
went alone to walk. I strolled along upon the shore
of the bay towards the light-house a mile or more,
and never did I meet with so delightful a scene.
There was no wind stirring, or not enough to make a
ripple on the wave, and the hardly perceptible swell
of the tide cast its waters upon the pebbles without a
sound. You know the appearance of a bay when the
light is shed obliquely upon it — looking like one im-

mense sheet of liquid silver, and if you have ever
seen a boat pass across it at such a moment, and seen
that beautiful phenomena of the phosphorus dripping
like fire from the oars and gilding the foam before
the prow, you can have some idea of the scene I then
witnessed. Now and then a sloop stole languidly
across the bay, hardly appearing to move, and presenting an alternate light and shade as the moon
struck upon the flapping sail or the helmsman tacked
to take advantage of the hardly perceptible breeze
which swept him slowly from the land. I declare it
did seem like enchantment. The clock struck one,
but I felt no disposition to go home, and, as the air
was pure and balmy, the thought struck me that it
would be a pleasant hour to bathe. Accordingly I
undressed, and swam along the shore slowly for about
half a mile in the cool, refreshing waters, with sensa-
tions which must be felt to be understood. After this
delightful exercise I walked home, and, seating myself by the window where I could look at the moon,
fell asleep, and did not wake till near morning."

This fancy, that he was peculiarly affected by
the light of the moon, was the first suggestion
of his wild tale, " The Lunatic's Skate," one of
his most imaginative stories, and not unworthy
of comparison with the weird fictions of Edgar
Poe.

In the summer term of his sophomore year
Willis was again suspended for a few weeks,
this time in common with a majority of his

class and in consequence of what was known
as "the Conic Sections Rebellion." The class
had been assured by the tutors that they would
not have to learn the corollaries to the propo-
sitions in that branch of mathematics, and
when the objectionable corollaries were, notwithstanding, imposed upon them, the mercury
then standing at 90° and the annual examinations at hand, eighty-four members bound
themselves by a solemn pledge not to recite
them. The government were firm, and the
recalcitrant sophomores were suspended in pla-
toons, day after day. Horace Bushnell was a
ring-leader in this revolt, which included the
" professors " equally with the worldly. All the
suspended men were taken back at the end of
the term.

In some recollections of Willis by his classmate, Hugh Blair Grigsby, published in the
latter's journal, the "Norfolk Beacon," in the
autumn of 1834, he says : —

" The first notice that the public had of his budding genius was a little poem in six verses, the two
first lines of the first verse being, —

> ' The leaf floats by upon the stream
> Unheeded in its silent way.'

We cannot recall the whole stanza ; but our fair readers may remember that their albums contained, some
time since, a beautiful vignette representing a lady

resting in her bower, listening to the notes of a
pretty songster perched above her. This engraving
was taken from these lines in this poem : —

> ' The bird that sings in lady's bower,
>   To-morrow will she think of him ? ' "

Grigsby says that this poem took the prize offered by the " New York Mirror." He also recalls a division-room composition, of a humorous character, read by Willis in the winter of
1824–25, about an old man planting a cabbage
on his wife's grave, which produced great merriment in the class. In the same year verses
signed " Roy," mainly on scriptural subjects,
began to appear in the poet's corner of the
" Boston Recorder," where they jostled the selections from Watts or original contributions
from the pens of " Maro," " Eliza," and " The
Green Mountain Bard." Some of these *juvenilia* were too imperfect to merit preserving,
and were never put between covers. Others,
like " Absalom," " The Sacrifice of Abraham,"
and " The Burial of Arnold," were among his
most successful things. They were widely quoted and admired, copied about in the newspapers, inserted in readers and collections of
verse, and have done as much to upbear his
memory as any of his later writings. They
were not all contributed to the " Recorder."
Some came out in " The Christian Examiner,"

"The Memorial," "The Connecticut Journal,"
"The Youth's Companion," and "The Telegraph." It was customary for the editors of
weekly and monthly periodicals, who ordinarily
paid their contributors nothing, to stimulate
Columbia's infant muse by an annual burst of
generosity in the shape of a prize for the best
poem printed in their columns during the year,
— a device now relegated to the juvenile and
college press. Several of these honors fell to
Willis's share. Lockwood, the publisher of an
annual gift-book, "The Album," paid him fifty
dollars for a prize poem, and he got unknown
sums for his "Absalom," "prize poem desig-
nated by the judges of original poetry in the
'Christian Watchman,'" as announced in the
issue of that paper for March 30, 1827; and
for "The Sacrifice of Abraham," similarly des-
ignated by the judges in the "Boston Recorder" for 1826. He was also invited to write
for the "Atlantic Souvenir," published in Philadelphia, Goodrich's "Token," and Hill's "Lyceum" in Boston, Bryant's new magazine in
New York, and a paper recently started in the
same city and edited by a brother of Professor
Silliman; for the "Bristol Reporter," a "newspaper in Rhode Island," and other publications.

All this literary glory gave the young undergraduate great *éclat* in New Haven. He re-

ceived many invitations out, and was teased for verses by the owners of countless albums. He began to frequent the society of the town, where his rapidly developing social gifts soon made him a favorite. He was at this time a tall, handsome stripling, with an easy assurance of manner and a good deal of the dandy in his dress. His portrait, painted by Miss Stuart of Boston, a daughter of the famous portrait-painter, Gilbert Stuart, shows him with a rosy face, very fair hair hanging in natural curls over the forehead, a *retroussé* nose, long upper lip, pale gray eye with uncommonly full lid (a family trait), and a confident and joyous expression. He carried himself with an airy, jaunty grace, and there was something particularly spirited and *vif* about the poise and movement of his head, — a something which no portrait could reproduce. With naturally elegant tastes, an expansive temper, and an eagerness to see the more brilliant side of life, Willis could at all times make himself agreeable to those whom he cared to please. But he was quick to feel the chill of a hostile presence, and toward any one, in especial, who seemed to disapprove of him he could be curt and defiant. He had a winning way with women, who were flattered by his recognition of their influence over him and grateful for *les petits soins* which he never neglected.

Taken up more and more with social distractions, he ceased to apply himself to his college duties. Indeed, he had never felt much interest in the studies of the curriculum, excepting Latin, for which he had a taste and in which his scholarship was fairly good. Mathematics was his pet aversion. He did considerable miscellaneous reading, and cultivated a liking for the old British dramatists and Commonwealth prose writers, like Burton, Taylor, and Browne; his studies in whom he afterwards imparted to the readers of the "American Monthly." He wrote to his father, shortly before graduation, that he had devoted his whole time in college to literature.

Always more of a ladies' man than a man's man, fastidious too in the choice of acquaintances, he took small part in college affairs, and preferred the social life of the town. He was not a frequenter of Linonia, that forum whose decay furnishes an annual theme for lamentation to returning graduates at Commencement. But once he debated that perennial question, "Were the Crusades a Benefit to Europe?" and once he composed a comedy, which was acted in the society with applause, though not without scandal. The following reminiscences will find an echo in the breast of many an alumnus who in his salad days has sparkled out

in some " Coffee Club " or " Studio," or other
Ambrosial experiment of the kind : —

" I sunk some pocket money in a blank book
on reading Wilson's ' Noctes.'   Celestial nights I
thought *we* had of it, at old black Stanley's forbidden oyster house in New Haven ; and it struck me
it was robbery of posterity (no less !) not to record
the brilliant efflorescence of our conviviality.   Regularly on reaching my chambers (or as soon after
morning prayers as my head became pellucid), I attempted to reduce to dialogue the wit of our Christopher North, ' Shepherd ' and ' Tickler ; ' but alas !
it became what may be called ' productive labor.'
Either my memory did not serve me, or wit (I
should n't be surprised) reads cold by repentant daylight.   It was heavy work, as reluctant as a college
exercise, and after using up for cigar-lighters the
short-lived ' Noctes,' I devoted the remainder of the
book to outlines of the antique (that is to say, of old
shoes), my passion just then being a collection of
French slippers from the prettiest feet in the known
world (' known,' to me)."

Among the uncollected " Recorder " verses is
a series of three divertingly Byronic performances, " Misanthropic Hours," from which it
would seem that the poet, in his junior year,
had a momentary attack of cynicism, produced
by his discovery of the soullessness of " woman."
Most boys who tag lines have gone through this
species of measles.

> " I do not hate, but I have felt
> Indifferent to woman long :
> I bow not where I once have knelt,
> I lisp not what I poured in song.
> They are too beautifully made
> For their tame earthliness of thought;
> Ay, their immortal minds degrade
> The meaner work His hands have wrought."

The specifications of this painful charge were several. He had been walking with a beautiful girl one glorious night, with his soul uplifted by the influences of the hour, when she rudely jarred upon his mood by remarking that "their kitchen chimney smoked again." Another young woman, with whom he was viewing a Crucifixion in a picture gallery, had "coldly curled her lip and praised the high priest's garment." A third had profaned one of his religious hours.

> " I turned me at the slow Amen
> And wiped my drowning eyes, and met
> A trifling smile ! Think ye of *men* ?
> I tell you *man* hath heart : — no, no,
> It was a woman's smile. They tell
> Of her bright ruby lip, and eye
> That shames the Arabic gazelle ;
> They tell of her cheek's glowing dye,
> Of her arch look and witching spell :
> But there is not that man on earth
> Who at that hour had felt like mirth."

Worse than all, he had been watching by a corpse, in company with a young lady of his acquaintance, when

> " She trifled, ay, that *angel* maid,
> She *trifled* where the dead was laid ! "

These misogynistic musings called forth a remonstrance, — " Woman — to Roy," — by one of the " Recorder's " poetesses, who signed herself " Rob."   " Ye know her not," she sang,

> " An idle name
> Ye give to toys of fashion's mould,
> And well ye scorn those guilty ones
> Who curl their smiles of pride to heaven.
> Oh, seek her not in halls of mirth,
> But in those calm dwellings of earth," etc.

Meanwhile, rumors of his idleness and dissipation began to reach Boston, and caused his family much distress. These reports were absurdly exaggerated, and were warmly denied by his friends, who asserted that the head and front of his offending were an occasional moonlight drive to " the Lake " and a supper, with a glass of ale at " Barney's." Willis was gay in college, but very far from dissipated. In the select circles where he was made at home nothing like dissipation was tolerated. The society of the little university town was as simple as it was refined. He was cordially welcomed in such families as the Whitings, the Bishops, the Hubbards, and the entire Woolsey, Devereux, and Johnson connection in New Haven, Stratford, and New York. His winter holidays were spent partly at New York with his classmates Rankin and

Richards, partly at Stratford with the Johnsons, once at New London among the kinsfolk of his grandmother, Lucy Douglas; and once he traveled as far as Philadelphia. His "dissipations" in New Haven were picnics to East Rock, rehearsals of "The Lady of the Lake" at a seminary for young ladies, pie-banquets in Thanksgiving week, — paid for with verses, — and New Year's calls with their accompaniments of a cooky and a glass of wine.

That his head was a little turned by his literary and social successes is not wonderful. He had his share of vanity, and in his confidential letters to his parents and sisters he made no effort to conceal his elation. A passage from one of these, dated January 7, 1827, will give a good idea of his occupations and his frame of mind at this point in his senior year : —

"I stayed in Stratford till Friday, and then the Johnsons offered me a seat in the carriage to New York. This, of course, was irresistible ; and Friday night at ten o'clock I was presented to the mayor of the city, at a splendid levee. It was his last before leaving his office, and I never saw such magnificence. The fashion and beauty and talent of the city were all there, crowding his immense rooms to show their respect for his services. . . . I found many old acquaintances there and made some new ones, — among the latter, a Mrs. Brunson, as beautiful a woman as I

ever saw, and her sister, Miss Catherine Bailey, also
a most beautiful woman. I met the very accomplished Adelaide Richards there, who patronized me
and played my dictionary, and from whose father
and mother I received an invitation to dine on New
Year's day. At two or three o'clock I went *home* to
Mr. William Johnson's (who married Miss Woolsey's
sister), and in a glorious bed, with a good coal fire by
my side, slept off the fatigues of a sixty miles' ride
and four hours' dissipation.

"On Saturday evening I went to a genuine *soirée* at
the great Dr. Hosack's. This man is the most luxurious liver in the city, and his house is a perfect palace. You could not lay your hand on the wall for
costly paintings, and the furniture exceeds everything
I have seen. I met all the literary characters of the
day there, and Halleck, the poet, among them. With
him I became quite acquainted, and he is a most glorious fellow. More of him when we meet. . . . You
know on New Year's day in New York all the gentlemen call on all their acquaintances. I began at
twelve o'clock at the Battery, and went up to St.
John's Park, merely running in and right out again
till four, the dinner hour. I called on everybody.
William Woolsey went with me, and, by appointing
a rendezvous in every street, we kept along together.
At four I went to Mr. George Richards's to dine.
He is no relative of Robert's, and lives in the best
style in a large house on St. John's Park. We sat
down to dinner between five and six, and sat several
hours with a very large party. I got a seat next

to the beautiful Miss Adelaïde, and enjoyed it much. They live in the French style, and the last course was sugar-plums ! "

In another letter he says : —

" I was much flattered in vacation by the attentions of literary men and women ; the latter more particularly, who seemed to consider it quite the thing to find a poet who was not a bear, and who could stoop so much from the *excelsa* of his profession as to dress fashionably and pay compliments like a lawyer. I heard of a very *blue* young lady who said, ' La, how I should love to see Mr. Willis ! I am sure I should fall in love with a man who writes such sweet poetry.' She is both belle and bluestocking, they say."

One of the families in which Willis was an *habitué* was the household of Mrs. Apthorp, a widow with four lovely daughters, who conducted one of the seminaries for young ladies for which New Haven was famous. This was the original of Mrs. Ilfrington's school in " The Cherokee's Threat." Willis was much ridiculed by the reviewers for his very high-colored description of this educational establishment, and in particular for declaring that " in the united pictures of Paul Veronese and Raphael " he had " scarcely found so many lovely women, of so different models and so perfect, as were assembled in my sophomore year," in this Connecticut " sugar-refinery." His lines " On the Death of a Young

Girl " were written on the occasion of the death
of one of this family, some years after. The
"Lines to Laura W——, Two Years of Age " —
one of two selections from Willis in Emerson's
" Parnassus " — were addressed to a little New
Haven girl, the sister and biographer of Theodore Winthrop. Another friend of Willis's was
a Mrs. De Forest, widow of the American consul at Buenos Ayres, a lady of fortune, who came
to New Haven, and bought a house facing the
green, where she gave fashionable parties. She
was herself a beautiful woman, and her daughters, Julia and Pastora — *matre pulchra filiæ
pulchriores* — were great belles among the students in Chevalier Wikoff's day, who describes
one of them as a " perfect blonde," and the other
as a " matchless brunette."

The religious impressions which had been
stamped upon Willis's mind by the Andover revival were gradually obliterated by the preoccupations of undergraduate life. He did not definitely renounce his profession, and remained till
graduation in communion with the college church.
But the state of his soul gave deep anxiety to his
good parents, who looked upon him, as he did
upon himself, as a backslider. In a letter to his
father during a season of " ingathering " in the
college, stimulated by the eloquent preaching of
Professor Fitch, he wrote as follows : —

"My own experience makes me very much alive to the frequent fallacy of the hopes which are experienced in revivals. I understand your anxiety for me, and I understand the feelings which prompted mother's most tender and affectionate addition to your letter. If I perish it will not be because I do not *know* my duty, for there are few who have been better instructed. But my feelings are most peculiar and most trying. I am under one ceaseless and enduring conviction of sin ; one wearing anxiety about my soul, without making any visible progress. I know what you will write about it. I could anticipate every word you can say upon the point. But so it is, and I have done with *all* discussion of it."

At the completion of the senior examinations Willis delivered the valedictory poem to his class, "with a simplicity and feeling which thrilled the audience," says one who was present. Portions of this were printed in his " Sketches " and in subsequent editions of his poems. It is one of the hardest things in the world to write a good occasional poem, and Willis's Class Day address does not differ much from other performances of the kind. It is in blank verse, laboriously didactic, and expresses the usual conventional sentiments and noble moral reflections proper to the occasion. It is by no means as good as another occasional poem of his, " The Death of Arnold," written upon the burial of the class champion, and first printed in the " Connecticut Journal."

Willis spent the senior vacation — a halcyon period of six weeks that formerly intervened between Class Day and Commencement — in a trip through New York State and Canada; taking what is now known as the grand tour, and gathering impressions which he ultimately worked into the texture of his vivid sketches of " Niagara, Lake Ontario, and the St. Lawrence." He traveled by the Erie Canal, then newly opened through an almost unbroken wilderness, dotted here and there with stripling cities, Utica, Palmyra, Rochester, — the last only a few years old.

" The burnt stumps of the first settlers are all over the town: you find them close by the doors and in the yards of the people, and you may look between elegant blocks of stone and brick buildings and see the *natural forest* within five minutes' walk. It is complete mushroom. We saw Colonel Rochester, who first settled it. He and his wife were sitting at their front door, enjoying the evening under trees which twelve years ago were the depth of the wilderness."

There was a perpetual novelty in these contrasts. He saw the country, as it were, in the making. The canal-boat went only four miles an hour, and the voyager could get out, when so minded, to stretch his legs and pick the wild flowers along the tow-path. Odd experiences relieved the monotony of this quiet sail along the amber Mohawk, " bonniest stream that ever dimpled." One Sunday, at the request of old General Wadsworth of Geneseo, who happened to be aboard and took a great fancy to Willis, the latter preached a sermon to the passengers assembled in the cabin, and passed among them, in consequence, as a young minister who " had geten him yet no benefice." And here is a little idyl perhaps worth recording : —

" On Sunday morning I saw a girl on a hillside in the wildest part of the Mohawk Valley, milking. So I leaped ashore, to the great amusement of the passengers, and ran up to give her a lecture. She was quite pretty, and blushed when I asked her if she knew it was wicked to milk on Sunday. She had a pretty little clean foot, probably washed by the wet grass, and held up the milking-pail for me to drink with considerable grace. I should have begged a kiss if the boat had not been in sight. I have just been called up to look at Palmyra. It is curious to sail through the centre of a town, and see people in the windows above you and on the steps of the houses, crowding to see the strange faces on board. They look so much at home and you come so near them that you can hardly believe you shall be in ten minutes in the depth of the forest again."

At Utica he found a host of friends, was re-

ceived with Western hospitality, and had twenty
or thirty invitations to dinners and parties. A
Utica belle whom he had known in New Haven
made up a picnic in his behoof to Trenton Falls,
the scenery of which he described so admirably
in " Edith Linsey." It was his hap to visit
Trenton on the very day when a Miss Suydam,
a young lady from New York, fell over the falls
and was killed. From Auburn he drove out on
a visit to another fair acquaintance, Miss Adele
Livingston, whose country house on Skaneateles
Lake he found to be a " little palace of cultivation and refinement " dropped down unexpectedly in the wilderness. This was " Fleming
Farm " in " Edith Linsey," though it would
probably be a mistake to identify the heroine of
that tale with Willis's hostess. With her he
took a horseback ride round the head of the lake,
and then he returned to his canal. At Niagara
he encountered a pleasant party of Boston and
Salem people, and was asked to attach himself to
their train on the way up Ontario and down the
St. Lawrence. Among them was a " Miss E.
M——" (Emily Marshall?), a famous beauty,
who figures in Willis's " Niagara " sketch in a
romantic and perilous adventure behind the fall.
" I am sorry I may not mention her name," he
says, " for in more chivalrous times she would
have been a character of history. Everybody

who has been in America, however, will know
whom I am describing." At Montreal he fell
in with Chester Harding, the artist, with whom
he afterwards became intimate at Boston, and
who painted an excellent portrait of Willis, now
owned by Mr. Charles A. Dana. In September
he went back to New Haven to take his degree
and say good-by, and then college life was over
and the world before him.

Willis always looked back with tenderness to
his college days. Years after, in his "Slingsby"
papers, contributed to an English magazine, he
made New Haven and the university the scene
or background of some of his best stories and
sketches of American life, such as "Edith Linsey," "F. Smith," "Scenes of Fear," "Larks
in Vacation," and "The Cherokee's Threat."
These, however, are not college stories in the common meaning of the term. The heroes of these
amusing and often incredible adventures are undergraduates, but they have the easy *savoir faire*
of men of the world, and the incidents of the
narrative are mainly enacted outside the college
fence, and consist for the most part of love-mak-
ing, driving stanhope, and touring about the
country in an independent manner. The academic life of the time offered but a meagre field
to the romancer, nor indeed is the case much altered since. There have been loud calls, at pres-

ent subsiding, for an " American Tom Brown."
A few patriotic Harvard graduates have re-
sponded, but their success has been such that
the alumni of other colleges have congratulated
themselves that no one has been moved to perform the same office for their own *Almæ Ma-
tres.* It may be doubted whether the four years
of a college course are a broad enough base to
support a full-length novel. A man is not born
in college, and he seldom dies or marries there.
The struggle which decides his final success or
failure is fought on other fields. As to the life
itself, though engrossing enough to those who
lead it, as stuff for fiction it is scant, — a life of
pleasant monotony, varied by contests for honors
and prizes which seem paltry to the man, and
made exciting by that most fatuous of pursuits,
college "politics." Nevertheless, it has unique
features of its own, peculiar developments of
sentiment and humor which appeal to the imagination. To these, the man who has lived it and
found it sweet will often attempt to give shape,
as he looks back upon it in less happy years,
even though he may understand well enough that
such fragmentary experiences want the unity
and importance required in a continuous fiction. As experiments of this nature, Willis's college stories should be regarded. It must be confessed that he idealized a good deal. His geese

were always swans, and he practiced an airy exaggeration provoking to the statistician or the literal minded. He speaks, for example, in an off-hand way of "the thousand students of the university," though the number never reached half a thousand at any time when he was a student. But in the incidental glimpses of the life which he described, in the atmosphere which he flung around it, he was true to the spirit of that life, — the gay, irresponsible existence of half-idle, half-earnest youth, whose friendships are warm and unquestioning, to whom the world is new, the future full of promise, and every girl a Venus. There is a glamour over it all — "the golden exhalations of the dawn " — and romance is the proper medium in which to present it.

"Bright as seems to me this seat of my Alma Mater, however," wrote Willis in "Edith Linsey," " and gayly as I describe it, it is to me a picture of memory, glazed and put away; if I see it ever again it will be but to walk through its embowered streets by a midnight moon. It is vain and heartbreaking to go back after absence to any spot of earth, of which the interest was the human love whose home and cradle it had been. There is nothing on earth so mournful and unavailing, as to return to the scenes which are unchanged, and look to return to ourselves and others as we were when we thus knew them."

On leaving college, Willis signalized his en-

5

trance upon a literary career of forty years by collecting and publishing a score of his juvenile poems, in a thin volume entitled "Sketches," and dedicated to his father. It contained, among other things, four of the scriptural pieces which had done more than anything else to give him reputation. This vein he continued to cultivate, and added others in later volumes till they reached the number of eighteen. Even in his last years he wrote one more scriptural poem for the "New York Ledger," at the persuasion of the enterprising Mr. Bonner, reinforced by the proffer of a hundred dollars. As there is little difference in value between the earliest and latest of these, it may be well to speak of· them here collectively. It is not hard to explain the vogue which they obtained, or the reason why many people at this day, who know nothing else of Willis, have read his Scripture poems. One still encounters, here and there, a good old country lady who reads little poetry, but who can quote from "Absalom" or "Jephthah's Daughter" and thinks them quite the best product of the American Parnassus. They made good Sunday reading. They appealed to an intensely biblical and not very literary constituency; to a public familiar with the Old and New Testaments alike, and familiarized also with the life and scenery of the East through Bible commentaries and the lectures of missionaries who had traveled in Palestine. They were pleased to meet again the most striking episodes and affecting situations in the sacred narratives, set forth in easy verse, embroidered prettily, and with the sentiments and reflections proper to the subject all duly marshaled before them. It lent concreteness to the story to learn that in the room of Jairus's daughter,

> "The spice lamps in the alabaster urns
> Burned dimly and the white and fragrant smoke
> Curled indolently on the chamber walls;"

or that the Shunamite's little son, on his way to the field, passed

> "Through the light green hollows where the lambs
> Go for the tender grass;"

or that the scene of Christ's baptism

> "Was a green spot in the wilderness
> Touched by the river Jordan. The dark pine
> Never had dropped its tassels on the moss
> Tufting the leaning bank, nor on the grass
> Of the broad circle stretching evenly
> To the straight larches had a heavier foot
> Than the wild heron's trodden. Softly in
> Through a long aisle of willows, dim and cool,
> Stole the clear waters with their muffled feet,
> And, hushing as they spread into the light,
> Circled the edges of the pebbled tank
> Slowly, then rippled through the woods away."

For the merely literary quality of these poems, independent of their sacred associations, not very much can be said. They were certainly remarkably mature work for a college boy, pure in taste, delicate and correct in execution. But there is a slightly hollow ring to them, as of verse exercises on set themes. The inspiration is at second hand, from books and not from life. As other juvenile poets have gone to their classics for a subject, Willis went to his Bible. He drank at Siloa's fount instead of Helicon, and tuned the psaltery instead of the lyre. We have evidently not reached the real Willis yet. In general the experiment of paraphrasing the narrative portions of the Scriptures has not been successful. Something is lost when the impressive simplicity of the original is blown out into wordy and sentimental verse. This process of spinning rhetorical commonplaces from brief texts is well illustrated in the following passage from " Lazarus and Mary : " —

> " But to the mighty heart
> That in Gethsemane sweat drops of blood,
> Taking for us the cup that might not pass —
> The heart whose breaking chord upon the cross
> Made the earth tremble and the sun afraid
> To look upon his agony — the heart
> Of a lost world's Redeemer — overflowed,
> Touched by a mourner's sorrow! Jesus wept!"

This is what Lowell called " inspiration and water." Alfred de Vigny, a fine spirit and good poet, has tried the same thing in French and succeeded little, if at all, better than the Yankee collegian. The inadequacy of Willis's Scripture renderings is made more apparent by the fact that his blank verse is not a good vehicle for strong feeling. It is correct and flowing, sometimes musical, but seldom energetic. It favored his tendency to diffuseness and it often degenerates into a kind of accentless *oratio soluta*, which is only verse because it scans, and only blank verse because it does not rhyme.

Upon the whole the most genuine expression of Willis's talent in this early volume was in the piece entitled " Better Moments," which remains one of his best, because one of his most spontaneous poems.

It makes one realize the startling growth of the United States in the last fifty years, to remember that Willis had already won a " national reputation " by his poetry when he left college. The air was much thinner then, American literature much scantier, the population so small and so comparatively homogeneous, that the suffrages of a few hundreds of readers in New York, Boston, New Haven, and Philadelphia, and the praises of a few dozen journals were enough to bestow fame. What undergraduate nowadays, however clever or precocious, could hope to make his voice heard beyond the limits of the college yard?

It remains only to mention that the presence in New Haven of the two poets Percival and Hillhouse, when Willis was a student there, was not without influence on his literary development. Percival went to West Point as Professor of Chemistry in 1824 and did not come back to New Haven until 1827, but Hillhouse resided constantly at his beautiful home in the outskirts of the city, "Sachem's Wood." His Master's Oration, "The Education of a Poet," and his Phi Beta Kappa poem, "The Judgment," had given him great fame in the university as an orator and poet. "'Hadad' was published in 1825," wrote Willis, "during my second year in college, and to me it was the opening of a new heaven of imagination. The leading characters possessed me for months, and the bright, clear, harmonious language was, for a long time, constantly in my ears." Of its author he said, "In no part of the world have I seen a man of more distinguished mien. . . . Though my acquaintance with him was slight, he confided to me, in a casual conversation, the plan of a series of dramas, different from all he had attempted, upon which he designed to work with the first mood and leisure he could command."

CHAPTER III.

1827–1831.

BOSTON AND THE AMERICAN MONTHLY.

THE profession of letters was Willis's manifest destiny. Family tradition, his inborn tastes and talents, the course of his studies, and his achievements hitherto, all pointed that way. Yet in the then state of the American press it took no small amount of self-confidence to decline a paying profession and launch upon the uncertain currents of literary life. His next four years were spent in Boston and were years of apprenticeship in his life-work as an editor and journalist. He continued to write and publish verses, but his hand was acquiring cunning, through constant practice and frequent failure, in the production of that light, brilliant prose which made him the favorite periodical writer of his day ; and he was also learning how to conduct a magazine. He still made occasional contributions to the " Recorder " — among others the New Year's verses, then essential to every well-regulated paper — for 1828 and 1829. But

his first editorial engagement was with Samuel
G. Goodrich, the well-known bookseller and publisher, who had removed from Hartford to Boston in 1826.   One of the first books which he
had published in Boston was Willis's " Sketches,"
and he now employed the author of it to edit
" The Legendary " for 1828 and " The Token "
for 1829.   Goodrich was a fine example of Yankee enterprise and versatility.   He was one of
the pioneers of " the trade " in America, entering the field at the same time with the Harpers.
Under the pen-name of " Peter Parley," he
wrote or edited a long list of books for the
young, histories, travels, biographies, tales, works
of natural history, school text-books, etc.   He
had himself some pretensions as a poet, by virtue of " The Outcast and Other Poems," 1841.
He was an extensive traveler, and he became in
1851 United States consul at Paris.   It was
the fashion among a certain set in Boston to
abuse " Peter Parley " and laugh at his literary
claims.   But he was a very successful publisher,
and in selecting his editorial assistants, he had a
keen eye for the kind of talent that takes, and
the kind of work that pays.   In his interesting
" Recollections of a Lifetime " he gives contrasted sketches of the two principal contributors to his annuals — Willis and Hawthorne.
Goodrich's perceptions were, perhaps, not of the

finest, but he was a shrewd observer of matters within his ken, and his recollections of Willis are worth repeating.

"The most prominent writer for ' The Token ' was N. P. Willis. His articles were the most read, the most admired, the most abused, and the most advantageous to the work. In 1827 I published his volume entitled ' Sketches.' It brought out quite a shower of criticism, in which praise and blame were about equally dispensed : at the same time the work sold with a readiness quite unusual for a book of poetry at that period. One thing is certain, everybody thought Willis worth criticising. He has been, I suspect, more written about than any other literary man in our history. Some of the attacks upon him proceeded, no doubt, from a conviction that he was a man of extraordinary gifts and yet of extraordinary affectations, and the lash was applied in kindness, as that of a school-master to a loved pupil's back. Some of them were dictated by envy, for we have had no other example of literary success so early, so general, and so flattering. That Mr. Willis made mistakes in literature and life, at the outset, may be admitted by his best friends ; for it must be remembered that before he was five-and-twenty he was more read than any other American poet of his time ; and besides, being possessed of an easy and captivating address, he became the pet of society and especially of the fairer portion of it. As to his personal character, I need only say that, from the beginning, he has had a

larger circle of steadfast friends than almost any
man within my knowledge. It is curious to remark
that everything Willis wrote attracted immediate attention and excited ready praise, while the productions of Hawthorne were almost entirely unnoticed.
Willis was slender, his hair sunny and silken, his
cheek ruddy, his aspect cheerful and confident. He
met society with a ready and welcome hand and was
received readily and with welcome."

It is needless to pursue the contrast which the
writer goes on to draw between Willis and the
other and greater Nathaniel, who was then " the
obscurest man of letters in America." The publisher's sympathies were obviously with his more
lively and popular contributor, and he is puzzled
to understand why such articles as " Sights from
a Steeple," " Sketches beneath an Umbrella,"
" The Wives of the Dead," and " The Pro-
phetic Pictures," should have " extorted hardly
a word of either praise or blame " when originally published in " The Token," while " now
universally acknowledged to be productions of
extraordinary depth, meaning, and power." He
is inclined to attribute it to a " new sense " in a
portion of the reading world — obtained unluck-
ily too late to profit the publisher of " The Token " — " which led them to study the mystical."
To Goodrich's personal description of Willis
may be added the following little portrait by

Dr. Holmes, who remembers him well, as he looked during this Boston period.

"He came very near being very handsome. He was tall; his hair, of light brown color, waved in luxuriant abundance, and his cheek was as rosy as if it had been painted to show behind the footlights, and he dressed with artistic elegance. He was something between a remembrance of Count d'Orsay and an anticipation of Oscar Wilde. There used to be in the gallery of the Luxembourg a picture of Hippolytus and Phædra, in which the beautiful young man, who had kindled a passion in the heart of his wicked stepmother, always reminded me of Willis."

"The Legendary" described itself as consisting of original pieces in prose and verse; tales, ballads, and romances, chiefly illustrative of American history, scenery, and manners. It was designed as a periodical, but only two volumes were issued, one in the early, and one in the later part of 1828. "The work proved a miserable failure," said Goodrich, though numbering among its contributors Mrs. Sigourney, Miss Sedgwick, Halleck, Pierpont, Willis, Gaylord Clark, George Lunt, Grenville Mellen, and others less known to this generation. Willis wrote the two prefaces and contributed half a dozen poems of no importance, unless we except "The Annoyer," which had considerable currency, and three prose papers, "Unwritten

Poetry," " Unwritten Philosophy," and " Leaves
from a Colleger's Album." These last were
very juvenile and he never reprinted them. The
first two were tales with a moral, one depicting
the restorative influences of nature on a heart
crushed by bereavement, the other describing a
scholarly recluse, who lived alone with nature
and his books, and finally educated and married
his landlady's daughter. The story in both
instances is very slight, overladen with sentiment, descriptive digressions, and philosophy,
that might better have stayed "unwritten." In
short, they are tedious — which Willis in his
later work never was. " Unwritten Poetry "
included, however, a description of Trenton
Falls and a fine rhapsody about water which he
rehabilitated afterwards and incorporated with
" Edith Linsey." Both of these had the honor
— in the then paucity of our literature — to
be selected by Mary Russell Mitford for her
" Stories of American Life by American Authors." " Leaves from a Colleger's Album "
was a first experiment of another kind, a humorous sketch of a trip on the Erie Canal,
utilizing the experiences of his senior vacation,
and, in particular, the incident of his reading
a sermon in the cabin of the canal boat on
Sunday. It contains, in the person of Job
Clark, the nucleus of Forbearance Smith in the

" Slingsby " papers — the nearest approach that
Willis ever made to the genuine creation of a
character. He was always thus economical of
his material, repeatedly working over the same
stuff into new shapes.

" The Token " belonged to the class of illustrated publications known as Annuals. It was
the age of Annuals, Gift Books, Boudoir Books,
Books of Beauty, Flowers of Loveliness, and
Leaflets of Memory. The taste for these ornate combinations of literature and art was imported from England, where the Ackermans had
published " The Forget-Me-Not," the earliest
specimen of the kind, in 1823. Carey & Lea
of Philadelphia brought out the first American
Annual, " The Atlantic Souvenir," for which
Willis had been asked to write, when in college,
and to which he actually did contribute a copy
of birth-day verses, " I 'm twenty-two — I 'm
twenty-two," in the volume for 1829. These
were written, he affirmed, " in a blank leaf
of a barber's Testament, while waiting to be
shaved." They were also inserted in the "London Literary Souvenir " for the same year, by
Alaric A. Watts, a copious editor of Annuals,
whose middle initial was cruelly asserted by
Lockhart to stand for *Attila*. The rage for
Annuals soon became general and lasted for
about twenty years. Goodrich enumerates some

forty of them, bearing such fantastic titles as
The Gem, The Opal, The Wreath, The Casket,
The Rose, The Amulet, The Keepsake, Pearls
of the West, Friendship's Offering. And these
are probably not half the list. There were
religious Annuals, juvenile Annuals, oriental,
landscape, botanic Annuals. Most rummagers
among the upper shelves of an old library have
taken down two or three of them, blown the
dust from their gilt edges, ruffled the tissue
papers that veil " The Bride," " The Nun,"
" The Sisters," and " The Fair Penitent," and
wondered in what age of the world these remarkable "embellishments" and the still more
remarkable letter - press which they embellish
could have reflected American life. There is
a faded elegance about them, as of an old ball
dress : a faint aroma, as of withered roses,
breathes from the page. Those steel-engraved
beauties, languishing, simpering, insipid as fashion plates, with high-arched marble brows, pearl
necklaces, and glossy ringlets — not a line in
their faces or a bone in their bodies : that
Highland Chieftain, that Young Buccaneer,
that Bandit's Child, all in smoothest *mezzotint*,
— what kind of a world did they masquerade
in ? It was a needlework world, a world in
which there was always moonlight on the lake
and twilight in the vale; where drooped the wil-

low and bloomed the eglantine, and jessamine
embowered the cot of the village maid; where
the lark warbled in the heavens and the night-
ingale chanted in the grove 'neath the mould-
ering ivy-mantled tower; where vesper chimes
and the echoes of the merry bugle-ugle-ugle
horn were borne upon the zephyr across the
yellow corn; where Isabella sang to the harp
(with her hair down) and the tinkling guitar of
the serenader under her balcony made response;
a world in which there were fairy isles, en-
chanted grottoes, peris, gondolas, and gazelles.
All its pleasantly *rococo* landscape has vanished, brushed rudely away by realism and a
" sincere " art and an " earnest " literature.

In these Gems and Albums, the gemmy and
albuminous illustrations alternated with romantic tales of mediæval or eastern life and with
" Lines on Seeing ——," or " Stanzas occasioned
by " something. " The May-Flowers of Life,"
for example, " suggested by the author's having
found a branch of May in a volume of poems
which a friend had left there several years ago."
In the Annual dialect a ship was a " bark," a
bed was a " couch," a window was a " casement,"
a shoe was a " sandal," a boat was a " shallop,"
and a book was a " tome." Certain properties
became gemmy by force of association, as sea-
shells, lattices, and Æolian harps. In England

L. E. L. and in America Percival and Mrs.
Sigourney were perhaps the gemmiest poets.
But much of Willis's poetry was album verse,
with an air of the boudoir and the ball-room
about it, a silky elegance and an exotic perfume
that smack of that very sentimental and artificial school.   This passage from "The Declara-
tion" is in point : —

> "'T was late and the gay company was gone,
> And light lay soft on the deserted room
> From alabaster vases, and a scent
> Of orange leaves and sweet verbena came
> From the unshuttered window on the air,
> And the rich pictures, with their dark old tints,
> Hung like a twilight landscape, and all things
> Seemed hushed into a slumber.   Isabelle,
> The dark eyed, spiritual Isabelle,
> Was leaning on her harp."

"The Token," begun in 1828 and continued
to 1842, was edited by Goodrich every year except 1829, when Willis had charge of it.   Like
other Annuals it contained, in spots, some good
art and good writing.   There were delicately
designed and engraved vignette titles or presentation plates by Cheney, the Hartford artist.
There was an occasional contribution, in prose,
from Longfellow or Mrs. Child — then Miss
Francis, and likewise a contributor to "The Legendary."   Many of Hawthorne's "Twice-Told
Tales" came out in "The Token."   Mrs. Sigour-

ney's " Connecticut River" divided with Willis's "The Soldier's Widow" the $100 prize offered by the publisher for 1828. Among the contributors to Willis's volume (1829) were John Neal, Colonel William L. Stone, Mrs. Sigourney, Mrs. Hale, the Rev. T. H. Gallaudet, Willis's Albany friend, J. B. Van Schaick, and Goodrich himself. The Rev. G. W. Doane — afterward Bishop Doane — gave his well known verses, " What is that, Mother?" Willis gave five poems of his own, the only noteworthy one among which was " Saturday Afternoon," written to accompany the frontispiece, engraved by Ellis from a painting by Fisher, and representing children swinging in a barn. This had more the character of a simple, popular ballad than anything else which he had written, and was liked by many readers who cared little about his more elaborate verse. Another poem in "The Token," "Psyche before the Tribunal of Venus," he wrote for the engraving by Cheney from a drawing of Fragonard. A college tale, " The Ruse," was a slight advance on the experiments in " The Legendary;" the dialogue was handled more freely, but the story was weak as a whole, hardly worth mentioning, certainly not worth preserving. Willis continued to contribute verses to "The Token" after he had resigned its editorship. " To a City Pigeon," " On a

Picture of a Girl leading her Blind Mother through the Woods," and doubtless other pieces were printed in subsequent numbers. He wrote for other Annuals, at various times : " The Power of an Injured Look," for " The Gift," a Christmas book, 1845 ; an article " On Dress," for "The Opal," 1848, and edited "The Thought Blossom," a memorial volume, as late as 1854. " The Torn Hat " was contributed to " The Youth's Keepsake " for 1829, and "Contemplation " was written in 1828 to accompany an engraving in " Remember Me," a religious Annual published in Philadelphia. But he had no very high opinion of the class of literature that they cultivated, and spoke of them as " yearly flotillas of trash."

In the spring of 1829 he entered upon his first serious venture as a journalist, by starting the " American Monthly Magazine," which ran two years and a half — from April, 1829, to August, 1831. Mr. Thomas Gold Appleton describes Willis's undertaking as " a slim monthly, written chiefly by himself, but with the true magazine flavor." Appleton and his friend Motley, then students in Harvard, were both contributors. For a young *littérateur*, only a year and a half out of college, without capital, without backing, almost without experience, the establishment of a monthly magazine was certainly an enterprise of some boldness. His expectations, however, were modest enough, and his preliminary card, " To the Public," casts some light on the conditions of literary journalism at that time. He says that he cannot pay much for contributions, like the English magazines which he took for his model. " The difficulties of transmission over such an immense country and the comparatively small proportion of literary readers limit our circulation to a thousand or two, at the farthest." He had, moreover, " the ebb of a boyish reputation " against him. Notwithstanding he launched upon his voyage with excellent pluck and vigor. He conducted his magazine with little assistance, writing himself from thirty to forty pages of printed matter every month in the shape of tales, poems, essays, book reviews, and sketches of life and travel. Boston was not yet the Boston of Emerson, Longfellow, Lowell, and Holmes, but it had already as fair a claim to the title of literary metropolis as New York. Everett and Channing were great names. Dana, Pierpont, and Sprague were among its poets. These men were not available for Willis's purposes, but he rallied to his support a number of younger men, such as Richard Hildreth, the historian, George Lunt, the poet, Park Benjamin, Isaac McLellan, the Rev. George B. Cheever, Albert Pike,

afterwards the Arkansas poet and fire-eater,
and Rufus Dawes, — then a budding genius,
subsequently a preacher of erratic doctrines, —
J. O. Rockwell, Mrs. Sigourney, and others
whose names have fallen silent. Next to the
editor's own graceful work, the most notable
things given to the public through the columns
of the " American Monthly " were Pike's
" Hymns to the Gods," poems of a richly classical inspiration, which have often provoked
comparison with Keats's odes; and which, if
their workmanship were equal to their imaginative fervor, would justify the comparison.

Willis led off in the opening number with
a carefully written, but not very characteristic,
essay on " Unwritten Music." It was thought
monstrous fine by his friends, but suggests, it
must be confessed, that dreariest product of the
human mind, — a prize composition. As a
study of the harmonies of nature, it was much
too general in its reflections and descriptions to
please a modern taste, wonted to the sharp and
full detail of Thoreau and his successors. The
editorial articles, prose and verse, in the " American Monthly " were too many to be mentioned
here individually. There were stories, " The
Fancy Ball," " The Elopement," " P. Calamus,
Esq.," and others which their author never recognized so far as to give them any place in his

collected writings. Others, as " Baron von Raff-loff," " Captain Thompson," " Incidents in the Life of a Quiet Man," etc., were the rough drafts of later tales, such as " Pedlar Karl," "Larks in Vacation," and " Scenes of Fear." " Albina M'Lush " was the best of these. " The Death of the Gentle Usher " contained an elo-quent passage on the night heavens, which ob-tained a better setting in " Edith Linsey." " An Inkling of Adventure " lent its name and noth-ing else to the first published collection of Wil-lis's " Slingsby " stories. Then there were sketches of travel in New York State and Can-ada, partly reminiscences of senior vacation and partly memorials of holidays from the editorial desk, spent at Saratoga, Lebanon Springs, or elsewhere: " Notes upon a Ramble," " Letters of Horace Fritz, Esq.," and " Pencillings by the Way," — a title afterward used to better advan-tage. Parts of these were similarly refurbished for later employment. The secret of that skill-ful blending of gayety and sentiment, the quick, light transitions, which make much of the charm of Willis's best stories and sketches, like " F. Smith," or " Pasquali," he had not yet learned. In these earlier efforts the serious parts drag and the humorous parts are flashy and thin. Be-sides the monthly " table " there were editorial articles of that rambling, chatty description pe-

culiar to the period, and which the " Noctes " had
done as much as anything to introduce : "Scrib-
blings," " The Scrap Book," " The Idle Man,"
" Tête-à-tête Confessions," etc., in which the editor takes the reader into his confidence and
his sanctum, makes him sit down in his red morocco *dormeuse*, reads him bits of verse from his
old scrap-books and his favorite authors, calls
attention to his japonica, his smoking pastille,
his scarlet South American trulian (a most familiar bird with Willis — he gets it in again in
" Lady Ravelgold "), and his two dogs Ugolino
and L. E. L., whose lair is in the rejected MSS.
basket.   He fosters an agreeable fiction that he
writes with a bottle of Rudesheimer and a plate
of olives at his elbow, and he says now and then
in a hospitable aside " Take another olive," or
"Pass the Johannisbergh"; this to his imaginary interlocutor, Cousin Florence, or Tom Las-
celles, or The Idle Man, an epicure and dandy,
" who eats in summer with an amber-handled
fork to keep his palm cool."

These amiable coxcombries of Willis gave
dire offense to the critics, and especially to Joseph T. Buckingham, the veteran of the Boston
press and editor of the " Courier," then the
most influential Whig newspaper in Massachusetts.   He published epigrams on Willis, with
very blunt points, administered fatherly rebukes

to him for his affected English, and objected
strongly to Ugolino, L. E. L., and the trulian.
Willis retorted in kind, and a good-natured war
raged between the " Courier " and the " American Monthly," though their editors were pri-
vately the best of friends. In his " Specimens
of Newspaper Literature," Buckingham paid a
glowing and, indeed, extravagant compliment to
the talents of his young adversary. Willis's experience in editing 'the " American Monthly "
was of great advantage to him. He had a natural instinct for journalism, and he soon acquired
by practice that personal, sympathetic attitude
toward his readers, and that ready adjustment
of himself to the public taste, which made him
the most popular magazinist of his day and de-
fined at once his success and his limitations.
For its purposes Willis's crisp prose was admirable: "delicate and brief like a white jacket,
— transparent like a lump of ice in champagne,
— soft-tempered like the sea-breeze at night."
It had an easy, conversational grace, the air of
" the town," the tone of good society. In his
review of Lady Morgan's "Book of the Boudoir," he made a plea for that *negligé* style
which he practiced so daintily himself. " We
love this rambling, familiar gossip. It is the
undress of the mind. There are few people
who possess the talent of graceful trifling, either

in writing or conversation. Study may make
anything but this. It is like *naïveté* in character, — nature let alone." There was a great
deal of good writing in Willis's "American
Monthly" articles; bright thoughts expressed
in exquisite English, here and there a page
which Charles Lamb or Leigh Hunt might have
been glad to claim. Some of these he rescued
from the old files of the magazine and inserted
in his later work. The chapter on "Minute
Philosophies," "A Morning in the Library,"
and "The Substance of a Diary of Sickness"
were used again in "Edith Linsey," and a spirited description of Nahant in one of the "tables" did duty in "F. Smith." But many a
nice bit was too small for resetting and remained
lost in the ephemeral context, — many such a
scrap as this little picture of summer in town:

"Was ever such intense, unmitigated sunshine?
There is nothing on the hard, opaque sky but a mere
rag of a cloud, like a handkerchief on a tablet of
blue marble, and the edge of the shadow of that tall
chimney is as definite as a hair, and the young elm
that leans over the fence is copied in perfect and mo-
tionless leaves like a very painting on the broad side-
walk."

The "New England Galaxy," which was also
under Buckingham's management, was edited
for a time by one William Joseph Snelling, who

made quite a stir in Boston newspaper circles.
He had been an under-officer in the army and
stationed somewhere in the Northwest, but came
to Boston about 1830 and devoted himself to
sensational journalism and in particular to a
crusade against gamblers. His life was threat-
ened for this, and he converted his office into a
sort of arsenal. In 1831 he published a slash-
ing lampoon, " Truth: a New Year's Gift for
Scribblers," in which he blackguarded American
writers in general and paid his respects to Willis as follows: —

> " Muse, shall we not a few brief lines afford
> To give poor Natty P. his meet reward ?
> What has he done to be despised by all
> Within whose hands his harmless scribblings fall ?
> Why, as in band-box trim he walks the streets,
> Turns up the nose of every man he meets,
> As if it scented carrion ?   Why of late
> Do all the critics claw his shallow pate ?
> True he 's a fool ; — if that 's a hanging thing,
> Let Prentice, Whittier, Mellen also swing."

Some of this delicate banter was exhumed and
quoted a few years later by Captain Marryat,
in the article in the " Metropolitan " which led
to the affair of honor between that warrior and
Willis. The latter answered Snelling " con-
temptuously but effectively," Goodrich reports,
" in some half dozen verses inserted in the 'Statesman,' and addressed to *Smelling* Joseph. The

lines stuck to poor Smelling for the remainder
of his life." The pasquinader himself afterwards went to New York and conducted a meat-
axe publication, "The Censor." Goodrich adds,
that he "fell into habits of dissipation, which
led from one degradation to another, till his
miserable career was ended," — a victim, no
doubt, to the angry muse. Willis also contrived
to offend Mrs. Lydia Maria Child by a satirical
review of her "Frugal Housewife" and by harp-
ing on a sentence from that authority, "hard
ginger-bread is nice." She took this very much
to heart, and when she afterwards had charge
of the literary department of the "Traveller"
showed an abiding hostility toward her whilom
critic. He early attained to the dignity of parody. "The Annoyer" was travestied in the
"Amateur" and a humorous imitation of "Albina
M'Lush" was also printed. Mere literary criticism, however unfair, need not greatly disturb
any one. But Willis was subjected, in Boston,
to personalities of a very annoying character.
He was constantly in receipt of anonymous letters calling him a puppy, a rake, etc. He was
attacked in the newspapers for his frivolity, his
dandyism, and his conceit. Private scandal,
circulated by word of mouth, concerning his
debts and his alleged immoralities, sometimes
got into print. It would not be easy to explain

why so kind a man as Willis, one always so
eager to oblige and so prone to say good-natured
things about everybody, should have excited so
much wrath, not only at this time, but all
through his life, by his harmless literary fopper-
ies and foibles, did we not remember that he
was successful, that he was a favorite in society,
and, above all, that he wore conspicuously good
clothes. There was also something about his
airy way of writing and the personality it suggested that was and is peculiarly exasperating
to a certain class of serious-minded people who
resent all attempts to entertain them on the part
of any one whom they cannot entirely respect.
Willis carried it off lightly enough, though, of
course, it must have stung him. He knew, he
said, "how easy it is to despise the ungentle-
manly critic and forget the poor wrong of his
criticism."

In intervals of work on the "American Monthly" he contributed frequently to the "Boston
Statesman," having been engaged, together with
Lunt and Dawes, to write something for it every
week, "short or long, prose or verse," at the
rate of five dollars an article, an arrangement
that lasted for some months. This seems now
beggarly pay, but Nathaniel Greene of the
"Statesman" was, according to Willis, the only
editor in the country who, as early as 1827, paid

anything at all for verse. During these early
years of journalistic life Willis sojourned awhile
in the pleasant land of Bohemia. He was a
member of a supper club, which included two
representatives of each profession. Washington
Allston and Chester Harding were the artists;
Willis and Dawes the men of letters; Horace
Mann and five or six more completed the tale.
Willis was a frequent lounger in Harding's studio, and some years after he was delighted to
come across his tracks at Gordon and Dalhousie
castles, where Harding was known. Willis was
fond of fast horses, and used to drive his friends
out to Nahant, for a spin on the hard beach
along the edge of the surf. This was the scene
of "F. Smith," one of his most perfect and
characteristic stories. With Dawes and others
he resorted, not seldom, for a game supper, to
an ancient and once somewhat stately hostelry,
known as the "Stackpole House," where the
wines were excellent and the landlord good-hu-
mored and disposed to trust, — the original,
doubtless, of Gallagher in " The Female Ward,"
a story written long afterwards, but whose incidents and descriptions are assignable to this
period.

Willis's position in Boston was in some respects a difficult one. His family connection
were plain, good folks, not " in society," — not,

at least, in the literary society, which was Unitarian, or in the so-called aristocratic society,
which was mainly either Unitarian or Episco-
palian. He himself was socially ambitious, and
these were the circles which he wished to frequent. "The pale of Unitarianism," he wrote,
"is the limit of gentility." He was a great favorite with Mrs. Harrison Gray Otis, the "lady
autocrat" and leader of the *ton* in the Puritan
capital for many years. He was constantly at
her house when she was in town, and was invited
to be one of her party when she went to Saratoga in the summer. Nor was this a passing
fancy with Mrs. Otis, but stood the test of time
and separation. She made him a long visit at
Idlewild during the latter years of his life. But
the Park Street Church people, among whom he
had been brought up, looked askance upon his
fashionable associations. The old stories of his
college dissipations were revived, while rumors
of his Boston irregularities reached the ears of
his New Haven acquaintances. Willis himself
took no notice of these slanders, but they were
warmly resented by his friends. His brother-in-
law, Joseph Jenkins, wrote to Mr. D. W. Whit-
ing of New Haven: "Nat is a good fellow. He
is not dissipated in any way; nor traveling the
Tartarean turnpike, as the good New Haven people suppose. He is attending to his magazine,

and doing his duty as well as any of us."
Though Willis did not make the impression of
a man of very scrupulous morality, he was certainly not given to any serious dissipations. It
was not in his temperament to run into physical
excesses. His senses were delicate, and he always respected them. He never, for example,
used tobacco; he was never a hard drinker. In
youth he affected a moderate conviviality and
had an æsthetic liking for champagne. In middle age he was accustomed to mix a little spirit
with his water, expressing a horror for the pure
element, on the whimsical ground that it tasted
of sinners ever since the flood. In this Boston
period, his offenses were probably limited to
running up bills at livery stables and inns, with
a too sanguine expectation of being able to pay
them from the proceeds of his literary work.
Edward Beecher, who had been a tutor at Yale
during his college course, was at this time pastor
of the Park Street Church. Finding himself
unwilling to conform his life to the strict rules
of that society, Willis called on Mr. Beecher
and stated the manner of his supposed conversion in a revival at Andover, and the influences
that had induced him to join the church. He
said that he was sincere in the act, but was con-
vinced afterward that he was mistaken in his
conviction, and that he had not experienced the

change that qualified him for church member-
ship; and he requested Mr. Beecher to obtain
for him an honorable dismission. Mr. Beecher
sympathized with him in his feelings, and made
an effort to satisfy his request, but failed, as
the church then believed that there were but
three ways out of it, death, dismissal to another
church, or excommunication. Accordingly, at
a church meeting on April 29, 1829, in which
Mr. Beecher took no part, the following sentence
was passed : —

" Whereas certain charges have been made against
Brother N. P. Willis, which, in the opinion of this
church has been fully proved, namely : Absence from
the communion of this church and attendance at the
theatre as a spectator; and whereas he has neglected
to appear before the church to answer the said
charges, although duly notified ; and has not given to
the church satisfactory evidence of penitence, but has
evinced by a letter laid before the church an entirely
different state of feeling; therefore voted, That Mr.
Nathaniel P. Willis be, and he hereby is, in the name
and by the authority of the Lord Jesus Christ, ex-
communicated from this church."

Deacon Willis was naturally grieved by this
turn of affairs, although he acquiesced silently
in the church's decision. Theatre going, indeed,
was an offense against family, as well as church
discipline. Naturally, also, the object of this

significavit always afterwards thought and spoke with some bitterness of "the charity of a sect in religion." He never renounced definitely his Christian belief. He never became skeptical; was not at any time, in fact, a thinker on such themes and subject to the speculative doubts which beset the thinker. He remained through life easily impressible in his religious emotions. "Worldling as I am," he wrote many years after, "and hardly as I dare claim any virtue as a Christian, there is that within me which sin and folly never reached or tainted." But this ended his connection with organized Christianity, and he ceased for a long time to be a church-goer.

His position in Boston was also made painful by an unsuccessful love affair. He had paid court to Mary Benjamin, a woman of uncommon beauty of person and graces of mind and character, the sister of Park Benjamin and afterwards the wife of the historian Motley. She returned his feeling and the two were engaged to be married, but the engagement was broken through the determined opposition of the lady's guardian, Mr. Savage. Willis carried this thorn in his side for years, and it gave him many hours of bitter homesickness while abroad. In a letter written a few days after landing in England, in the summer of 1834, he said: —

"I loved Mary B., and never think of her without

emotion; but with all the world in France, Italy, and England treating me like a son or a brother, I am not coming home to fight my way to her through bitter relatives and slander and opposition. They nearly crushed me once, and I shall take care how they get another opportunity. Still, after three years' separation, I think I never loved any one so well, and if my way were not so hedged up, it would draw me home now."

To Mary Benjamin was addressed the lovely little poem, "To M——, from Abroad," with its motto from Metastasio, —

"L'alma, quel che non ha, sogna et figura."

By 1829 Willis had accumulated verses enough to fill another slender volume of "Fugitive Poetry." Of the forty-three pieces in this, the "Dedication Hymn," written to be sung at the consecration of the Hanover Street Church in Boston, has the best title to remembrance. It possesses a brief energy seldom attained by Willis. As late as 1856, his old English friend, Dr. William Beattie, wrote to him: "Your beautiful 'Hymn' was sung in one of our cathedral towns, at the consecration of a new church, by an overflowing congregation. Surely this is a fact worth noting. Miss Rogers was the first who told me of it, and often have I repeated 'The perfect world by Adam trod,' etc." "The An-

noyer" and "Saturday Afternoon" have been
already mentioned. "Contemplation"—

> "They are all up, the innumerable stars"—

had the feeling, though not the artistic touch, of
Tennyson's "St. Agnes," and came near to being
a fine poem.   There were five sonnets, one of
them — an acrostic to Emily Marshall — with a
good closing couplet, —

> "Life in thy presence were a thing to keep,
> Like a gay dreamer clinging to his sleep."

" A Portrait," also, which Willis did not repub-
lish, contained an effective passage, beginning

> "I go away like one who 's heard,
> In some fine scene, the prompter's word," etc.

There were two more scriptural pieces, and the
remainder of the book was of no importance.
Many of its contents were written before those
of the earlier volume of " Sketches."

The "American Monthly" proved a failure
financially, owing, doubtless, to a lack of the
right business management, for which Willis
had no faculty, and with which, in truth, he had
nothing to do.   At the close of the summer of
1831 the magazine suspended publication, and
its editor, shaking off the dust of his feet against
the New England metropolis, fled to more genial
climes.   He left behind him the squibs of his
brother journalists, the cackle of the tea-tables,

and some $3,000 of debts incurred through the failure of his enterprise. He never quite forgave Boston. In a letter to his mother from England, September 12, 1835, he wrote: —

" They have denied me patronage, abused me, misrepresented me, refused me both character and genius, and I feel that I owe them nothing. I have never suffered injustice except from my countrymen, and I have in every other land found kindness and favor. I would not write this for another human eye, but you know how unjustly I have been treated, and can understand the wound that rankles even in so light a heart as mine. The mines of Golconda would not tempt me to return and live in Boston."

The " New York Mirror " of September 10, 1831, contained the following item: " We take much pleasure in announcing to our readers that the ' American Monthly Magazine ' has been united to the ' New York Mirror,' and that Nathaniel P. Willis, Esq., will, from this period, be an associate editor of the joint establishment." This announcement was followed in the next week's issue by " A Card to the Public," in which the new editor promises that, " having transferred the only literary undertaking in which he has any interest to the proprietor of the ' Mirror,' his whole time and attention will hereafter be given to this work." The " Mirrors " of September 10th and 17th published, furthermore, two letters from Saratoga, written by Willis in August, and containing some characteristic verses, "The String that tied my Lady's Shoe," and " To ——," —

> " 'T is midnight deep : I came but now
> From the bright air of lighted halls ; "

as also a " Pencilling by the Way," descriptive of Providence and Brown University, where he had just been delivering a Commencement poem. On September 25th the editorial page for the first time bore the heading, " Edited by George P. Morris, Theodore S. Fay, and Nathaniel P. Willis."

The journal with which he had now connected himself — and with whose successors, under different names, he continued to be identified until his death, thirty-six years later — was a weekly paper, published on Saturdays, and "devoted to literature and the fine arts." It had been founded in 1823 by Samuel Woodworth, author of " The Old Oaken Bucket," and General George P. Morris, but Woodworth had withdrawn some time before Willis joined it. Morris, with whom Willis now began a business partnership that lasted, with slight interruptions, for the rest of their lives, and a personal friendship almost romantic in its tenderness and fidelity, was the most popular song writer of his

generation in America, — a sort of cis-Atlantic
Tom Moore, whose songs, adapted to the piano,
were on all the music-racks in the land. "Near
the Lake where droops the Willow" was a universal favorite in the days of gem-book min,
strelsy. "My Mother's Bible" was dear to the
great heart of the people, and the air of "Woodman, spare that Tree" was heard by wandering
Americans ground out from every hurdy-gurdy
in the London streets. Unless a clever letter
in the "Mirror" of March 2, 1839, is wholly a
hoax, this last-mentioned song compared in popularity with "Home Sweet Home," having suffered
translation into French ("Bûcheron, épargne mon
arbre"), German ("Haue nicht die alte Eiche
nieder"), Spanish, Portuguese, and Dutch; the
German version being even introduced by an
essay, "Ueber Morris's Entwickelung, Denken
und Wirken." "The Amaranth" for 1840, an
annual, edited by Nathaniel Brooks and dedicated to Morris, contains Greek and Latin renderings of his "Woodman," as well as of Wilde's
almost equally familiar and far better lyric, "My
Life is like the Summer Rose." Morris was a
bustling, affable little man, with a shrewd, practical side to him. He was a good business manager, and as Willis had no talent in that kind, the
association was mutually advantageous. Morris's
intellectual stature was not great, and Willis,

who loved the man, was unable to admire the poet. He praised his songs in print, but there was more of friendship than critical sincerity in his praise. He had been in correspondence with Morris before, and had contributed occasionally to the "Mirror," having sent it a poem in competition for a twenty-dollar prize when he was still in college. He now began to decant into its columns a number of his "American Monthly" articles, a circumstance which not only shows how local the circulation of the latter must have been, but sheds a curious light on the methods of journalism at that epoch. The old "New York Mirror" had a reputation for brightness in its time and a circulation then considered large, but as compared with the great magazines of to-day it seems a very primitive affair, with its "Original Essays," its "Popular Moral Tales," "Desultory Selections," and "Extracts from an Unpublished Tragedy," its poems "For the ' Mirror,' " by Isidora and Iolanthe, and its solemn "Answers to Correspondents." Now and then there is a contribution of more pronounced individuality, a poem by Halleck, a story by Paulding or Fay. Theodore S. Fay, the other editor, was a man of parts. He was the author of several once popular novels, "The Countess Ida" and "Hoboken," *tendenz* romances against dueling, "Ulric," a poetical romance, and "Nor-

man Leslie," which was afterwards dramatized,
and was founded on a famous murder trial in
which Burr and Hamilton had figured as counsel. Fay contributed to the " Mirror " satirical
letters on New York society, " The Little Genius,"
and in 1832 published a volume of his " Mirror "
articles under the title of " Dreams and Reveries
of a Quiet Man." In 1833 he went abroad, and
his letters from Europe, " The Minute Book,"
appeared in the paper side by side with Willis's
"Pencillings." He was appointed secretary of
legation at Berlin in 1837, and minister resident
at Berne in 1853. His novels have now gone
quite out of sight, but many of his short tales
are really very clever, — written in a rattling
style, with abrupt, jerky dialogues, — and may
be read even now without much effort. Another
name connected with the " Mirror " was that of
William Cox, an English printer employed upon
the paper, whose " Crayon Sketches by an Amateur," published in 1833, were highly commended
by Willis. He, too, was abroad during Willis's
and Fay's sojourn in Europe, and wrote letters
from England to the " Mirror," whose foreign
correspondence was thus uncommonly varied.
The first thought of sending Willis abroad occurred while the three editors were supping
together at Sandy Welsh's oyster saloon. Long
and earnestly they revolved the question of ways

and means.   At length $500 were scraped to-
gether as *viaticum*, and it was agreed that Willis was to write weekly letters at ten dollars the
letter.   The investment proved a good one both
for the " Mirror " and for its traveling editor.
With this slender capital in his pocket he em-
barked at Philadelphia October 10th, the only
passenger on the merchant brig Pacific, bound
for Havre.   He was young, sanguine, eager to
see life, but in his most hopeful mood he could
hardly have foreseen the dazzling experiences of
his next four years, or the far-reaching consequences which the trip thus lightly undertaken
were to have for him.

Before sailing he had found time to visit Philadelphia, Baltimore, Washington, and Mount
Vernon, and make a " Pencilling " of them for
the " Mirror."   Another letter gave his impressions of New York, now become his American
address.   He had also put to press the poem delivered before the " Society of United Brothers,"
at Brown University, on September 6th, the day
before Commencement, together with a few other
pieces written since 1829.   The dedication was
" To one of whom, in this moment of departure
for a foreign land, I think sadly and only — to
my mother."   The name-poem was one of those
conventional performances with which unlucky
recipients of invitations to " speak a piece " be-

fore Phi Beta Kappas, United Brothers, or other
such academic bodies, are wont to dazzle the
young alumni. It was in blank verse, of course,
and dealt with the usual commonplaces about
ambition, content, the beauty of human love, and
the folly of skepticism and contempt. It showed
more maturity than the poem delivered before
his own Alma Mater four years before, but it
was much the same sort of thing. Of the remaining contents of the book two were Scripture
sketches and four were of a more ambitious description than Willis had previously attempted.
These were " Parrhasius," " The Dying Alche-
mist," " The Scholar of Thebet Ben Chorat," and
" The Wife's Appeal " to her husband to " awake
to fame." The theme of all these and the cen-
tral thought of this whole volume is the vanity
of an inordinate thirst for knowledge, power, or
fame. " Parrhasius," the story of an old Olyn-
thian captive who was tortured to death by the
Athenian painter that he might catch the expression of his last agony for his picture of
Prometheus, comes the nearest to success. Willis had read the tale in Burton's " Anatomy of
Melancholy." " The Scholar of Thebet Ben
Chorat " was the story of a young Bedouin who
grew mad and died from too close application to
astrology, on which science Willis seems to have
crammed up for the nonce, if one may judge

from the profusion of his foot-notes. But in truth these poems were little better than wax-work. The sweet and natural lines, " To a City Pigeon," were worth all the rest of the book.

CHAPTER IV.

1831–1834.

LIFE ABROAD.

WHATEVER may have been the effect of Willis's career in Europe upon his character, its influence on his literary fortunes was most propitious. Foreign travel furnished just the stimulus that he wanted. As a writer he was at all times very dependent on his supplies. If they were fresh and abundant his writing was correspondingly so; if life stagnated with him his writing wore thin. Place is comparatively indifferent to men of deep or intense genius, to a philosopher like Emerson or a brooding idealist like Hawthorne. They strike root anywhere, and it is no great matter from what corner they look forth upon the world. The life of the soul, the life of nature, the problems of the conscience, may be studied in Concord or Salem as well as anywhere else. A profound insight, a subtle imagination will interpret the humblest environment into philosophy and poetry. And yet even these are not quite free of their surroundings. To all but sworn Emersonians " English Traits " is probably the most intelligible and satisfactory of Emerson's writings. " The Marble Faun " is not Hawthorne's greatest romance, but there is a richness about it, a *body*, that comes simply from its material, and is not to be found in " The Scarlet Letter " or " The House of the Seven Gables."

As for Willis, his genius, such as it was, was frankly external. His bright fancy played over the surface of things. His curiosity and his senses demanded gratification. He needed stir, change, adventure. He was always turning his own experiences to account, and the more crowded his life was with impressions from outside, the more vivid his page. He had the artist's craving for luxury, and was fond of quoting a saying of Godwin : " A judicious and limited voluptuousness is necessary to the cultivation of the mind, to the polishing of the manners, to the refining of the sentiment, and to the development of the understanding." This taste for the sumptuous had been starved in Willis at home. Not only were literature and society in America far more provincial then than now, but life was plainer in every way. The rapid growth of wealth has obliterated the most striking contrasts between cities like New York and Boston,

on the one hand, and cities like London and
Paris, on the other. In every foreign capital
nowadays one finds his simple republican com-
patriots grumbling at the absence of American
conveniences, cursing the steamboats, the railway carriages, the hotels, the luggage system,
the portable baths and bed-room candles, and
proclaiming loudly that the Americans are the
most luxurious people on the face of the earth.
In Europe, and especially in England, circumstances threw Willis into a new world. He
shared for a time in the life of the titled aristocracy and the idle rich, and he took to it like one
to the manner born. He was at home at once
amid all that gay ease and leisure. The London clubs, the parks, the great country houses,
Almack's and the Row, the beautiful haughty
women, the grace, indolence, and refinement,
hereditary for generations, seemed no more than
the birthright of this New England printer's
son, from which some envious fairy had hitherto
shut him out.

"I have now and then a fit of low spirits," he says,
in a letter from Marseilles, April 28, 1832, "though
generally the excessive excitement of new scenes and
constant interest occupies me quite. It is like an in-
toxication to travel in Europe. I feel no annoyance,
grumble at no imposition, am never out of temper.
Fatigue is the only thing that bears me down. I

want leisure and money. I shall come back, I think,
to America after my engagement with Morris is over,
and marry and come out again. As to settling down
for these ten years, I cannot think of it without a
sickness at my heart. I wish to heaven I could keep
a journal and publish after I got home. This writing and sending off unrevised is the worst thing in
the world for one's reputation. However, I see a
world of things that I cannot put into letters, and I
feel every day that my mind is ripening and laying
up material which I could get nowhere else. You
can have no idea of the stirring, vivid habit one's
mind gets into abroad. Living at home forever would
never be of half the use to me."

Willis arrived at Havre November 3d, and
went on by diligence to Paris, where he spent
between five and six months. He had taken out
with him a number of good letters, some from
Martin Van Buren among the rest. The American colony in Paris was then small and select.
It was under the wing of Lafayette, who was
very polite to Willis during his stay. Cooper
was there and his *protégé*, Horatio Greenough,
the sculptor, who had come from Florence to
execute a bust of Lafayette. Morse, the artist,
too, who, on his return trip to America in a
Havre packet, in the year following, was to hit
upon his invention of the electric telegraph.
And lastly, Willis's fellow-townsman, Dr. Howe,

then a zealous young philanthropist, who had won much glory by his recent campaign in Greece, and was now attending medical lectures at the French capital. Willis took lodgings with Howe until the latter, having been appointed president of the American committee for the relief of the Poles, went off on his dangerous mission of distributing supplies among the insurgent bands in Polish Prussia, an enterprise which ended in his capture and confinement for six weeks in a Prussian prison. All these gentlemen Willis had the good fortune to meet in familiar and cordial intercourse. Cooper asked him to breakfast with Morse and Howe, and walked and talked with him in the gardens of the Tuileries. The acquaintance thus pleasantly begun between the two authors was afterwards renewed at home, though, from accidents of geography, they never became really intimate.

Willis also made desirable acquaintances among the foreigners resident in Paris. Morse took him to call upon Sir John Bowring, editor of the " Westminster Review," the translator of much of the national poetry of the Russians and Hungarians, and afterwards the English governor of Hong Kong at the time of the Opium War. He made acquaintance, too, with Spurzheim, the phrenologist, who took a cast of his head ; with General Bertrand, who had been with

Napoleon at St. Helena; and with the Countess
Guiccioli, who presented him with a sonnet by
herself, and an autograph note from Shelley.
The glamour of " Childe Harold's Pilgrimage "
was still over Europe, and everywhere the American traveler looked eagerly for his footprints.
Mr. Rives, the minister of the United States at
Paris, was very attentive to his young countryman, and presented him to the king, with two
other American gentlemen, Mr. Ritchie and Mr.
Carr.   The latter was American consul at Tangiers.   He took a great liking to Willis, made
him a number of presents, and offered to appoint
him his secretary, and take him to Morocco.
This offer Willis was at first inclined to accept.
It was a tempting one in many particulars, and
in a birthday letter to his mother, January 20,
1832, he thus explained its advantages : —

" Mr. Carr takes me into his family and pays all
my expenses.   We go to the old palaces of the Aben-
cerrages, perhaps the most romantic country in history, and one very little written about, and it will
double the value of my journey to Morris at the same
time that it secures me from any reverse of fortune.
He means to spend his summers in Spain, which is
right opposite Tangiers at two hours' sail, and next
fall he will run down to Italy and the Sicilies, thus
giving me every opportunity I want.   I have letters
from Lord James Hay to his brother-in-law, the gov-

ernor of Gibraltar, and one from Lord Fife to the
governor of the Ionian Islands."

Why he did not embrace this golden chance
remains uncertain, though he hints at a possible
difficulty in the fact that his friend, the consul,
was a notorious duelist, who had shot seven or
eight men and had a very pretty wife. However, before he left Paris, Mr. Rives attached
him to his own embassy, a courtesy which proved
of the greatest service to him. It entitled him
to wear the uniform of a secretary of legation,
and the diplomatic button gave him the *entrée*
to the court circles of every country he visited.

Willis saw Paris at an interesting moment.
The Polish revolution had just failed, and the
city swarmed with refugees. Louis Philippe
was already growing unpopular, and there were
continual small *émeutes* on the Boulevard Mont-
martre, at the Porte Saint Denis, and in other
quarters, led by Polytechnic students and put
down without much trouble by the troops. It
was a cholera year and people were dying by the
hundreds daily. Meanwhile the gay world went
on much as ever. Carnival was kept with the
usual elaborate follies. There were masked balls
at the palace. Malibran and Taglioni were on
the stage. Paris, with its novelties and splendors, exercised the same fascination over Willis
that it exercises proverbially over his compa-

8

triots. He was never tired of promenading and sight-seeing. His lodgings were in the Rue Rivoli, facing the Tuileries. Sismondi, the historian, had the apartment under him. In a private letter he thus describes his daily occupations : —

"I have bought a coffee maker and cups, and a loaf of sugar and a pan, etc., etc., and my hostess's daughter, Christine, brings me my bread and butter, and I breakfast gloriously alone, the doctor (Howe) being always at the hospitals in the morning. I breakfast and write all along the forenoon till twelve, and then see sights and hear lectures till dark, dine at five or six, and either go to some party in the evening, or stay at home and study with Zelie."

He had no fear of the cholera and firmly believed that it was not contagious. He was advised that good living, frequent bathing, a cheerful frame of mind, and regular habits were the best preventives. He even went boldly through the cholera wards of the Hôtel Dieu, and sent a harrowing description of them to the " Mirror." But towards spring the pestilence gained more and more. The theatres were shut, all gayeties suspended, and thousands fled the city daily. The upper classes, who had thus far escaped, began to be attacked. The streets were almost deserted, people went about holding camphor bags to their nostrils, and the panic became universal. Finally, toward the middle of April, while dancing at a party, Willis was seized with violent pains in the stomach, vomiting, and chills. He ran out of the room to an apothecary's, swallowed thirty drops of laudanum, took a carriage home, and a prescription of camphor and ether, and went to bed. These instant remedies, he had no doubt, were all that saved him, and on April 16th he started for Italy.

It is unnecessary for the biographer to follow him step by step in his saunterings through Europe. These are fully recorded in his letters to the " Mirror," which covered a period of four years, the first appearing in the issue of February 13, 1832, and the last on January 14, 1836. He began them on the voyage out, as soon as he had recovered from his first seasickness, and he continued them until about six months before his return home. The title " Pencillings by the Way," he had used before, but he retained it and added the sub-caption, " First Impressions of Europe." Both described well the character of these letters, which were written hastily, often on the wing, and sent off in many cases without revision, to catch the next packet for America ; in which, moreover, the writer aimed to " record impressions, not statistics." There were one hundred and thirty-nine of them in all, and they were designed to appear weekly so far as pos-

sible. But by reason of irregular postal facilities, they averaged less than one a fortnight,
and sometimes a month or more elapsed between
two of them. They were read with eagerness
in America, and Morris asserted that they were
copied into five hundred newspapers. Their
popularity is explained in part by the fact that
Europe was much farther off from us in those
days than it is now. The voyage by sailing-ves-
sel was tedious, and few Americans went abroad
for pleasure. Willis, to be sure, professed himself astonished by the numbers of his countrymen whom he met in Italy and elsewhere, but
these were but a handful compared with the annual horde of tourists who rush back and forth
in the steamers, and do Great Britain and the
continent in three months. It is also true that
the literature of travel was not then so abundant.
The time has gone by for first impressions of
countries. The reader now demands a more
minute and authoritative study of some single
corner of the map. Yet this does not serve to
account altogether for Willis's success in his
" Pencillings." There were already plenty of
books by American travelers in Europe, such as
they were, which have long been obsolete. Who
ever hears nowadays of James's " Travels," for
instance, published in 1820; or of Austin's "Letters from London," 1804 ; or of " A Journal of

a Tour in Italy by an American," 1824; to say
nothing of innumerable " Americans in Paris,"
and " Americans in London," of later dates ?
The truth is that Willis's rapid sketches were
capital writing of their kind, and the work of a
born " foreign correspondent." He was a quick
and sympathetic, though not a subtle observer,
had an eye for effect, and a journalist's instinct
for seizing the characteristic features of a scene
and leaving out the lumber. Few of his letters
are in the least guide-bookish. His raptures in
stated places for admiration, such as galleries,
palaces, and cathedrals, are sometimes conventional, and doubtless his passing judgments on
famous works of art are often either at second
hand or incorrect. His education had not prepared him to pronounce on these, and he had
not the patience to cultivate a critical appreciation of them. But in the crowd and out of
doors — whither he gladly escapes — he is always
happy, and there are many pictures, scattered
here and there through these excellent letters,
which for sharpness of line and brightness of
color have not been excelled either by Hawthorne, in his " Note-Books," or by Bayard Taylor, in his numerous views, afoot or otherwise, or
by Henry James, in his more penetrating and
far more carefully finished studies.

Willis did not sit down in Europe, like Long-

fellow, and become the interpreter to the New
World of the Old World's romantic past.   He
was never much of a scholar.   The literature
and legends of the countries he traveled had little to give him, though he possessed just enough
of the historic imagination for the proper equipment of a picturesque tourist.   In general it was
the present that interested him : all this stirring
modern life, the strange manners and dresses,
the changing landscapes, the gay throngs in the
streets, the pretty women and notable men at
the drive or the ball.   Nor was his attitude that
of criticism, but rather of intense personal enjoyment.   He had gone out ready to be pleased,
and he was pleased.   He gave, in consequence,
a somewhat rose-colored view of Europe to his
readers at home.   Not that the disagreeable
side escaped his notice, but he was having his
holiday and he gave a holiday account of it, and
his engaging egotism lent a personal interest to
his descriptions.   The " Edinburgh Review,"
in a just but rather heavy notice of " Pencillings," complained of the scantiness of useful information in them.   Useful information was a
thing which Willis eschewed.   He took small
interest in politics, public institutions, industrial
conditions, etc. ; and he knew that they would
bore nine out of ten among his readers.   He
lumped them jauntily under the head of " sta-

tistics," referred the anxious inquirer concerning
them to the cyclopædias, acknowledged with delightful candor that he himself was an ornamental person, and went on with his sketches of
people and places. Yet "Pencillings by the
Way" was a book which so solid a man as Daniel Webster carried with him on a journey, and
which, says his biographer, "he read attentively
and praised. He said the letters were both instructive and amusing and evinced great talents
on the part of the author." They inspired the
young Bayard Taylor with his first longing to
travel. Thousands of Americans have taken
their impressions of Europe from them; and in
spite of all that has since been written by more
leisurely and better instructed observers, they
retain their freshness wonderfully, and present
to the reader of to-day vivid glimpses of the outside of European life, at a time when steam had
not yet made the byways of all countries acces-
sible.

Willis spent the summer and autumn of
1832 in the north of Italy, making Florence
his headquarters. Dr. Bowring had given him
in Paris a letter to Count Porro at Marseilles.
The latter had been with Byron in Greece,
where Count Gamba, the Guiccioli's brother,
was of his corps and served under him. He
gave Willis letters to "half the rank of Italy:"

among others, to the Marquis Borromeo, who owned the " Isola Bella " in Lake Maggiore. Porro assured Willis that Borromeo would give him the use of one of his palazzos, " as he has five or six and is happy when people he knows occupy his servants." The nominal position of *attaché* to the American legation at Paris obtained for him a private presentation to the Grand Duke of Tuscany, and an invitation to the ducal balls and the receptions at the Casino, both of which were given weekly. The Florentines did not entertain much at their houses, but the foreign residents did, and especially the English. Willis was dined by Jerome Bonaparte, the ex-King of Westphalia, who was living at the Tuscan capital with the title of Prince Montfort, and giving very exclusive parties. He resorted to the Saturday *soirées* of Prince Poniatowski, who professed love for Americans, and whose august name was afterwards borne by the favorite pony of the Willis children at Idlewild. In short, he was freely admitted to Florentine society and took part in its fashionable intrigues and dissipations. He secured lodgings in Florence in the same palazzo with Greenough, in the apartment just vacated by Cole, the American landscape painter. Through Greenough he saw a great deal of artist life in Italy. At Rome Green-

ough subsequently introduced him to Gibson,
the English sculptor, who presented him with a
cast of his bas-relief, Cupid and Psyche. Under the guidance of the two, Willis amused
himself by trying his hand, in an amateurish
fashion, at moulding in clay. He was flattered
by their assurances that he had a good touch,
and felt half inclined, for a moment, to exchange his dilettantish pursuit of letters for an
equally dilettantish pursuit of art. His dreams
of the possibilities of such a career took shape
long after in the novel of " Paul Fane." Greenough had moulded a bust of Willis at Florence,
and some years after he cut it in marble and
gave it to him. There is a story about this
which is authentic, and too pretty to leave untold. Mr. Joseph Grinnell of New Bedford
happened to be in Florence in the spring of
1830 and had employed Greenough to make
him a statue of his niece Cornelia, — then a
child of five years, — who became in time Willis's second wife. It was from a remnant of
the same block used for her statue that the
sculptor, unconscious of the omen, afterwards
carved the bust of her future husband. The
two fragments thus strangely reunited stand
now in the same drawing-room, the head of
the youthful poet, with its Hyperion curls,
and the full-length figure of the demure little

Quaker maiden, holding in one hand a drinking-cup and in the other a bird. From this portrait-bust of Willis is taken the engraving by Halpin in the illustrated edition of Willis's poems published by Clark, Austin & Smith, 1859. It was a fair likeness, but somewhat heavy and unideal. Its original had grown quite fat abroad. His inherited tendency to *embonpoint* was counteracted in later life by the emaciation of long illness. Even as a young man his height gave him a look of slenderness, though his face was full. The "Autocrat," apropos of dandies whose jaws could not fill out their collars, affirms that "Willis touched this last point in one of his earlier ambrotypes."

August found him at the Baths of Lucca, "The Saratoga of Italy," flirting, and recuperating from the exhausting effects of an Italian summer. In a private letter dated on the 20th, he announces his intention of starting for England to-morrow by way of Switzerland and the Rhine, returning to Italy in a few months in time for the Roman season.

"In London I mean to make arrangements with the magazines, and then live abroad altogether. It costs so little here and one lives so luxuriously too, and there is so much to fill one's mind and eye, that I think of returning to naked America with daily increasing repugnance. I love my country, but the *ornamental* is my vocation, and of this she has none. I shall pass the next summer, perhaps, in Germany at a university, and I mean to learn German thoroughly. You would be astonished at the facility of learning a language *in the country.* I speak French well and Italian passably, and you know how little I knew and how short a time I have been abroad."

This programme was altered for some reason. Instead of starting for England, he made a second visit to Venice, then returned to Florence, and when the autumn was far enough advanced to make it safe went on to Rome. In the letter just quoted he mentions that he has made the acquaintance of a young Mr. Noel, a cousin of Byron.

The winter of 1832–33 and the spring of 1833 were spent between Florence, Rome, and Naples.

Wherever he traveled he made friends. He was not without a title to his secretary's button, for his whole progress through Europe was a ticklish feat of diplomacy. Few of the people whom he met in society suspected what thin ice he was skating on, or dreamed for an instant that the dashing young *attaché* was dependent for his bread and butter on weekly letters to a newspaper. The failure of remittances from Morris sometimes put him in an awkward predicament, but he always managed to find a way out. In one of the letters which he made it a religion to write his mother on each recurring birthday — this one dated at Florence, January 20, 1833 — he relates some of his experiences of the kind: —

" I have dined with a prince one day and alone for a shilling in a cook-shop the next. I have twice been entirely destitute of money in places where I had not an acquaintance, and the instant before the last coin was out of my pocket, chances too improbable for a dream have provided for me. One was at Marseilles. I had relied on receiving a letter of credit when I got there. I was disappointed and was at the hotel a week, wondering whether I should find fate working its usual miracle for me. I had only two francs remaining, when a gentlemanly man, who had commenced conversation with me at table, asked me to his room and ended with offering me a seat in his carriage to Nice. The quarantine drove him back, but he had brought me two hundred miles on my route, and knowing my disappointment by my inquiries at the post office, he offered me the use of his banker to any amount and took drafts for the money on my partner in New York. This now is a thing that does not occur once in a century. I have corresponded with Doyne (that was his name) ever since. I find that he is a *religious man*, and from one of the first families in Dublin."

With all his taste for luxury, Willis knew how to make economies, and living was much cheaper then. He never affected a mystery, and in one

of his letters to the "Mirror" he explained
how it was that he could live in Florence on
three hundred dollars a year "exclusive of post-
age and pleasure," paying four dollars a month
for his apartment and attendance, breakfasting
for six cents, and dining "quite magnificently"
for twenty-five. Meanwhile a deal of gossip
about him was in circulation in America, and
the editor of the "Mirror" had to contradict,
inter alia, a rumor that his foreign collaborator
had married the widow of a British nobleman
and was faring sumptuously in Rome.

Having been invited by the officers of the
frigate United States to join them in a six
months' cruise up the Mediterranean, he repaired to Leghorn, from which port the United
States, with her consort the Constellation, set
sail on the 3d of June, 1833. Commodore
Patterson of Baltimore commanded the former
ship and Captain Reed of Philadelphia the latter. Both gentlemen were accompanied by their
wives and the commodore by his three beautiful daughters. These were all old friends of
Willis, and he had made acquaintance with the
other officers of the squadron in Italy. He
could not have seen the East under pleasanter
auspices, and the next half year was the richest
in literary fruit of his entire sojourn upon the
continent. The squadron loitered along like a

pair of pleasure yachts, touching at all the
more interesting ports. The bright shores of
the Mediterranean and the Levant passed in a
magic panorama before the eyes of the passengers, who sailed and danced and ate the lotus
day after day. Elba, Naples, and Sicily; Trieste
and Vienna; the Ionian Islands, Greece, and the
shores of the Dardanelles were visited in turn,
and at length in October the frigate dropped
anchor in the Golden Horn. Willis's "Pencillings" of Constantinople are among the best in
his portfolio, among the best, indeed, that have
ever been made of the surface of Oriental life.
Italy was hackneyed : the Rialto and Saint
Mark's, the Coliseum and the Vatican, Pompeii
and the Bay of Naples, had been described a
thousand times. But here he was off the track
of common tourists. His nature reveled in the
barbaric riches of the East and cheerfully
blinked the discomforts and the dirt. The mysteries of the seraglio and the slave market and
the veiled women in the bazaars piqued his
curiosity, and the poetry of the Turkish ceme-
teries and mosques appealed to his sentiment.
He was never weary of wandering through the
grand bazaar. "I have idled up and down in the
dim light and fingered the soft henna, and
bought small parcels of incense wood for my
pastille lamp, studying the remarkable faces of

the unconscious old Mussulmans, till my mind
became somehow tinctured of the East, and my
clothes steeped in the mixed and agreeable
odors of its thousand spices." Willis was a
born shopper and had a feminine eye for the
niceties not only of costume, but of upholstery,
pottery, and all kinds of purchasable knick-
knacks. He relished a fine appeal to his senses
and his fancy all in one. So he liked to go
through the street of the confectioners and
taste the queer sweetmeats with flowery names,
"peace to your throat" and "lumps of delight,"
and to inventory the merchants' stock in trade,
their gilded saucers, brass spoons, and vases of
rose water. He liked the opium-eating druggists, smoking their narghiles and fingering
their spice wood beads, the edges of their jars
"turned over with rich colored papers (a peculiar color to every drug), and broad spoons of
box-wood crossed on the top." He delighted to
cheapen amber and embroidered slippers in the
Bezestein, and best of all to lounge on the
cushioned divan, taking sherbet and aromatic
coffee and bargaining for attar of roses in the
octagonal shop of Mustapha, the perfumer to
the Sultan, whom he has introduced as a *deus
ex machina* into his story, "The Gypsy of Sardis." In the "Letters from under a Bridge,"
he affirms, whether seriously or not I cannot say,

that the English artist Bartlett, who was his col-
loborator in " American Scenery," encountered
old Mustapha in Constantinople, and that the
latter showed him Willis's card "stained to a
deep orange with the fingering of his fat hand,
unctuous from bath hour to bath hour with the
precious oils he traffics in." He questioned
Bartlett about America, " a country which to
Mustapha's fancy is as far beyond the moon as
the moon is beyond the gilt tip of the seraglio," and finally gave him a jar of attar of jas-
mine to send to Willis. " The small gilt bottle,
with its cubical edge and cap of parchment, lies
breathing before me." Then there was the street
of the booksellers, where " the small brown reed
stood in every clotted inkstand," and the bearded
old Armenian bookworm, interrupted in eating
rice from a wooden bowl, took down an illuminated Hafiz, "and opening it with a careful
thumb, read a line in mellifluous Persian." Willis also struck up an acquaintance with Dr. Millingen, the Sultan's physician, who had attended
Byron in his last illness. He spent two days
with him, by invitation, at his house on the Bosphorus, and picked up a smattering of Romaic
from Mrs. Millingen, who was a Greek.

After five weeks at Constantinople, the frigate
weighed anchor for Smyrna. There he found
an old schoolmate, Octavus Langdon, a Smyr-

niote merchant, who entertained him very hospitably, and invited him to join a party for a
few days' tour in Asia Minor. The party consisted of Willis and his host, an American mis-
sionary named Brewer, and two other gentlemen,
and their adventures included a night in a real
Oriental khan at Magnesia, and a visit to the
site of ancient Sardis. A beautiful girl, of
whom Willis caught a glimpse, through a tent
door, in a gypsy encampment on the plain of
Hadjilar, was the original of his " Gypsy of
Sardis." At Smyrna he said good-by to Commodore Patterson and his other friends on the
United States; and the ship which had been his
home for more than six months sailed away to
winter at Minorca, leaving him "waiting for a
vessel to go — I care not where. I rather lean
toward Palestine and Egypt, but there are no
vessels for Jaffa or Alexandria."

By this time Willis's literary reputation had
penetrated to the London press, though not as yet
to the London public, possibly through scattered
copies of his " Mirror " letters ; and while staying at Smyrna he received "an offer of a thousand dollars a year to write for the London
' Morning Herald.' But the articles were to be
political, and that I had modesty enough to
think beyond my calibre. I was to live abroad,
however, and go wherever there was a war or

9

the prospect of one. I would much rather write about pictures and green fields." The not unpleasant hesitation as to his next move was ended at last by the departure from Smyrna of the Yankee brig Metamora, bound for his native Portland with a cargo of figs and opium. The skipper, a Down-Easter, agreed to take him as a passenger, and land him at Malta. At Malta, accordingly, he arrived late in December, after being nearly shipwrecked in a Levanter, and was put ashore through a heavy sea in the brig's long boat, narrowly escaping being carried all the way to America. The letter to the " Mirror " in which this part of his travels was recorded was lost, and the " Pencillings " leap at once from Smyrna to Milan. He afterwards rewrote the episode, turning it into a capital story (" A Lost Letter Rewritten," in the " Mirror " for May 14 and June 11, 1836), which figures in his collected writings as " A Log in the Archipelago." The startling conjunction of East and Down East on board the Metamora suggested, no doubt, some of the incidents in " The Widow by Brevet," a tale which moves between the poles of Constantinople and Salem, Massachusetts.

From Malta he made his way *via* Italy, Switzerland, and France to England, arriving at Dover on the 1st of June, 1834.

While at Florence, Willis had been introduced by Greenough to Walter Savage Landor, who was then living in his villa at Fiesole. Landor entertained him hospitably, and, at parting, made him a present of a Cuyp, for which Willis had expressed admiration, and gave him some valuable letters to people in England. One of these was to the Countess of Blessington, and with it Landor intrusted to his American guest the manuscript of his " Citation and Examination of William Shakespeare," for delivery to the same lady, under whose superintendence it was duly published the following autumn. He also put into his hands a package whose temporary disappearance was the cause of some blame attaching to Willis. Landor's own story of the transaction, told in an addendum to the first edition of " Pericles and Aspasia," is as follows : —

" At this time an American traveler passed through Tuscany and favored me with a visit at my country seat. He expressed a wish to reprint in America a large selection of my ' Imaginary Conversations,' omitting the political. He assured me they were the most *thumbed* books on his table. With a smile at so energetic an expression of perhaps an undesirable distinction, I offered him unreservedly and unconditionally my only copy of the five printed volumes, interlined and interleaved in most places, together

with my MS. of the sixth, unpublished.   He wrote to
me on his arrival in England, telling me that they
were already on their voyage to their destination."

It seems from Willis's public explanation in
" Letters from under a Bridge," that he received
the volumes, which were in a dilapidated condition, at the moment of starting, and not knowing how to add them to his baggage he — rather
carelessly, perhaps — " sent them with a note to
Theodore Fay, who was then in Florence, requesting him to forward them to America by
ship from Leghorn."   Fay accordingly committed
them to a Mr. Miles, an American straw-bonnet-
maker, who did send them to New York, where
Willis expected to follow in the course of the
summer and take charge of them.   Instead of
doing this, he spent the next two years in England, and meanwhile wrote to Landor that the
package had been left with Miles, to forward it
to America.   Landor " called in consequence at
the shop of this person, who denied any knowledge of the books."   These, however, after a
brief stay in New York, were consigned to Willis at London, " and Fay and Mr. Landor both
happening there together, the explanation was
made, and the books and manuscripts restored
unharmed to the author," but not in time to keep
Willis from going down " to posterity astride
the finis of ' Pericles and Aspasia.'   I trust," he

continues, " that his [Landor's] biographer will either let me slip off at Lethe's wharf, by expurgating the book of me, or do me justice in a note." In spite of which trust the biographers have been a little hard on Willis in the matter. Sidney Colvin, heartened, probably, by the " Quarterly's " onslaught, denounces him as " that most assiduous of flatterers and least delicate of gossips," and says that he gave Landor occasion to repent of his hospitality by consigning his books to America and then basely lingering on in England " in obsequious enjoyment of the great company among whom he found himself invited : " while Forster, after declaring that Willis's " fuss and fury of boundless hero-worship found in Landor an easy victim," adds that " Landor will perhaps be thought not without excuse for the way in which he always afterwards spoke of Mr. N. P. Willis." But whatever inconvenience the latter may have caused in this business, he certainly made the *amende honorable* in the letter to Landor from which Mr. Forster quotes : —

" I have to beg," he writes, " that you will lay to the charge of England a part of the annoyance you will feel about your books and manuscripts. I was never more flattered by a commission and I have never fulfilled one so ill. They went to America *via* Leghorn, and I expected fully to have arrived in New York a month or two after them."

Landor was a man of noble courtesy and most generous nature, although, to put it mildly, often unreasonable. The delay and uncertainty about his precious manuscripts were certainly vexatious and may, very likely, as his biographer implies, have influenced " the way in which he always afterwards spoke " of the man who, innocently enough, made him the trouble. But up to the time of this little misunderstanding, his feelings toward Willis, as expressed in their correspondence, were exceedingly cordial; as will sufficiently appear from the following letter, undated, but written, probably, during the winter of 1834–35 : —

My dear Sir, — By a singular and strange coincidence, I wrote this morning and put into the post office a letter directed to you at New York. And now comes Mr. Macquay, bringing me one from you, delightful in all respects. I know not any man in whose fame and fortunes I feel a deeper interest than in yours. Pardon me if I am writing all this illegibly in some degree, for certainly I shall scarcely be in time for the post with all the agility both of hand and legs. For I am resolved to transcribe an ode to your President in spite of the resistance his [MS. illegible] has met with, — indeed, the more am I resolved for this very reason. I envy you the evenings you pass with the most accomplished and graceful of all our fashionable world, my excellent friend, Lady Blessington. Do not believe that I have written any paper in the magazine. Whatever I write I submit to Lady B. My "Examination of Shakespeare" I published for a particular and private purpose, which, however, it has not answered. I should not be surprised if it procured me a hundred pounds or more within seven years. Had I known of your being in England I should have ordered a copy to have been sent to you. Pray tell Lady Blessington I have at last received her Byron from Colonel Hughes. It came a week ago. I think better of him than I did, and thank her for it. Nevertheless, I suspect she has given him powers of ratiocination which he never attained. I must now try to recollect my verses. So adieu, and believe me,

Ever yours most sincerely,

W. S. LANDOR.

Pray write to me when you find time.

The verses accompanying this letter were the rough draft of the ode "To Andrew Jackson," numbered CCLXXXVIII. in Landor's miscellaneous poems. On his side Willis could not thank Landor enough for his introduction to Lady Blessington. "She is my lode star and most valued friend," he writes, "for whose acquaintance I am so much indebted to you that you will find it difficult in your lifetime to diminish my obligations."

In England Willis fell at once upon his feet. While traveling on the Continent, his intimacies had been principally among Englishmen and

Americans, and though well received in the native society of Florence by virtue of his diplomatic credentials, he had remained, after all, a stranger and a looker-on. A foreign language imperfectly learned is a barrier to complete intercourse even in the most cosmopolitan society. In France and Italy he had made acquaintances; in England he made friends and formed domestic ties which bound him to the country as long as he lived. He did not fancy the French and Italians, though he found their cities interesting to visit; but he liked the English and they treated him well. No American author except Irving and Cooper had received from them a tithe of the attentions which they accorded to Willis; and Cooper, though personally well liked, had offended British prejudices by his pugnacious writings and was more popular in Paris than in London. The next two years of Willis's life were perhaps the acme of his social and literary career, and he always looked back to them as the brightest spot in his memory. The experience was not altogether healthy for him, though it was stimulating at the time. He was not spoiled by success, but he was naturally a little intoxicated by it, and a little dazzled by the courtly splendors of the circles to which he was now admitted. When he went back to America, he did so reluctantly, and with the hope of returning soon to make his home in England. He found the change to the plainer conditions of American life a chilling one, and he had acquired habits and standards which did not fit in easily with the requirements of a journalist's career in a new country.

As soon as he reached Dover he began to have that feeling of being at home once more which is familiar to American travelers who make their first entrance to England by way of the Channel. Everything was new, and yet nothing was strange. The blazing coal fires — it was June — the warm carpets, the quiet coffee-room with the London newspapers on the table, the subdued, respectful servants, the mother-tongue again, the plain richness of the furnishings, the snugness and comfort, — the Anglo-Saxon knows by these that he is once more in Anglo-Saxondom. Arrived at London, he lost no time in delivering his note of introduction from Landor to Lady Blessington, who immediately asked him to dinner and presented him to the *beaux esprits* who frequented Seamore Place. For this charming woman her young *protégé* conceived at once the strongest admiration, tinctured, it may be, by a tenderer sentiment. Her wit and beauty, her cordiality and social graces, had drawn about her a court of statesmen, authors, and notabilities of all kinds, over whom she presided like the queen of a Parisian *salon.* It was natural that Willis should have formed, or at least should have politely expressed, an exaggerated estimate of her literary gifts. To posterity, who have not the advantage of her personal acquaintance, Lady Blessington's writings seem of very little importance, with the possible exception of her " Conversations with Lord Byron," whose subject lends it a certain claim to remembrance. At her house Willis met Bulwer, Moore, Lord Durham, Disraeli, James Smith, Galt, Procter, Fonblanque of the " Examiner," and many other distinguished men whose portraits he has given in the " Pencillings " with a sharpness of outline which makes them increasingly valuable as their figures recede into history. It is not at all strange that an enthusiastic and fanciful young American, without antecedents, ushered all at once into a roomful of people about whom all the world was talking, should have been a little imposed upon by these exalted personages. He was not in a critical mood, and it may be freely conceded that he had too high an opinion of Barry Cornwall's poetry, and of the electroplated novels of the authors of " Pelham " and " Vivian Grey ; " and that he exclaimed more than was necessary over the varied accomplishments of that gorgeous dandy — Byron's *Cupidon déchainé* — the Count d'Orsay.

Still he kept his head fairly well. Fortunate in his introductions, he was the man to make the most of his chances. His talent for society and his easy assurance put him quickly *de niveau* with his new acquaintances. He was not at all above owning that the English nobility, for example, impressed his imagination. He liked to stay at their houses; he enjoyed the wealth, the grandeur, the historic associations that surrounded them. His appetite for luxury was gratified by the perfection of all their appointments in the art of living. The fineness of their manners pleased his aristocratic tastes and he could not sufficiently admire the high-bred women and the simple, cordial, dignified gentlemen with whom he dined or drove through the cultivated landscapes. But Willis was no snob or vulgar tuft hunter. His enjoyment of his privileges was accompanied with an entire reserve of his self-respect. He liked the company of those whom Dr. Johnson was wont to call " the great." But though he loved a lord, he preferred a commoner, if the commoner was preferable. The Duke of Richelieu, whom he had met at Lady Blessington's, and previously at the French court, he described as " the inheritor of nothing but the name of his great ancestor, a dandy and a fool."

" What a star is mine! " he wrote in a letter to his

sister Julia, three days after his landing in England. "All the best society of London exclusives is now open to me — *me!* a sometime apprentice at setting types — *me!* without a sou in the world beyond what my pen brings me, and with not only no influence from friends at home, but a world of envy and slander at my back. Thank heaven, there is not a countryman of mine, except Washington Irving, who has even the standing in England which I have got in *three days* only. I should not boast of it if I had not been wounded and stung to the quick by the calumnies and falsehoods of every description which come to me from America. But let it pass! It reconciles me to my exile at least, and may drive me to adopt the mother country for my own. In a literary way, I have had already offers from the 'Court Magazine,' the 'Metropolitan Monthly,' and the 'New Monthly' of the first price for my articles. I sent a short tale, written in one day, to the 'Court Magazine' yesterday, and the publishers gave me eight guineas for it at once. They all pay in this proportion, and you can easily see, with my present resources of matter, how well I can live. I lodge in Cavendish Square, the most fashionable part of the town, paying a guinea a week for my lodgings, and am as well off as if I had been the son of the President, with as much as I could spend in the year. Except my family now, I have forgotten everybody in America. [Here follows the passage about Mary Benjamin already quoted in chapter III.] I never can return, however, till I can pay my debts, and it will take me long to lay up three thousand dollars. When I can do it, I shall, and make America a farewell visit for years."

Willis followed up his advantages assiduously. He went constantly to Lady Blessington's, exchanged calls with Moore, breakfasted with Procter and also with that entertaining diarist, Henry Crabb Robinson, to whom he brought a letter from Landor, and in whose rooms in the Temple he met Charles and Mary Lamb. His Parisian acquaintance, Dr. Bowring, was back in London and introduced him to a number of people. At an evening party at the Bulwers' he met Sir Leicester Stanhope, who had been with Byron in Greece, and with whose beautiful wife Willis became quite a favorite, composing his verses " Upon the Portrait of the Hon. Mrs. Stanhope " to accompany an engraving of her in Lady Blessington's " Book of Beauty." At the Stanhopes' he met that famous pair of beauties, " the Sheridan girls," Mrs. Norton and her sister, Lady Dufferin, to the former of whom he had addressed a poem written at Paris in 1832 and printed in the " Mirror " of July 7, 1834.

It was the height of the London season, and the opera was in full blast, with Grisi singing and Fanny Elssler in the ballet. Willis was admitted to the Alfred Club, and invitations to dinners and parties began to pour in upon him.

All these gayeties he described in his letters to Morris, which, losing somewhat, it may be, in picturesqueness, gained greatly in personal interest during his stay in England. It was in the course of this first summer in London that he got acquainted with Mary Russell Mitford, who invited him to spend a week at Reading, and with whom he maintained for some time a friendly correspondence. A letter to Miss Jephson, July 23, 1834, gives her first impression of him : —

" I also liked very much Mr. Willis, an American author, whose ' Unwritten Poetry ' and ' Unwritten Philosophy ' you may remember in my American book,[1] and who is now understood to be here to publish his account of England. He is a very elegant young man, and more like one of the best of our peers' sons than a rough republican."

The generally agreeable impression which Willis made in English society was not without its exceptions. During this same summer in London he had been taken by a friend to see Miss Harriet Martineau. She was then on the point of embarking for that trip in America, her

---

[1] The book here mentioned was her compilation, *Stories of American Life by American Authors*, printed in 1830, to which reference was made in chapter III. A number of Willis's letters to Miss Mitford are published in *The Friendships of Mary Russell Mitford*, from one of which the above passage is taken.

very outspoken narrative of which afterwards
caused so many heart-burnings in this conntry.
Her vinegary reminiscences of Willis, as recorded in her autobiography, though rather long,
are perhaps worth reproducing here, not only
for their liveliness, but because any contemporary impression, however unjust and mistaken,
helps to fill out a complete picture of the man,
and there were plenty of people who disliked
Willis cordially.

"I encountered," she says, "one specimen of
American oddity before I left home, which should
certainly have lessened my surprise at any that I
met afterwards. While I was preparing for my
travels, an acquaintance one day brought a buxom
gentleman, whom he introduced to me under the
name of Willis. There was something rather engaging in the round face, brisk air, and *enjouement* of
the young man; but his conscious dandyism and un-
paralleled self-complacency spoiled the satisfaction,
though they increased the inclination to laugh. Mr.
N. P. Willis's plea for coming to see me was his
gratification that I was going to America, and his
real reason was presently apparent: a desire to increase his consequence in London society by giving
apparent proof that he was on intimate terms with
every eminent person in America. He placed himself in an attitude of infinite ease, and whipped his
little bright boot with a little bright cane, while he
ran over the names of all his distinguished country-

men and countrywomen, and declared he should send me letters to them all. This offer of intervention went so very far that I said (what I have ever since said in the case of introductions offered by strangers), while thanking him for his intended good offices, that I was sufficiently uncertain in my plans to beg for excuse beforehand, in case I should find myself unable to use the letters. It appeared afterwards that to supply them and not to have them used suited Mr. Willis's convenience exactly. It made him appear to have the friendships he boasted of without putting the boast to the proof. It was immediately before a late dinner that the gentleman called; and I found on the breakfast-table next morning a great parcel of Mr. Willis's letters, inclosed in a prodigious one to myself, in which he offered advice. Among other things, he desired me not to use his letter to Dr. Channing if I had others from persons more intimate with him; and he proceeded to warn me against two friends of Dr. and Mrs. Channing's, whose names I had never heard and whom Mr. Willis represented as bad and dangerous people. This gratuitous defamation of strangers whom I was likely to meet confirmed the suspicions my mother and I had confided to each other about the quality of Mr. Willis's introductions. It seemed ungrateful to be so suspicious: but we could not see any good reason for such prodigious efforts on my behalf, nor for his naming any countrywomen of his to me in a way so spontaneously slanderous. So I resolved to use that packet of letters very cautiously, and to begin with one which

should be well accompanied. In New York harbor
newspapers were brought on board, in one of which
was an extract from an article transmitted by Mr.
Willis to the 'New York Mirror,' containing a most
audacious account of me as an intimate friend of the
writer. The friendship was not stated as a matter of
fact, but so conveyed that it cost me much trouble to
make it understood and believed, even by Mr. Willis's own family, that I had never seen him but once,
and then without having previously heard so much as
his name. On my return the acquaintance who
brought him was anxious to ask pardon if he had
done mischief, events having by that time made Mr.
Willis's ways pretty well known. His partner in the
property and editorship of the 'New York Mirror'
called on me at West Point, and offered and rendered
such extraordinary courtesy that I was at first almost
as much perplexed as he and his wife were when
they learned that I had never seen Mr. Willis but
once. They pondered, they consulted, they cross-
questioned me, they inquired whether *I* had any notion what Mr. Willis could have meant by writing of
me as in a state of close intimacy with him. In like
manner, when, some time after, I was in a carriage
with some members of a picnic party to Monument
Mountain, a little girl seated at my feet clasped my
knees fondly, looked up in my face, and said, ' O
Miss Martineau! You are *such* a friend of my
Uncle Nathaniel's!' Her father was present; and I
tried to get off without explanation. But it was impossible, — they all knew how very intimate I was

10

with Nathaniel; and there was a renewal of the amazement at my having seen him only once. I tried three of his letters; and the reception was in each case much the same, — a throwing down of the letter with an air not to be mistaken. In each case the reply was the same, when I· subsequently found myself at liberty to ask what this might mean. 'Mr. Willis is not entitled to write to me: he is no acquaintance of mine.' As for the two ladies of whom I was especially to beware, I became exceedingly well acquainted with them, to my own advantage and pleasure; and, as a natural consequence, I discovered Mr. Willis's reasons for desiring to keep us apart. I hardly need add that I burned the rest of his letters. He had better have spared himself the trouble of so much manœuvring, by which he lost a good deal, and could hardly have gained anything. I have simply stated the facts, because, in the first place, I do not wish to be considered one of Mr. Willis's friends; and, in the next, it may be useful, and conducive to justice, to show, by a practical instance, what Mr. Willis's pretensions to intimacy are worth. His countrymen and countrywomen accept, in simplicity, his accounts of our aristocracy as from the pen of one of their own coterie; and they may as well have the opportunity of judging for themselves whether their notorious 'Penciller' is qualified to write of Scotch dukes and English marquises and European celebrities of all kinds in the way he has done."

The simple American reader will have a

chance to make up his mind, on independent evidence, of how far Willis was qualified to write of Scotch dukes, etc. ; but meanwhile it is not true that the audacious article in the " Mirror " of September 6, 1834 (which was not an "article," by the way, but an extract from a private letter to Morris), conveyed any implication of an intimacy between Willis and Miss Martineau. On the contrary, it expressly says that his acquaintance with the lady was of only one day's standing.

" I was taken yesterday," it begins, " by the clever translator of ' Faust' to see the celebrated Miss Martineau. She has perhaps at this moment the most general and enviable reputation in England, and is the only one of the literary *clique* whose name is mentioned without some envious qualification."

After some entirely respectful mention of her manner and appearance, the letter then goes on to say : —

" There is no necessity of bespeaking for so distinguished a visitor as Miss Martineau the warmest attentions of our country. She goes with high anticipations, and whatever she may find to object to in our society and institutions, it will be done, there cannot be a doubt, in a spirit of womanly and simple candor. She is sped on her way by the best wishes of the best hearts in England. I trust she will be met over there by wishes and welcomes as warm and as many."

Any one who knew Willis would have felt sure that his "prodigious efforts" on Miss Martineau's behalf sprang from his always good-natured and sometimes even officious eagerness to be of service. And most who knew him would probably have admitted that there was some mixture of a "desire to increase his consequence" in his offer of introductions. Motives are usually mixed in this bad world and Willis was seldom indifferent to opportunities for ingratiating himself with people worth knowing. But even so, it would have been more gracious in the lady if, after accepting his offers and the attentions of his partner at West Point, she had taken his professions for what they were worth, and omitted this spiteful mention of him in her book. Had he lived to read the passage, he would probably have consoled himself with the reflection that it was better to win smiles from beauty than approbation from a strong-minded Unitarian female with an ear-trumpet, or, as he politely paraphrased it in his letter to Morris, a "pliable, acoustic tube."

The last fortnight in August he was ill of a bilious fever, during which his new friends proved very kind. Lady Blessington called daily in her carriage at his lodgings (over the shop of a baker, who gratified Willis by being overwhelmed at her ladyship's condescension), and Dr. William

Beattie, the king's physician, attended his interesting patient devotedly and refused to take any fee. This excellent gentleman, who was the anonymous author of " Heliotrope " and a prolific contributor to the Annuals, became a firm friend of Willis and his correspondent for many years after his return to America. He was an intimate of Samuel Rogers and of Thomas Campbell, whose life he afterwards wrote, and he introduced Willis to both of them.

By September the latter was sufficiently convalescent to be ordered into the country. He had received an invitation from the Earl of Dalhousie, whom he had met in Italy, to make him a visit at Dalhousie Castle, near Edinburgh, and accordingly he set out for Scotland on the second of the month. Lady Charlotte Bury, a " scribbling woman," had given him a letter to her brother, the Duke of Argyle, and he carried a score beside to other people in Scotland. At Dalhousie, the feudal castle of the Ramsays, nobly situated on a branch of the Esk, Willis was heartily welcomed, and passed a most agreeable fortnight. The earl had been governor of the Canadas in 1831; Lady Dalhousie was an invalid, and both of them were quiet, domestic people, kindly and simple, living with the profuse and even splendid hospitality proper to their rank, but without ostentation of fashion or gay-

ety. The house was full of guests, among them
the countess's niece, Lady Moncrieff, a lovely
widow of twenty-five, who was very polite to
Willis during his next winter in London. The
earl's son, Lord Ramsay, was home from Oxford
and initiated Willis into the mysteries of shooting over the stubble. This young gentleman
succeeded to his father's title in 1838, was a member of Sir Robert Peel's ministry from 1843 to
1847, and in the latter year was made Governor-
General of India. It was during his viceroyalty
that the Burmese war was fought, the Punjaub
annexed, and the railway begun from Calcutta to
Bombay.

After leaving Dalhousie, Willis spent a few
days in Edinburgh, where he breakfasted with
Professor Wilson, dined with Jeffrey, and danced
till three o'clock in the morning at the Whig
ball given in honor of Lord Grey. An attack
of scrofula in his left leg, which he chose to describe in his correspondence with his English
friends as " gout," was aggravated by this last
dissipation, and after two or three days more of
poultices and plasters at Edinburgh, he took
steamer to Aberdeen. " The loss of a wedding
in Perthshire, by the way, a week's deer-shoot-
ing in the forest of Athol, and a week's fishing
with a noble friend at Kinvara (long standing
engagements all), I lay at the door of the

Whigs." He was laid up four days at Aberdeen, but finally recovered so far as to take coach seventy miles across country to Lochabers, a small town on the estates of the Duke of Gordon, to whom he brought a letter from Dalhousie. At Gordon Castle he found a distinguished company and passed ten days of unmixed enjoyment. There were thirty guests, among whom were Lord Aberdeen, who had been foreign secretary under Wellington; his son, Lord Claude Hamilton, a handsome young Cantab, who invited Willis to visit him at the university for a day's hunt; Lord Aberdeen's daughter, Lady Harriet Hamilton, " eighteen and brilliantly beautiful; " Lord and Lady Stormont, Lord Mandeville, Lord and Lady Morton, the Duchess of Richmond and her daughter, Lady Sophia Lennox, " the palest, proudest, and most highborn looking woman I ever saw." This Lady Sophia Lennox was probably the original of Mildred Ashly, the disdainful beauty in " Paul Fane." She seems to have impressed Willis as the type and embodiment of English aristocracy. In a letter to Lady Blessington, written from Gordon Castle and printed in Madden's " Life of Lady Blessington," he says, " There is a Lady Something, very pale, tall and haughty, twenty-three and sarcastic, whom I sat next at dinner yesterday, — a woman I came as near an antipa-

thy for as is possible, with a very handsome face
for an apology." The same letter gives his opinion of his host and hostess more unreservedly
than he could venture to do in " Pencillings."
The duke he describes as " a delightful, hearty
old fellow full of fun and conversation." Willis's letters from Gordon Castle were perhaps
more criticised than any other part of his " Pencillings" for their alleged violation of the sanc-
tities of private life. They are, nevertheless,
among the very best passages in his correspondence and, taken together, they present a brilliant picture of what is, doubtless, so far as material conditions go, the most perfect life lived
by man; the life, namely, of a chosen party of
guests, in late September, at the country seat of
a great British noble.

From this pleasant province in the land of
Cockayne, Willis departed toward the last of
the month and, after a tour of the Highlands,
returned October 6th to Dalhousie, where he
passed a few days more and then set out for
England. He had meant, on his way back to
London, to call upon Wordsworth and Surrey,
having letters to both of them, and to pass some
days by appointment with Miss Mitford at Reading. But continued trouble with his ankle altered
his plans, and, after spending a few weeks at the
country house of a friend in Lancashire — whose

acquaintance he had made in Italy — and of another in Cheshire, he returned hastily to London by way of Liverpool and Manchester, and on the 1st of November took up his quarters there for the winter. At this stage of his journeyings " Pencillings by the Way " come to an end. A number of supplementary letters descriptive of London life, of the Isle of Wight, of Stratford-upon-Avon, Charlecote, Kenilworth, Warwick Castle, etc., were published at irregular intervals in the " Mirror " under the general heading " Loiterings of Travel." With letters from Washington and the paper on " The Four Rivers," they make up the " Sketches of Travel " in their author's collected works.

CHAPTER V.

1834–1836.

LIFE ABROAD (CONTINUED).

WILLIS took lodgings at No. 2 Vigo Street. During the next ten months, which he spent in London and its vicinity, he found himself something of a lion. His articles in the English magazines had begun to be talked about in the clubs, and society people who had known him abroad or in London only as a dandy *attaché* were surprised to learn that "that nice, agreeable Mr. Willis" was identical with "Slingsby," the brilliant American *raconteur* of the "New Monthly." He had contributed in the summer and autumn of 1834 a number of sketches — "By a Here and Thereian" — to the "Court Magazine:" "Love and Diplomacy," "Niagara and So On;" to Captain Marryat's "Metropolitan:" an episode of Italian travel, "The Madhouse of Palermo;" and to Colburn's "New Monthly:" "Incidents on the Hudson," "Tom Fane and I," "Pedlar Karl," "The Lunatic," and "My Hobby — Rather" (the same as "The

Mad Senior " in " Scenes of Fear "). The *nom
de plume* of Philip Slingsby he borrowed from
the luckless wanderer in Irving's " Sketch-
Book." He followed these up during 1835–
36 with " F. Smith," " Love in the Library "
(" Edith Linsey "), " The Gypsy of Sardis,"
" The Cherokee's Threat," " The Revenge of the
Signor Basil," and " Larks in Vacation." For
his " Slingsby " papers Willis got double pay :
Colburn gave him a guinea a page, and Morris,
in his contract with whom he had reserved the
right to print twelve sketches a year in the English magazines, published them simultaneously
in the " Mirror," and paid for them at the same
rate as for original articles. They were forwarded to him in proof-sheets or in duplicate
MSS., so as to arrive in advance of the English
periodicals, which sometimes, however, reached
America first, because of the uncertainties of the
mail-carriage by sailing packet. To the " New
Monthly " Willis also contributed a number of
short poems, " Thoughts in a Balcony at Day-
break," " The Absent," " Chamber Scene," and
" To —— " (" Were I a star," etc.). He wrote
for it after his return to America and after it
was united with " The Humorist " in 1837, under the editorship of Theodore Hook. His last
contribution to it was " The Picker and Piler,"
in the April number for 1839.

Lady Blessington's kindness continued after his return to London, and he was taken up by other fashionable bluestockings, dined and wined, fêted and caressed to a degree that may well have made him giddy. The two rival *salons* to Lady Blessington's were Holland House and the residence of the Dowager Lady Charleville in Cavendish Square. It does not appear that Willis was invited to the former, but he went to the reunions at Charleville House, though not so constantly as to Seamore Place. Through Lady Blessington's influence he was admitted to the Travellers' Club, which was the resort of the ultra fashionable; and, on Sir George Staunton's nomination, to the Athenæum, which had more of a literary tinge than the Alfred or the Travellers'. Sir George Staunton also presented him at court, a favor which Mr. Vail, the American minister, who disliked Willis for some reason, had declined to render. Another friend gave him a perpetual ticket to the opera. Among his patronesses were the Countess of Arundel and Lady Stepney, who wrote bad novels but gave good dinners. Lady Blessington's biographer, Madden, who saw a great deal of him in those days, has recorded his recollections of him as follows : —

" I had the pleasure of meeting Mr. Willis on many occasions at Gore House, to which reference is made in the rather too celebrated ' Pencillings by the Way,' and also at the *soirées* of the late Lady Charleville in Cavendish Square. Mr. Willis was an extremely agreeable young man in society, somewhat over-dressed and a little too *demonstratif,* but abounding in good spirits, pleasing reminiscences of Eastern and Continental travel and of his residence there for some time as *attaché* to a foreign legation. He was observant and communicative, lively and clever in conversation, having the peculiar art of making him-self agreeable to ladies, old as well as young, *dégagé* in his manner, and on exceedingly good terms with himself and with the *élite* of the best society, wher-ever he went."

The secret of Willis's agreeableness to ladies lay in his unfailing deference. It is extraordi-nary how many women much older than himself cherished a warm affection for him. He had considered the meaning of Bacon's saying, " No Youth can be comely, but by Pardon," and sev-eral of his stories are studies on the thesis that there is a beauty in age which may inspire pas-sion. One in particular, not found among his collected writings, deals with this speculation : " Poyntz's Aunt," published in " The Ladies' Companion " of December, 1842, where the hero falls violently in love with a woman of sixty, to whose niece the family expected him to pay his court.

Willis saw more " life " in London than was quite good for him, and went into companies which were less select than the Gore House coterie, although, to say truth, Lady Blessington herself was looked upon by " the best people" as a trifle off color. Her house was frequented by men who were entirely irreproachable, but the English ladies were shy of visiting there. This was due mainly to her rather unusual relations with the Count d'Orsay. In obedience to the wishes of the Earl of Blessington, his daughter by a former marriage had been compelled to wed the count under penalty of forfeiting her inheritance. The poor girl reluctantly espoused the brilliant stranger provided for her by her father's eccentric caprice ; but the match was unhappy, and was almost immediately followed by a separation ; notwithstanding which, D'Orsay continued to live in the closest intimacy with his wife's stepmother after the earl's death, and in time under the same roof with her. This last arrangement, which was, to say the least, odd, and caused much scandal in British society, had not, however, gone into effect when Willis first came to London. Lady Blessington had not as yet moved to Gore House, but was living in Seamore Place, while D'Orsay had lodgings in Curzon Street. Nor did the latter's formal separation from his wife take place till 1838. Another

intimate friend of Willis in London was that
very unconventional, not to say rapid, woman,
Lady Dudley Stuart, the daughter of Lucien
Bonaparte, " a lady of remarkably small person,
with the fairest foot ever seen," under whose
bonnet " burn the most lambent and spiritual
eyes that night and sleep ever hid from the
world." She had about her a semi-foreign society, not without its fascinations, of artists, actors, opera-singers, refugee nobles, and adven-
turers of more or less shady antecedents. In his
" Sketches of Travel " Willis described a very
free and easy supper party, following a private
concert given by Lady Antrobus, at which he
and Lady Dudley Stuart assisted, together with
Grisi, Lablache, Rubini, and other members of
the Italian opera troupe then in London. Of
course neither Lady Antrobus nor Lady Stuart
was mentioned by name in this account.

But Willis's acquaintance was by no means
confined to the Blessington set, or to the Bohe-
mian circle that surrounded Lady Dudley Stuart,
but included many families of unquestioned position. The Ramsays, for instance, were solid
people, above any suspicion of queerness, and the
earl's niece, Lady Moncrieff, whom Willis visited in London, was decidedly " evangelical."
There were two households in particular which
were like homes to him during the last year and

more of his stay in England. These were Shirley Park, near Croydon in Surrey, the residence of the Skinner family, and the Manor House of the Shaws at Lee, in Kent, only a ten miles' drive across country from Shirley Park. The Hon. Mrs. Fanny Shaw was a daughter to Lord Erskine and a sworn friend of Willis. Mrs. Mary Skinner was wife to an Indian nabob, a leader of fashion, and a woman of intellectual tastes, who patronized letters and entertained literary people, a kind of Mrs. Leo Hunter, in short. Willis was introduced to her at Lady Simpkins's by Sir John Franklin, in February, 1835, and met her again at a dinner given by Longman, the publisher, at Hampstead, where were present, among others, Moore, Joanna Baillie, Jane Porter, and Miss Pardoe. The last was a very pretty woman, author of " Beauties of the Bosphorus," and other books more remarkable for their sumptuous illustrations than for their literary quality. She was a poetess, too, after her fashion, and once addressed a tribute in verse " To the Author of Melanie," which was printed in the " Mirror " of October 17, 1835. Both Mrs. Shaw and Mrs. Skinner treated their young guest with the most delicate and considerate kindness. They made him offers of pecuniary help, of which, fortunately, he had no need to avail himself, as his letters to the " Mirror" and his "New Monthly" stories (which added fifteen or twenty guineas a month to his "poor two hundred a year") brought him in returns which were ample for his occasions. The Skinners had a town house in Portland Place, and their carriage in London was always at Willis's service. Both of these ladies regarded him as a son or a younger brother. Bruce Skinner, a son of Willis's hostess, named one of his children after him. At Shirley Park and at the Shaws' he met a number of very charming people, and his time there was spent in drives, lawn-parties, etc. In the library at Shirley Park two nieces of Walter Scott, the Misses Swinton, copied for him "Melanie" and "Love in the Library," which he was preparing for the press. An extract from a very confidential letter from Willis to Mrs. Skinner may be worth transcribing, to show the terms of frank and cordial familiarity on which he lived with these excellent people. After a brief history of his life and a statement of his financial situation, the letter concludes as follows : —

"There is a passage in your note which pleased me. You say if you had a daughter you would give her to me. If you *had* one I certainly would take you at your word, provided this *exposé* of my poverty did not change your fancy. I should like to marry in England, and I feel every day (more and

11

more) that my best years and best affections are running to waste. I am proud to *be* an American, but as a literary man, I would rather live in England. So if you know any affectionate and *good* girl who would be content to live rather a quiet life, and could love your humble servant, you have full power of attorney to dispose of me, *provided* she has *five hundred* a year, or as much more as she likes. I know enough of the world to cut my throat sooner than bring a delicate woman down to a dependence on my brains for support, though in a case of exigency I could always retreat to America, and live comfortably by my labors. Meantime I am the only sufferer by my poverty, and am *not* poor, for no man is so who lives upon his income. *Comprends-tu?* My dear friend, I have told you what I have told no other person in the world. Most men and women would think it incredible that an *attaché* to a legation could keep up appearances on two hundred a year, or pity him if he could ; and I never thought anybody worth the confidence — save only yourself. I would tell Miss Porter just the same, or Mr. Swinton, but who else? No one! so *gardez cela!*

"I enjoyed the ball at the Ravenshaws' exceedingly, and am so much obliged to you for introducing me to Praed, whom I like."

"I have one or two homes in England," wrote Willis to his mother, July 22, 1835, "where I am loved like a child. I had a letter the other day from Honorable Mrs. Shaw, who fancied I looked low-spirited at the opera. 'Young men have but two causes of unhappiness,' she says, ' *love* and *money*. If it is *money*, Mr. Shaw wishes me to say, you shall have as much as you want ; if it is *love*, tell us the lady, and perhaps we can help you.' Where could be kinder friends ? I spend my Sundays alternately at their splendid country house and Mrs. Skinner's, and they never can get enough of me. I have a room always kept for me at both places, and there is universal rejoicing when I come and mourning when I go. I am often asked whether I carry a love philter with me ; yet with all the uncommon honors and favors shown me in England, I assure you I never asked or made interest directly or indirectly for any acquaintance or any favor since I landed at Dover. *What has come* has come of its own accord."

Miss Porter and Miss Pardoe were both domesticated at Shirley Park, and he met there at different times, as fellow guests, Lady Franklin, Lady Sidney Morgan, author of once popular French and Italian travels, and the brilliant young orator, poet, and wit, Winthrop Mackworth Praed. Of the latter Willis wrote in the " Home Journal " many years later : " We were followers together in the train of the admired belle (a visitor under the same hospitable roof) whom I afterward brought home with me to Glenmary." Willis attributed to his religious poetry the honor of his first acquaintance with Joanna Baillie, Jane Porter, and the Byrons.

For the authoress of " The Scottish Chiefs," especially, he formed an enduring attachment, and she regarded him with an almost motherly affection. A lifelong correspondence was kept up between them, and at the death of Admiral Robert Ker Porter at St. Petersburg in 1842, among the MSS. found in his sea-chests were ninety letters from Willis to his sister. The letters from Miss Porter, among Willis's private papers, show that she was an equally indefatigable, though a not very legible correspondent. Willis encountered Ada Byron at an evening party in London, and thought her " earnest and sweet." Lady Byron, who was a Unitarian, was much interested by the spirited sketch of Dr. Channing in a series of papers on American literature which Willis had contributed to the "Athenæum," and she expressed her favorable opinion of them in a letter to Miss Baillie, as also her pleasure that her daughter had made the author's acquaintance. Miss Baillie gave this note to Willis for his autograph book. Byron's sister, Augusta Leigh, he also met in London society. She gave him an autograph letter of Byron, and on the appearance of " Melanie and Other Poems," in March 1835, he sent her a copy, and received an acknowledgment in which she said that the book contained " some of the most touching and exquisite lines I ever read." The venerable Joanna

Baillie wrote him, on the same occasion, a letter filled with the most graceful compliments.

Among other London acquaintances of Willis's at this time were John Leech, the artist, and Martin Farquhar Tupper, the proverbial philosopher, who afterwards visited him in America. A few extracts from a manuscript diary irregularly kept by Willis from June, 1835, to March, 1836, will serve to show the nature of his daily engagements and occupations: —

"June 30. Breakfasted with Samuel Rogers. Met Dr. Delancey, of Philadelphia, and Corbin, *ditto.* Talked of Mrs. Butler's book, and Rogers gave us suppressed passages. Talked of critics, and said that ' as long as you cast a shadow, you were sure you possessed *substance.*' Coleridge said of Southey: 'I never think of him but as mending a pen.' Southey said of Coleridge: ' Whenever anything presents itself to him in the shape of a duty, that moment he finds himself incapable of looking at it.'

" Went to the opera with Hon. Mrs. Shaw and heard Grisi in ' I Puritani,' and saw Taglioni : both divine. Visited Lady Blessington's box and Lady Vincent.

" After to a party at Mrs. Leicester Stanhope's. Saw Guiccioli, and was stuffed to the eyelids by Lady Mary Shepard about my shorter and scriptural poems.

" July 1. Mrs. Skinner drove Jane Porter and myself to Harrow to hear the speeches. . . .

"In the evening to a party at Lady Cork's, and after to Lady Vincent's *soirée.*"

Lady Cork was the aged but still beautiful Dowager Countess of Cork and Derry; who in her youth, as Miss Moncton, had been a favorite of Dr. Johnson, and whose *soirées* in New Burlington Street, between 1820 and 1840, were crowded with talent and fashion.

"2.   Sat to Rand for my picture.   Went to Lady Dundonald's *fête champêtre* at her beautiful villa in Regent's Park.   D'Orsay and all the world there.

"3.   Dined with Tyndale and Greenfield at the Wyndham Club.   Took tea with Jane Porter and went to a ball at the Longmans', Hampstead.

"4.   Went to Lee on a visit to Hon. Mrs. Shaw.

"5.   Drove to Lady Hislop's to tea.

"6.   Duke de Regina, Vail, Gen. and Mrs. Talmadge dined with the Shaws.

"7.   Returned to town.   Dined with Mrs. Channon.   Lady D. Stuart, Counts Battaglia, Vodiski, De Grognon, and Miss Cockaine present.   Came home ill.

"8.   Dined with Mrs. S., and went to Lady Dudley Stuart's *soirée.*

"9.   Dined with Dr. Beattie and met Thomas Campbell.   Praised my poetry to the skies and quoted from ' Melanie,' —

' She died
With her last sunshine in her eyes.'

Spoke of Scott's slavishness to men of rank, and after said it did not interfere with his genius.   Said it sank a man's heart to think he and Byron were dead and there was nobody left to praise or approve. Why should he write now? Told story of the man at the deaf and dumb who did not know him as a poet. Abused the nobility bitterly. Said they were ungrateful, and thought they honored you by receiving a favor from you. Said he was sorry for his vindication of Lady Byron. Story of dining with Burns and a Bozzy friend who, when C. proposed the health of *Mr.* Burns, said, 'Sir, you will always be known as *Mr.* Campbell, but posterity will talk of *Burns.*' He was playful and amusing, and drank gin and water. Went after in uniform to the grand Coliseum ball. Seven thousand people present.

" 10. Grand review in Hyde Park. Went to a *déjeuner* at Mrs. Wyndham Lewis's on the Park. Talked to Miss Caton and the Duchess of St. Albans. Music after the review. Malibran sang.

" Received a congratulatory letter from Edward Everett.

" Party at Mrs. F.'s, Lady Franklin's sister. Stupid.

" 11. Went to the Duchess St. Albans's *fête* at Holly Lodge. The duke flew a falcon and killed a pigeon. Fireworks, dinner in a tent, dancing, singing, etc., etc., there. Mrs. Marjoribanks brought me home."

This *fête* furnished some items for Willis's story of " Lady Ravelgold."

" 12. Dined with Mrs. Joanna Baillie at Hampstead. She gave me some of the wedding cake of

Ada Byron. Said that her husband, Lord King, was hated by his own father and mother and often in want of money, but an excellent person and beloved by his own second brother, who had received from the father all that was not entailed. On the death of the father, Lord K. had nine thousand a year. Mrs. Baillie said that Lady Byron had given to the present Lord B. her whole jointure when he came to the title.

" Went to Lady Blessington at ten, and had a long talk with Countess Guiccioli, who said she wished nevermore to be spoken of in good or ill. The evil was remembered and the good forgotten. She made a point of never reading the papers.

" Thence to Charles Kemble's *soirée.* Countess d'Orsay there."

And thus the journal proceeds with its daily count of dinners, balls, *soirées*, garden parties, and opera-going, the diarist finally recording himself as " fatigued to death with dinners and dissipations." In fact the pace began to tell upon him. Following the last entry that I have copied here, for July 12th, comes the first draft of a poem, " Thoughts on the Balcony of Devonshire House at Sunrise after a Splendid Ball : "

> " Morn in the East ! How coldly fair
>   It breaks upon my fevered eye !
> How chides the calm and dewy air ;
>   How chides the pure and pearly sky !
> The stars melt in a brighter fire, —
>   The dew in sunshine leaves the flowers, —

They from their watch in light retire,
While we in sadness pass from ours."

This is one of Willis's most genuine utterances.
The same revulsion of feeling is expressed in
" Better Moments " and " She was not There."
There were two men in him, the worldling and
the poet; and when worn with fashionable dissipation he was sensitive to the rebuke of the
midnight heaven or of that " awful rose of
dawn " which God makes for himself in the
" Vision of Sin." But the mood, though sincere, was not lasting. " Recovered my spirits,"
runs the entry for July 15th, " after a causeless
depression for a week."

Toward the end of July he escaped to the
country and " passed a month at Shirley Park
and the Manor, Lee, alternately reading and ly-
ing on the grass in delightful idleness, with the
kindest friends and the greatest contentment."
At Shirley Park there were archery *fêtes*, the
Archbishop*ess* of Canterbury, " lords and ladies
in abundance, and poets and travelers *ad libi-
tum*. It is midsummer," continues the letter
from which I quote (August 5th), " in cool and
breezy England, five o'clock in the afternoon,
and a beautiful day. The house is in the middle of a park (nothing but grass and trees) as
large as the Common in Boston, the soft velvet
greensward closely shaven all around the house,

and a lovely archery ground on the edge of the lake just beneath my window, with red and gold targets, and a dozen young girls and beaux with beautiful bows and quivers shooting with all the merriment conceivable. There is a beautiful daughter of Sir Henry Brydges beating everybody, and my friend Mrs. Shaw, and Lady Encombe, and quantities of nice people."

At Shirley Park he had a letter from Jane Porter, inclosing an invitation to him from Sir Charles Throckmorton, a Catholic gentleman in Warwickshire, at whose country seat she was staying. Willis joined her there on September 10th, but meanwhile something else of great importance to him had happened. While visiting at the Skinners' he had met his fate in the person of Miss Mary Stace, a daughter of General William Stace of Woolwich. He saw her first at a picnic on the grounds of Lord Londonderry, at North Cray, and " thought her the loveliest girl he had ever seen." At Shirley Park — whither she came as a guest — he was thrown much in her company, and after a week's acquaintance made her a proposal of marriage, and was accepted. On the 1st of September he went to Woolwich on a visit to the Staces, and in the course of a day or two asked the general for his daughter's hand. It was agreed that the engagement should be short, like the courtship, and that the wedding should come off on the 1st of October. Mary Stace, who became Mrs. Willis on the day fixed, was a girl of uncommon beauty and sweetness. In appearance she was of the purest Saxon type, a blonde, with bright color, blue eyes, light brown hair, and delicate, regular features. She had a gentle, clinging, affectionate disposition, adored her husband, had been religiously and carefully educated, and possessed the true Englishwoman's sense of the importance of the male sex and the due subordination of woman. Her family were most worthy and substantial people, and strictly evangelical. General Stace was the Royal Ordnance Storekeeper at Woolwich Arsenal. He had been commissary to the British navy in Egypt, and commissary of ordnance at the battle of Waterloo, and had been rewarded for gallant service in that famous action. He gave Willis, as a souvenir, a military cloak and an eagle clasp taken from the body of a French officer after the battle, which are still preserved in the family. His son-in-law described him as honest, hearty, and plain-spoken, with the common soldierly weakness for telling post-prandial stories of his campaigns. Mrs. Stace was Irish, a great singer, and a friend of Tom Moore, who used to listen to her songs by the hour. There were five other children besides Mary. Two of the sons were in the army, and afterwards there were three Colonels Stace. The general agreed to give his daughter £300 a year, which, with the £300 or £400 which Willis counted upon making by literary work, would do, wrote the latter to Mrs. Skinner, for a poet. Having completed the arrangements for his marriage, he set out from London, September 10th, by the Tantivy coach for Sir Charles Throckmorton's seat of Coughton Court. This was a fine old Elizabethan mansion near Alcester, and Willis spent ten days there very agreeably, visiting, in company with Miss Porter and his host, Warwick Castle, Kenilworth, Stratford, and other points of interest in the neighborhood. Of these jaunts an ample narrative is given in " Sketches of Travel," originally communicated to the " Mirror." Thence he returned to Woolwich, receiving on his departure an invitation from the hospitable baronet to bring his wife and stay a fortnight with him. At Woolwich he was again joined by Miss Porter, on the 25th, who came for a week's visit to the Staces and to be present at the wedding. From Coughton Court the expectant groom had written to his friends announcing his engagement, and received in reply many expressions of good wishes. Among others, Lady Blessington wrote as follows : —

ANGLESEY-NEAR-GOSPORT, *September* 19, 1835.

MY DEAR MR. WILLIS, — Yours of the 16th has been forwarded to me here, and I lose not an hour in replying to it. I congratulate you with my whole heart on your approaching marriage, and wish you all the happiness you so well deserve, and which a marriage well assorted will alone bestow. I predict the happiness I wish you, for you would not, I am sure, make an unworthy choice, and the distaste which the scenes you have gone through during the last year must have engendered in your mind will have taught you still more highly to appreciate the society and affection of a pure-minded and amiable woman, on whom your future happiness will depend. I think you have acted most wisely, and am sure that the rational plans you have laid down will insure your felicity. A residence *near* London, which gives you the opportunity of enjoying its numerous advantages, without weakening your mind by a too frequent contact with its dissipations, is, of all others, the one I would select for a literary man, and I shall look forward with pleasure to seeing you at Seamore Place in your new and more respectable character of a Domestic Man, which, be assured, will bestow more happiness on you than all the futile successes ever acquired in the heartless maze of fashion and folly, in whose vortex you have been whirled during so many months. A Man of Genius is out of his natural sphere in such a circle; he loses his identity and blunts the fine edge of his sensibility. You have retired in time, and will, I am persuaded, have reason to bless the gentle and benign influence that has attracted you from it to the pure and healthy atmosphere of domestic life. Be assured, my dear Mr. Willis, that out of the circle of your immediate family you have no friend more truly interested in your welfare or more anxious to promote it than I am, of which no proof in my power shall ever be wanting. I shall be in London on the 22d, and shall have great pleasure in seeing you. Your secret shall be safe with me, you may be sure. I hope the little tale will be sent for your correction in a day or two. Pray have "Ion" left at my house. Mr. Talfourd requested that it might not leave my possession, so that in lending it to you I disobeyed his request.

The old Earl of Dalhousie wrote a letter of hearty congratulation.

"Wherever you go or sit down at last," it said, "think of us as being with you in our minds' eye at least, and if it shall please God that, in the course of time, we ever meet again, it will be truly a day of joy here, for from hence I move no more."

His son, the young Lord Ramsay, had jestingly promised to be Willis's groomsman some day at Niagara, and the former now reminded him of it, and asked him to stand up with him, and Ramsay sent the following excuses some three weeks after the wedding : —

YESTER, *October* 23, 1835.

I promised to play my part as best man, my dear Willis, at *Niagara,* and to have descended from that to Woolwich would have been a sad *bathos*, so that it was perhaps as well that your notice was too short to allow of the possibility of my being with you before the 1st of October. Still I can congratulate you as well at a distance as with my own lips, and though the romance which we proposed for ourselves is gone, I am very happy to congratulate you on the prose reality.

I had written all this to you three weeks ago, and directed my frank to the Athenæum Club, a place which I took it into my head you frequented, when, this morning, the letter was returned by the porter with a "*non est inventus*" written on it. This to save my character.

Furthermore, your example was so good an one, and, fortunately, so *contagious*, that I have fallen a victim, and am going to be married, and as this is *not* a lady's letter, it will be as well not to keep the most important part of the intelligence for the post-script, but to tell you at once that it is to Lady Susan Hay. If I were to dash out into a rhapsody you, whose experience of such a situation is of so recent a date, might easily forgive me, but I will take mercy even on you. I am happy, — happy now, and if I am not happy always in time to come, Heaven knows how utterly it will be my own fault.

When next summer brings visiting time we shall meet, I trust, in Scotland, and exchange at once news, visits, and congratulations.

May I beg, even though a stranger, my compliments to Mrs. Willis, and believe me

Ever yours sincerely,   R<small>AMSAY</small>.

Mrs. Skinner wrote, in a letter to Jane Porter : —

"Mary Stace is a sweet, gentle, affectionate, lively
girl, — natural, so that you may see at once there is
no deceit in her and no guile. She is religious, accomplished, sings sweetly, is pretty, and will make
Willis more happy than any other woman I know.
He will have no heart-burnings, no misgivings with
her, for she is true and sincere. You will love her.
She was so religious, good, and depend-on-able that I
told her she should be my daughter-in-law."

In his letters to his folks at home announcing
his betrothal, Willis insisted a good deal on this
point of his *fiancée's* religiousness, and he evidently shared the belief commonly held and
proclaimed among men of the world, that religion, like a low voice, is an excellent thing — in
woman ; a theory which some women resent as a
covert insult to their understandings, and some
men as an open insult to their religion, and
which may be described as the converse of the
proposition that a reformed rake makes the best
husband.

"I should never have wished to marry you," he
wrote to his betrothed, about a fortnight before the
wedding, "if you had not been religious, for I have
confidence in no woman who is not so. I only think
there is sometimes an excess in the ostentation of
religious sanctity, and of that I have a dread, as you

have yourself, no doubt. Miss Porter," he adds, "is sincere and *refined* as few professedly religious people are."

In another letter he says : —

"Mine is not a love such as I have fancied and written about. It is more sober, more mingled with esteem and respect, and more fitted for every-day life. It had well need be, indeed, for I have taken it in lieu of what has hitherto been the principal occupation of my life. I am to live for you, dear Mary, and you for me, — if you like! That is to say, henceforth dissipation (if we indulge in it) will be *your* pleasure, not mine. I have lived the last ten years in gay society, and I am sick at heart of it. I want an apology to try something else. I am made for something better, and I feel sincerely that this is the turning-point of both mind and heart, both of which are injured in their best qualities with the kind of life I have been leading. Do not understand me that I am to make a hermit of myself, however, or a prisoner of you. You will have always friends enough, and society enough, and change of place and scene enough. In short, I shall exact but one thing, — four or five hours in my study in the morning, and you may do what you like with the rest."

They were married in Plumstead Church, by the Rev. Mr. Shackleton, on the 1st of October. "It was a kind of April day," writes Willis, "half sunshine, half rain," — recalling, somehow, the coincidence in Julia Mills's diary between the checker-board tavern-sign and checkered human existence on a similar occasion in David Copperfield's life, — " but everybody was kind, the villagers strewed flowers in the way, the church was half full of people, and my heart and eyes were more than full of tears." The bridal pair were driven in Mr. Stace's carriage to Rochester, posted next day to Dover, and crossed the Channel on the 3d. They passed a fortnight at the Hôtel Castiglione in Paris, and then returned to England, where they spent the winter, partly in London and partly at Woolwich, and in visits to the Shaws, Skinners, and other friends. Willis was busy in getting out the first and second English editions of " Pencillings " and the " Inklings of Adventure." He presented his bride to his " swell " acquaintances in London, and was himself introduced by his brothers-in-law to numbers of military people, dined at the Artillery Mess, and was given the freedom of the Army and Navy Club. He set up an " establishment," a cabriolet and a gray cab-horse, " tall, showy, and magnificent." He had taken into service a young fellow named William Michell, the son of his landlady, a bright and handsome lad, who now made a very presentable tiger. William went to America with his master in the spring, remained in his service during his residence at Glenmary, and

came back with him, in 1839, to England, where
he ultimately got employment as a machinist,
having a good education and a knack at me-
chanics.

In May, 1836, after many leave-takings, Willis sailed with his wife for America. His "Lines
on Leaving Europe," —

     " Bright flag at yonder tapering mast," —

dated in the English Channel, express the feelings at once of regret and of hope with which
he set his face homeward after an absence of
four years and a half. These spirited lines are
among the very few poems of Willis which
seem destined to last. They have the real lyrical impulse, and it is not easy to read them
without emotion. Emerson, who gives part of
the poem in "Parnassus," omits the closing
stanza, in which the poet touchingly bespeaks a
welcome for his English bride.

   " Room in thy heart ! The hearth she left
     Is darkened to lend light to ours.
  There are bright flowers of care bereft,
     And hearts — that languish more than flowers.
  She was their light — their very air ;
  Room, mother, in thy heart ! place for her in thy prayer ! "

Willis published three books while in England. "Melanie and Other Poems" appeared
March 31, 1835. It was divided into three
parts and included a selection from the three

volumes of verse published in America, but un-
familiar to the British public, besides some half
dozen new poems, dated, said the author, in his
prefatory note, from "the corner of a club [the
Travellers'] in the ungenial month of January."
It was introduced by Barry Cornwall, who
speaks of the poet as "a man of high talent and
sensibility," and then goes on with some reflections of a friendly nature on American literature and the desirableness of cultivating kinder
feelings between England and America. Wilson, who reviewed "Melanie" very favorably in
"Blackwood's," made Procter's introduction to
it the theme of much elaborate ridicule, in the
well-known style of "Maga," when rending a
cockney author. He affected to have gathered
an impression from the title-page, — which described the poems as "edited" by Barry Cornwall, — that Willis was dead, and that Procter
was performing the office of literary undertaker
for "poor Willis's remains." "Alas! thought
we, on reading this title-page; is Willis dead?
Then America has lost one of the most promising of her young poets. We had seen him not
many months before in high health and spirits
and had much enjoyed his various and vivacious
conversation. . . . But why weep for him, the
accomplished acquaintance of an hour?" He
goes out on the street and tells the first friend

he meets that Willis is dead. "Impossible,"
answers the friend; "day before yesterday he
was sitting very much alive in the Athenæum
Club: here is a letter from him franked Ma-
hon," etc. Another Scotch professor — Aytoun
— who belonged, like Wilson, to the Tory light
artillery, was moved to write a parody of "Melanie." The same humorist also paid his respects to Willis in one of his "Ballads of Bon
Gaultier," — a strenuous piece of North British
playfulness, in which Willis and Bryant are
represented as sallying forth like knights er-
rant on the Quest of the Snapping Turtle: —

> "Have you heard of Philip Slingsby —
> Slingsby of the manly chest ?
> How he slew the snapping turtle
> In the regions of the west ? "

The two longest and most ambitious poems in
this volume were "Melanie" and "Lord Ivon
and his Daughter." The first is the story "told
during a walk around the cascatelles of Tivoli,"
of an English girl, "the last of the De Brevern
race," who betroths herself in Italy to a young
painter of unknown parentage; but at their
bridal at St. Mona's altar a nun shrieks through
the lattice of the chapel: —

> "The bridegroom is thy blood — thy brother!
> Rudolph de Brevern wronged his mother,"

and the bride thereupon " sunk and died, with-

out a sign or word." The stanza and style are
taken from Byron's and Scott's metrical romances. The very first line —

" I stood on yonder rocky brow" —

is a reminiscence of "The Isles of Greece."
The second poem, which is equally melodramatic in its catastrophe, is in blank verse and
in the form of a dialogue between the Lady Isi-
dore and her father, Lord Ivon. He tells his
daughter (with a few interruptions from her,
such as "Impossible!" and "Nay, dear father!
Was't so indeed?") how he had in vain wooed
her grandmother with minstrelsy and feats of
arms, and then her mother more successfully
with gold: marrying whom, he had begotten Isi-
dore, and afterwards, in remorse for having
dragged his young bride to the altar, had been
on the point of draining a poisoned chalice,
when she had anticipated him by running away
with a younger lover, leaving to his care the
babe, now grown to a woman, who dutifully concludes the dialogue with, "Thank God! Thank
God!" Both of these poems were imitative and
artificial, and the last not a little absurd. Willis had no genius for narrative or dramatic poetry, and when he tried to be impersonal and
"objective," he wrought against the grain. The
lyrical pieces in the book were almost all of
them graceful and sweet. He himself thought

that the best thing in the volume was "Birth-Day Verses," addressed to his mother on January 20, 1835. Similar in theme were the lines, "To my Mother, from the Apennines," written at an *auberge* on the mountains, August 3, 1832. The verses to Mary Benjamin, written in Scotland in September, 1834, have been already mentioned. They stand in his collected poems as "To M——, from Abroad," and were also incorporated in "Edith Linsey," under the title "To Edith, from the North." "The Confessional," dated Hellespont, October 1, 1833, was also meant for Mary Benjamin. This and "Florence Gray" had the note of travel. But a Boston poem, "The Belfry Pigeon," was the most popular of anything in the book and has retained a place in readers and collections to the present day. These shorter pieces, like all of Willis's truest poetry, were purely poems of sentiment. His description, in "Edith Linsey," of Job Smith's verses as "the mixed product of feeling and courtesy" applies consciously to his own. They were "the delicate offspring of tenderness and chivalry," airy, facile, smooth, but thin in content: not rich, full, concrete, but buoyed up by light currents of emotion in a region, to quote his own words again, of "floating and colorless sentiments." This disembodied character is a mark of almost all the American

poetry of the Annual or *Gemmiferous* period,
and is seen at its extreme in the unsubstantial
prolixity of Percival and the drab diffuseness of
Mrs. Sigourney. It was the reflection on this
side the water from Shelley, from Byron's earlier manner, from Wordsworth's most didactic
passages, and from the imitations of all these
by secondary poets, like Mrs. Norton and L. E.
L. Willis's verses were much better than Percival's or Mrs. Sigourney's — defter, briefer, more
pointed. But they had a certain poverty of im-
agery and allusion which belonged to the school,
a recurrence of stock properties, such as roses,
stars, and bells. He was ridiculed by the critics,
in particular, for his constancy to the Pleiades,
which would almost seem to have been the only
constellation in his horizon.

Toward the last of November, 1835, the first
edition of "Pencillings by the Way" was published. It was an imperfect one, made up hastily for the London market from a broken set of
the "Mirror," and gave only seventy-nine out of
the one hundred and thirty-nine letters since
printed in the complete editions. From this
imperfect copy the first American impression
(1836) was taken, and all in fact down to 1844.
The book reached a second English edition in
March, 1836, and a seventh in 1863. For this
first edition Willis received £250. He after-

wards testified, that from the republication of
the original " Pencillings," for which Morris had
paid him $500 a year, he had made, all told,
about $5,000. Their appearence in book form
had been anticipated by a severe criticism of the
original " Mirror " letters, written by Lockhart
for the "London Quarterly " of September, 1835.
This was echoed by the Tory press generally, and
it was their attacks which led to the issue of the
London edition and greatly stimulated its sale.
There were several reasons why the Tory papers
were " down on " Willis. In the first place he
was an American. In the next place he had been
admitted and made much of in English social
circles, where English men of letters, who were
merely men of letters, did not often go. And,
finally, he had spoken disrespectfully in these
letters of the editor of the "Quarterly " himself.
" Do you know Lockhart? " Wilson is made to
ask in Willis's report of their conversation at
Edinburgh. "No, I do not," replies his interlocutor. " He is almost the only literary man in
London I have not met; and I must say, as the
editor of the ' Quarterly,' and the most unfair
and unprincipled critic of the day, I have no
wish to know him. I never heard him well
spoken of. I probably have met a hundred of
his acquaintances, but I have not yet seen one
who pretended to be his friend."

This paragraph was enough to account for the
" Quarterly " article; but the personal grievance
was kept well out of sight, and Willis was taken
to task for his alleged abuse of the rights of
hospitality in reporting for a public journal private conversations at gentlemen's tables.   The
article was a very offensive one, written with
ability and with that air of cold contempt of
which Lockhart was master.   It sneered at Willis as a " Yankee poetaster," and a " sonnet-
eer of the most ultra-sentimental delicacy; " intimated that his surprise and delight at the
manners of the English aristocracy came from
his not having been familiar with the usages of
the best society at home, and accused him of
" conceited vulgarity " and " cockneyism " (an
awful word, under which the Scotch Tories con-
noted all possible offenses against sound politics
and good literature).   The passages that seem
to have given most offense to the critic were the
report of the conversation with Lord Aberdeen
at Gordon Castle and the remarks of Moore
about O'Connell at Lady Blessington's.   " It is
fortunate in this particular case," wrote Lockhart, "that what Lord Aberdeen said to Mr.
Willis might be repeated in print without pain-
ing any of the persons his lordship talked of;
but what he did say, he said under the impression
that the guest of the Duke of Gordon was a gen-

tleman, and there are abundance of passages in
Mr. Willis's book which can leave no doubt that,
had the noble earl spoken in a different sense, it
would not, at all events, have been from any
feeling of what was due to his lordship, or to
himself, that Mr. Willis would have hesitated to
report the conversation with equal freedom."
The article concludes as follows: "This is the
first example of a man creeping into your home
and forthwith printing, — accurately or inaccu-
rately, no matter which, — before your claret is
dry on his lips, — unrestrained *table-talk on delicate subjects, and capable of compromising in-
dividuals.*" Lockhart, as usual, contrived to
insult Willis's country, through her representative. "We can well believe," he said, "that
Mr. Willis has been depicting the sort of society
that most interests his countrymen.

'Born to be slaves and struggling to be lords,'

their servile adulation of rank and title, their
stupid admiration of processions and *levées*, and
so forth, are leading features in almost all the
American books of travels that we have met
with."

To this censure Willis replied, in substance,
in the preface to the first London edition of
"Pencillings," first, that from "the distance of
America, and the ephemeral nature and usual

obscurity of periodical correspondence," he had
never expected that the "Mirror" letters would
reach England; nor would they have done so,
had not the "Quarterly" "made a long arm over
the water," and reprinted all the offending portions; thereby forcing the author's hand and
compelling him to publish the entire collection
in justification of himself. Secondly, that his
sketches of distinguished people were neither
ill-natured nor untrue; that he had said nothing
in them which could injure the feelings of those
who had admitted him to their confidence or
hospitality. "There *are* passages," he allows,
" I would not rewrite, and some remarks on in-
dividuals which I would recall at some cost,"
but " I may state as a fact that the only instance in which a quotation by me from the conversation of distinguished men gave the least offense in England was the one remark made by
Moore, the poet, at a dinner party, on the subject of O'Connell. It would have been harmless,
as it was designed to be, but for the unexpected
celebrity of my ' Pencillings; ' yet with all my
heart I wish it unwritten." And finally, that
whatever violations of delicacy and good taste
might have been committed in the " Pencillings,"
the author of " Peter's Letters to his Kinsfolk "
was not the one to throw a stone at them. The
first plea in this defense was sincerely made, as

might be easily proved from Willis's private
letters. It *was* a disagreeable surprise to him
when the " Quarterly " reprinted passages from
the "Mirror" letters. And it is true that America was much farther away from England than
England was from America. Still, if Willis had
published anything that he should not have published, it was not a perfect excuse to say that he
had done it in a corner. As the event showed,
foreign correspondence in an American newspaper might reach England. But this apology
was not needed, for his second plea covered the
ground. There was, in truth, nothing malicious
or slanderous in " Pencillings ; " almost nothing
that could give pain even to the most sensitive.
The people described were, nearly all of them,
in a sense, public characters, accustomed to seeing themselves gossiped about in print. In one
or two instances Willis had been indiscreet, as
he freely admitted. But it is hard for one living in these times of society journals and " inter-
viewers " to understand why the papers should
have made such a pother over a comparatively
trifling trespass upon the reserves of private life.
The best proof of Willis's innocence in the matter is that the people whose hospitality and confidence he was charged with abusing took no
kind of umbrage at the liberty. On the contrary, Lord Aberdeen, Wilson, Dalhousie, and

others wrote to him in warm approval of his book. " With what feelings," said the " Quarterly " article, apropos of the description of Gordon Castle, " the whole may have been perused by the generous lord and lady of the castle themselves, it is no business of ours to conjecture." This point, however, need not be left to conjecture, as it is amply answered in the following letter to Willis from the Earl of Dalhousie, dated February 25, 1836 : —

. . . In the long evenings of winter we have beguiled the time with " Pencillings by the Way," and whatever critics and reviewers may say, I take pleasure in assuring you that we all agree in one sentiment, that a more amusing or more delightful production was never issued by the press. In what we know of it, it is true and graphic, and therefore in what is foreign to us, we think, must be so also. *The Duke and Duchess of Gordon were here lately and expressed themselves in similar terms.*

Lady D—— desires me to say that the reviews could not have done more for its success by their amplest praises, for it is now in every hand.

Our family has been much occupied by Ramsay's marriage this winter, he following your steps so closely. He has added greatly to his parents' happiness, and, I hope, to his own in life. Lady Susan Hay is a handsome woman, and an amiable, pretty creature. They have settled themselves at Coalstown, until called into a more active life, which I hope he looks forward to, and you have thought him fitted for. It is not unlikely that he will be chosen member for the East Lothian, in which he has made his residence, triangular between me and his father-in-law, Lord Tweeddale, about sixteen miles from me.

Pray let me hear from you, as your sincere attached friend, DALHOUSIE.

Lady Dalhousie had written some two mouths before : —

I feel that it is positive ingratitude not to offer our united thanks for your book, which we received in safety, and Miss Hathorne and I are now reading it aloud to Lord Dalhousie in the evening, with very great pleasure and amusement. Your descriptions recall to my mind admirably what I have seen, and paint to my mind's eye what I wish to see, and the happy sunshine which your own mind has shed over every person and thing you have met is refreshing and enlivening to us, living now much alone in this dark and gloomy December. The " Quarterly " we read with extreme wrath and indignation, and, believe me, it will afford us the most sincere pleasure if you will take, if you find them worthy of it, a few more of your spirited pencillings from D. Castle. . . . Believe me always very sincerely yours.

C. B. DALHOUSIE.

It has been said above that there was almost nothing in " Pencillings " that could give pain to any one ; but to this statement there are one or two exceptions. The first was the instance of

Moore and O'Connell, in which Willis acknowledged and regretted his imprudence. "This
publication, to my knowledge," says Madden in
his "Life of the Countess of Blessington," "was
attended with results which I cannot think Mr.
Willis contemplated when he transmitted his
hasty notes to America, — to estrangements of
persons who, previously to the printed reports of
their private conversations, had been on terms
of intimate acquaintance. This was the case
with respect to O'Connell and Moore. Moore's
reported remarks on O'Connell gave offense to
the latter, and aroused bad feelings between
them which had never previously existed, and
which, I believe, never ceased to exist."

It also appears from a letter from Willis to
Lady Blessington, and an unsigned note from
a friend of hers to Willis, both of which are
printed in Madden's "Life," that Fonblanque
resented the description of himself in "Pencillings," and had written the author a note in
terms which the latter thought "very unjustifiable." Fonblanque was an able and estimable
man, and Willis's portrait, or caricature, of him,
though not unkindly meant and applying merely
to his personal appearance, was certainly not
pleasant for the subject of it to see in print.

"I never saw," it runs, "a much worse face; sallow,
seamed, and hollow, his teeth irregular, his skin livid,

his straight black hair uncombed and straggling over his forehead ; he looked as if he might be the gentleman ' whose coat was red and whose breeches were blue.' A hollow, croaking voice, and a small, fiery black eye, with a smile like a skeleton's, certainly did not improve his physiognomy. He sat upon his chair very awkwardly, and was very ill dressed, but every word' he uttered showed him to be a man of claims very superior to exterior attraction."

With the exception of Lockhart, Moore, Fonblanque, and Captain Marryat, whose case will be mentioned presently, it does not appear that any one took offense at anything in "Pencillings." As to Lady Blessington, Lockhart's misgiving as to whether she would ever " again admit to her table the animal who has printed what ensues " was needless. It was she who saw the book through the press while Willis was in France on his wedding journey. He went to see her frequently during the remainder of his stay in London, and called upon her on his two subsequent visits to England ; and their friendship and correspondence continued unbroken till her death in 1849. His poem, " To a Face Beloved," originally printed in the " Mirror " of November 14, 1835, was addressed to her. It may well have been, however, that the noise made about the book, and the cause for complaint given to a few of the *habitués* of Gore House, put a certain constraint upon his visits there, and he probably absented himself from the dinners and receptions given by the mistress of the mansion, and which it had formerly been his chief pleasure to attend. In a letter to her from Dublin, January 25, 1840, he says: "I have, I assure you, no deeper regret than that my indiscretion (in 'Pencillings') should have checked the freedom of my approach to you. Still my attachment and admiration (so unhappily recorded) are always on the alert for some trace that I am still remembered by you. . . . My first pleasure when I return to town will be to avail myself of your kind invitation, and call at Gore House."

In spite of the " Quarterly's " attack — partly no doubt in consequence of it — " Pencillings by the Way " met, on the whole, with a generous reception from the English public, and even from the English press. Literary criticism in those days was largely influenced by political prejudice. It was useless for a Whig, a " Cockney," or an American, to hope for justice from the Tory reviews, The " Westminster " (Radical) was edited by Willis's friend, Dr. Bowring; the " Edinburgh " (Whig), by his acquaintance, Lord Jeffrey. The former accordingly greeted his book with warm approval, and the latter praised it with faint damns. On the other hand, " Fraser's," the lightest and brightest of the

Tory organs, received it with uproarious contempt. The notice of " Pencillings " in the February number of the magazine for 1836 was by
Maginn, — the " Odoherty " of the " Noctes,"
— a witty Irish blackguard, the hired bravo of
the Tory press, who spent his time, except when
drunk or in jail for debt, in writing lampoons
and rollicking songs for " Blackwood " and " Fraser," expressive chiefly of convivial joys and of
boisterous scorn of the Whigs. There was a flavor of whiskey and Donnybrook about whatever
Maginn wrote, and he wielded his blackthorn
with such droll abandon that his victims could
hardly help laughing, while rubbing their heads.
His onslaught on " Pencillings " began, " This
is really a goose of a book, or if anybody wishes
the idiom to be changed, a book of a goose.
There is not a single idea in it, from the first
page to the last, beyond what might germinate
in the brain of a washerwoman." He then goes
on to call the author a lickspittle, a " beggarly
skittler," a jackass, a ninny, a haberdasher, a
" namby-pamby writer in twaddling albums, kept
by the moustachioed and strong-smelling widows
or bony matrons of Portland Place ; " a " fifty-
fifth rate scribbler of gripe-visited sonnets," a
" windy-gutted visitor," and a " sumph," whatever that mystic monosyllable may import.[1] His

[1] It was doubtless this article which encouraged Bates in

writing is characterized as " chamber-maid gab-
ble," " small beer," " penny-trumpet eloquence,"
" Willis's bray," and " Niagara in a jordan."
President Jackson, whom Maginn supposes to
have appointed Willis *attaché* to the French embassy, is " that most open-throated of flummery-
gulpers, Old Hickory." Alluding to a passage
in Willis's " slimy preface," the reviewer says,
" that Willis should literally set his foot on
Lockhart's head is what we think no one im-
agines the silly man to have meant. The prob-
abilities are that if the imposition of feet should
take place between them, the toe of Lockhart
would find itself in disgusting contact with a
part of Willis which is considerably removed
from his head, and deemed to be the quarter
in which the honor of such persons is most peculiarly called into action." Such were the
amenities of criticism half a century ago. Of
course this animated billingsgate could not hurt
Willis in anybody's esteem, and called for no
reply. Maginn was a wretched creature and no
one minded what he said; though, to be sure,
the Hon. Grantley Berkeley thought it necessary, in this same year, 1836, to call him out
for a scurrilous attack upon himself and his
cousin, Lady Euston, in a notice of Berkeley's

the *Maclise Portrait Gallery* to describe Willis as a " sumph "
and " N(amby) P(amby) Willis."

novel, "Castle Berkeley." The latter, in his
very diverting "Life and Recollections," gives
a circumstantial history of this duel and of the
flogging which he administered to Fraser for
publishing the article, and of Maginn's shame-
ful treatment of poor Miss Landon.

But one of the notices provoked by "Pencillings" came near having serious consequences
for Willis. In a letter in the "Mirror" of
April 18, 1835, he had inserted a postscript,
after his signature, as he claimed, and meant
only for Morris's private eye, giving some information about the sales of books in London.
In this occurred, among other things, the sentence following: "Captain Marryat's gross trash
sells immensely about Wapping and Portsmouth,
and brings him five or six hundred the book,
but that can scarce be called literature."
Morris printed it with the rest of the letter, and
when it reached England the gallant captain
was naturally displeased by it. His revenge was
to publish in his magazine, the "Metropolitan"
for January, 1836, a review of "Pencillings,"
or rather a grossly personal review of the author
of "Pencillings." The article was less telling
than the "Quarterly's," simply because Marryat
did not drive so sharp a quill as the editor of the
"Quarterly." But the latter knew his business
as a reviewer and confined himself to the book

in hand. Marryat, on the contrary, traveled outside the record and helplessly allowed his private grievance to appear. He declared that Willis was a "spurious *attaché*," who had made his way into English society under false colors.

" He makes invidious, uncharitable, and ill-natured remarks upon authors and their works; all of which he dispatches for the benefit of the reading public of America, and, at the same time that he has thus stabbed them behind their backs, he is requesting to be introduced to them — bowing, smiling, and simpering." "Although we are well acquainted with the birth, parentage, and history of Mr. Willis, previous to his making his continental tour, we will pass them over in silence; and we think that Mr. Willis will acknowledge that we are generous in so doing." " It is evident that Mr. Willis has never, till lately, been in good society, either in England or America."

Finally he exhumed from some quarter the pasquinade of poor Joe Snelling, referred to in our third chapter, from which he printed the following lines by way of showing Willis's standing at home : —

> " Then Natty filled the ' Statesman's ' ribald page
> With the rank breathings of his prurient age,
> And told the world how many a half-bred Miss,
> Like Shakspere's fairy, gave an ass a kiss ;
> Long did he try the art of sinking on
> The muddy pool he took for Helicon ;
> Long did he delve and grub with fins of lead

At its foul bottom for precarious bread. . . .
Dishonest critic and ungrateful friend,
Still on a woman [1] thy stale jokes expend.
Live — at thy meagre table still preside,
While foes commiserate and friends deride ;
Yet live — thy wonted follies to repeat,
Live — till thy printer's ruin is complete ;
Strut out thy fleeting hour upon the stage,
Amidst the hisses of the passing age."

Marryat's article was a stupid one, ungrammatical and coarsely written. But its clumsy malice made it all the more exasperating. Lockhart was a gentleman and Maginn was an Irishman. The former took care not to say too much, and what the latter said was of no consequence. Both of them, besides, were clever writers, and a man of wit and spirit had rather be pricked by a rapier in the hand of a dexterous adversary than pounded on the head by an awkward bully with a bludgeon. Willis made a mistake in noticing Marryat's article at all, but he was stung by the implied insult to his parents, and his military friends persuaded him that his honor was touched. Accordingly he prepared an elaborate reply in the shape of a letter, dated January 10th, and sent it to Marryat at Brussels, whither the latter had gone about the middle of December, while his article was still in proof.

" Of that part of the paper which refers to the

[1] Mrs. Child.

merits of my book," Willis wrote, "I have nothing to say. You were at liberty, as a critic, to deal with it as you pleased. You have transcended the limits of criticism, however, to make an attack on my character, and your absence compels me to represent, by my own letter, those claims for reparation which I should have intrusted to a friend, had you been in England." The letter then proceeds to answer, in detail, the charges and innuendoes of the " Metropolitan." As to his seeking introductions, Willis declares, " I have never, since my arrival in England, requested an introduction to *any man.* . . . In the single interview which I had with yourself, I was informed by the lady who was the medium of the introduction, that *you wished* to know me." The letter concludes, apropos of Marryat's slur on Willis's birth and parentage, " You will readily admit that this dark insinuation must be completely withdrawn. My literary reputation and my position in society are things I could outlive. My honesty as a critic is a point on which the world may decide. But my own honor and that of my family are sacred, and while I live, no breath of calumny shall rest on either. I trust to receive, at your earliest convenience, that explanation which you cannot but acknowledge is due to me on this point, and which is most imperatively required by my

own character and the feelings of my friends."
As to the remark which had drawn the " Metropolitan " article upon him, Willis confesses that
it was an unjust one, but says that " it occurred
in a private communication to the editor of the
' Mirror ' and was never intended for publication."

Willis had this letter lithographed and sent
copies to seven of his particular friends, to clear
his character, as he said, in his own immediate
circle, of the aspersions in Marryat's article.
The reply to this demand was a long letter, under
date of January 21st, declining to make any apology until Willis had publicly withdrawn his remark in the " Mirror " about Marryat's gross
trash selling about Wapping, etc., which, said the
latter, amounted by implication to an attack on
his private character; denying, furthermore,
that *he* had attacked *Willis's* private character.
" The observations made by you upon my writings must be considered as more or less injurious
in proportion to the rank in society and estima-
tion of the person who made them. . . . It was
therefore necessary, in this instance, to point out
that the critic had not been accustomed to good
society. . . . Now this, if true, is no crime, and
therefore the remark can be no attack upon private character." Willis accepted this explanation, in a second letter to Marryat, and then

sent the entire correspondence to the " Times "
for publication.   Marryat was furious at this,
and wrote at once to Willis, " I refuse all explanation — insist upon immediate satisfaction —
and that you forthwith repair to Ostend to meet
me."   If the captain thought that his opponent
was a dandy poet, who would be afraid to face
his pistol, he mistook his man.   " The puppies
will fight," said the Duke.   Willis was no shot,
and the only weapon that he knew how to handle
was his pen, but he never showed any want of
personal courage.   The correspondence that followed this challenge was long and tedious.   The
documents in the case are a score in number and
need not be reproduced here.   The substance of
these various protocols and formalities was as
follows.   Willis answered Marryat's letter, ex-
plaining why he had thought right to publish
the first three letters that had passed between
them, accepting his challenge, in case he found
this explanation insufficient, but claiming his
privilege, as the challenged party, to name some
place in England for the meeting.   Meanwhile
a duplicate of Marryat's challenge had been
handed to Willis by the former's " friend," a
Mr. F. Mills, and Willis had referred him to
his friend, Captain Walker, and had agreed to
waive his right to name a place, and to meet
Marryat at Ostend.   Mr. Mills and Captain

Walker finally adjusted the matter and arranged a basis for an amicable settlement. But while these negotiations were pending, Marryat, on the receipt of Willis's letter of explanation, withdrew his challenge in a letter dated February 9th, which he sent to the " Times," along with his challenge and Willis's reply to it. The terms of this withdrawal Willis considered insulting, and the publication of the challenge after it had been agreed upon between the friends of the parties that Marryat " should entirely withdraw the offensive letter containing his challenge," he regarded as a further insult. He therefore wrote to the " Times," on the day following the appearance of these letters, that the differences between himself and Captain Marryat were *not* at an end ; and on February 17th he wrote to Marryat that his challenge still stood acc pted, insisting on his right to name England as the place of meeting, but offering in case of interruption there to give him a meeting on the other side of the Channel. Marryat accordingly came to England and — Mr. Mills having withdrawn from the affair — named as his second Captain Edward Belcher of the Royal Navy. Captain Belcher's ship was at Chatham and thither all parties repaired on the 27th of February. Willis's second declared to Captain Belcher that his principal " had come to fight, not to negotiate," but on a little discussion Captain Belcher found his principal in the wrong, and made him concede what was necessary, the following pronunciamento being signed by both seconds: —

CHATHAM.

Captain Marryat and Mr. Willis having placed the arrangement of the dispute between them in our hands, and both parties having repaired hither with the intent of a hostile meeting; we have, previously to permitting such to take place, carefully gone through the original grounds of quarrel, which do not appear to us of sufficient importance to call for a meeting of such a nature.

We are perfectly borne out in this opinion by the arrangement of the 8th of February entered into by the mutual friends of the parties, and on which we think Captain Marryat ought to have withdrawn his challenge of the 4th inst.

That the new quarrel arises from the publication of the challenge and subsequent letters, in which, in our opinion, Captain Marryat was not justified. We are further of opinion that both parties should mutually withdraw the offensive correspondence, the terms on either side being unjustifiable, and we conceive that they more honorably act in so doing than in meeting in the field.   EDWARD BELCHER.

F. G. WALKER.

Thus peacefully ended this tempest in a teapot. Willis had carried his point and had acted

throughout in a high-spirited and creditable
manner — barring the folly of entering into
"an affair of honor," in the first place. His
letters to Marryat are those of a gentleman,
while his adversary's language is invariably
hectoring and coarse. The quarrel, of course,
made a great deal of noise at the time in London literary and social circles. "The United
Service Gazette," the organ of the British
Army and Navy, took Willis's side in a long editorial in which much of the correspondence was
reprinted from the "Times." The latter journal, however, probably voiced the true sentiment of the community when it said: "We
confess that we have a great distaste for this
sort of squabbling, which exhibits, to say the
least, an extraordinary want of judgment in the
disputing parties."

From Chatham Willis posted at once to
Woolwich, thirty miles away, where he found his
wife in convulsions. He had left a farewell
letter for her, fully expecting to be killed in a
duel with Marryat, who was reputed a crack
shot. Two days later Willis went to London
and called out Mr. F. Mills, who had acted as
Marryat's "mediator," for an offensive letter in
the "Times." Mr. Mills named W. F. Campbell of Islay and Willis named John Tyndale,
between whom this subsidiary quarrel was soon

patched up, in a manner honorable to both. The assaults in the English magazines and the rumors of the Marryat affair of course found their way speedily to America, and were circulated and commented upon in the American periodicals according to their various prepossessions. " The cultivated old clergymen of the ' North American Review,' " as Poe used to call them, lent the support of that influential quarterly to Willis in an article by C. C. Felton, a very friendly review of the " Pencillings," and a defense of their author — a favor which Willis gratefully appreciated.

In March, 1836, he published in London " Inklings of Adventure," consisting of thirteen stories and sketches of American and European life, reprinted from the "New Monthly," " The Metropolitan," and the " Court Magazine," together with "Minute Philosophies" (from the " American Monthly ") and " A Log in the Archipelago," from the " Mirror." The book was handsomely published in three volumes, and dedicated to Edward Everett. For an edition of 1,200 copies Willis was paid £300, reserving to himself the copyright; and as he had received a guinea a page for the original articles, besides what Morris gave him for their republication in the " Mirror," they may be said to have been fairly profitable.

These " Slingsby " papers are exceedingly clever. With the possible exception of " Letters from under a Bridge " and portions of "Pencillings by the Way," they are the best work that Willis ever did ; and they compare well with such lighter fiction, in the way of short tales or sketches of travel and adventure, as has been produced in America since Willis's day. Whatever else they are, they are never dull and always readable. They are not read now only because the readers of light fiction habitually follow the market and inquire merely for the last thing out. Many of them were worked over from his " American Monthly " *juvenilia*, but his touch had grown firmer and he had purchased experience, as his motto declared, by his " penny of observation." These " Inklings " do not penetrate to the stratum of real character, of strong passion, and of the interplay of motives and moral relations in which all vital fiction has its roots. Their plots are commonly slight, their persons sketchy, their incidents not seldom improbable, their coloring sometimes too high. As transcripts of actual life such stories as " Pedlar Karl," " The Cherokee's Threat," and " Tom Fane and I," with the easy optimism of their conclusions and their cheerful avoidance of all the responsibilities imposed upon the dwellers in this workaday world,

are of course misleading and false. Their air
is the air of every day, but their happenings are
those of the wildest romance. Their charm —
and they have for many old-fashioned readers a
quite decided charm — does not lie in truth to
life, but in the vivacious movement of the narrative, the glimpses of scenery by the way, the
alternations of sentiment and gayety, neither
very profound, but each for the time sincere
and passing quickly into one another; and
finally in the style, always graceful, and in passages really exquisite. It has recently been
announced that style is " increasingly unim-
portant," but can this be true ? Not surely,
unless fiction is to become hereafter a branch
of social science and valuable only for its ac-
curate report of life. It will then be the novel-
ist's duty to obliterate himself in his message,
and any intrusion of his personality between
the reader and the subject will be an imperti-
nence. But it is hard to believe that the personal element is to lose its place in fiction and
be banished to the realm of autobiography and
lyric poetry. Style may be a purely external
part of an artist's equipment, but it is a necessary part all the same. A bad man or a weak
man may have it, but that does not make it
any the less indispensable for the good man
intending literature. Willis was born with it;

it showed in his manners, in his dress, in his writing. Whatever he did was done with an air.

The American parts of " Inklings," written for the English reader, are the best. They reproduce for us the life of gay society, when society was, or seemed, gayer, or at least fresher than at present. It was the era of expansion and hope before the financial panic of 1837. The great waterway lately opened through the state of New York had set people traveling. The beauties of American lakes, forests, and rivers were being discovered, but were as yet unhackneyed. Lake George, The Thousand Isles, and the St. Lawrence, did not swarm with tourists. Nahant was still a fashionable seaside resort and Niagara a watering-place, where people actually went to spend months, and not a fleeting show for bridal couples and a mill-race for manufacturers. Saratoga, and Ballston, and Lebanon were rival spas, the first a " mushroom village " merely, — " the work of a lath and plaster Aladdin," — when Congress Hall, with its big wooden colonnades, was in its glory. " A relic or two of the still astonished forest towers above the chimneys, in the shape of a melancholy grove of firs, and five minutes' walk from the door, the dim old wilderness stands looking down on the village." In which wilder-

14

ness was embosomed Barhydt's once famous hermitage, with its ear-shaped tarn and columnar pine shafts, whither one resorted for trout dinners, and where " the long, soft mornings, quiet as a shadowy elysium, on the rim of that ebon lake were as solitary as a melancholy man could desire."

This newness in life at the Springs, this background of primitive wilderness against which the drives and dances and piazza promenades of the fashionable frequenters were projected, has long since disappeared, and with it has gone a certain old school exclusiveness which once marked the society at American baths. That society, if not more aristocratic than at present, was at all events more select, simply by virtue of being smaller. Fewer people were in the habit of going into the country in summer, and fashionable circles in the cities were not so large but that " the best people " from all over the States might know each other at least by name. A reigning belle or a distinguished beau had a national reputation. Southern planters brought their families to Northern resorts and supplied an element which has been missed since the war.

" In the fourteen millions of inhabitants in the United States," Willis explains, " there are precisely four authenticated and undisputed aristocratic families. There is one in Boston, one in New York, one in Philadelphia, and one in Baltimore. With two hundred miles' interval between them, they agree passably, and generally meet at one or another of the three watering-places of Saratoga, Ballston, or Lebanon. Their meeting is as mysterious as the process of crystallization, for it is not by agreement. As it is not known till the moment they arrive, there is, of course, great excitement among the hotel-keepers in these different parts of the country, and a village that has ten thousand transient inhabitants one summer, has, for the next, scarcely as many score. The vast and solitary temples of Pæstum are gay in comparison with these halls of disappointment."

It is, for the most part, the life of this society which Willis so engagingly portrays in the "Slingsby" sketches. His heroes are devil-may-care young fellows, who wander about from one fashionable resort to another, composing love verses, flirting, dancing, eloping, or assisting at elopements. It was the era of the buck or beau, a joyous, flamboyant creature who wore figured waistcoats, was a knowing whip, danced with vigor, loved pink champagne, serenaded the ladies, was gallant in speech, dashing and confident in bearing, and never in the least *blasé*.

This freshness and youthfulness, this air of stir, adventure, excitement, hope, which was impressed upon American life, books, and society of that date are reflected from Willis's sparkling pages and give them even a sort of historical interest, apart from their claims as literature. There is a breath of morning wind in them. With the homelier side of life he had little concern, and his writing lacks gravity and simplicity. Whenever he grows serious, it is to grow sentimental. " F. Smith " is perhaps the most artistic of these sketches, and the most representative of its author's talent, in its quick interchange of poetic description, bright dialogue, light, malicious humor, and natural sentiment; neither mood in excess, nor dwelt on long enough to fatigue. It is a trifling episode — the caprice of a summer belle at Nahant. Its hero is the same " gentle monster " who reappears in many of the " Inklings " — in " Edith Linsey," "The Gypsy of Sardis," and "Niagara," a Green Mountain Frankenstein and Quixote in one, absent-minded and uncouth of aspect, but with a soul filled with enthusiasm for beauty and a delicate, chivalrous devotion to women. He is half hero and half butt, and introduced as a constant foil to Slingsby, the dandy exquisite and man of the world.

" Edith Linsey " was the most ambitious of the American sketches. It was a novel in outline, and had an original plot, the intellectual

passion of a young student for a girl who is
thought to be dying of consumption, and whose
disease has imparted an exaltation to her feelings, and a nervous, spiritual intensity to her
thoughts. The anti-climax comes when she unexpectedly recovers her health, and with it her
worldly ambitions, and coolly jilts her quondam
lover. There are passages in " Edith Linsey "
— particularly in the scenes between the lovers
in the library — of unusual thoughtfulness, eloquence, and emotional depth, but the story is
loosely put together, and interrupted by digressions, and in the latter part of it the author
seemed more concerned to deliver himself of
college reminiscences and descriptions of scenery
than to carry on his narrative with a firm hand.

" The Gypsy of Sardis " was the best of the
European sketches, and had a very moving,
though slightly melodramatic, conclusion. It
was a more highly finished study of Eastern
scenery and life than Willis had had leisure to
give in his " Pencillings." A comparison of the
two shows from what slight hints he worked up
the romance, — a momentary glimpse of a gypsy
girl at a tent door, and of an Arab in the slave
market at Stamboul, a ride up the Valley of
Sweet Waters, and a morning in the shop of
old Mustapha, the perfumer. " Love and Diplomacy " and " The Revenge of the Signor Basil "

were less successful, because more remote from their author's experience. He had not the kind of imagination necessary to transport him into alien characters and situations. His fancy required some contact with its object before it would take off the electric spark.

Willis's English had many excellent qualities. It was crisp, clean cut, pointed, nimble on the turn. He was good at a quotation, deftly brought in, unhackneyed, and never too much of it, a single phrase or sentence or half a line of verse maybe. There is a perpetual twinkle or ripple over his style, like a quaver in music, which sometimes fatigues. Is the man never going to forget himself and say a thing plainly? the reader asks. But the verbal prettinesses and affectations which disfigured his later prose do not abound in his earlier and better work. He had at all times, however, a feminine fondness for italics and exclamations, and his figures had a daintiness which displeased severe critics. Thus: "The gold of the sunset had glided up the dark pine-tops and disappeared, like a ring taken slowly from an Ethiop's finger." "As much salt as could be tied up in the cup of a large water-lily" is an instance of his superfine way of putting things. He likened Daniel Webster's forehead, among the heads at a Jenny Lind concert, to "a massive magnolia blossom, too heavy for the breeze to stir, splendid and silent amid fluttering poplar leaves." The "crushed orange blossom, clinging to one of the heels" of Ernest Clay's boots, was a touch which greatly amused Thackeray. And others have been amused by the fantastic headings which he invented for certain columns in the "Home Journal": "Sparklings of Tenth Waves: or Bits Relished in Recent Readings," "Breezes from Spice Islands, passed in the Voyage of Life," and the like, which read like the title of a sixteenth century pamphlet. An old lady in Hartford used to say that "Nat Willis ought to go about in spring, in sky-blue breeches, with a rose-colored bellows to blow the buds open." It is remarkable with what consent all who have had occasion to characterize Willis's diction hit upon the metaphor of champagne. "The wine of Bacon's writings," said Dr. Johnson, "is a dry wine." The wine of Willis's writings was certainly a *Schaumwein*. It had not the rich, still glow of burgundy, but a fizz and an up-streaming of golden bubbles, and when the spirit had effervesced the residue, as in his later writings, was rather flat.

During his stay abroad he made a few other contributions to literature which have not yet been mentioned. Among these were some miscellaneous papers in the "Mirror": "Notes from a Scrap Book " and " Fragments of Rambling Impressions," portions of which he afterwards republished in " Ephemera." Also a short tale of no value, " The Dilemma," from which he rescued the verses " To Ermengarde " for his collected poems. He contributed to the London " Athenæum " for January and February, 1835, a series of four articles on American literature, which do not appear in his " Complete Works." That pioneer of literature in the West, the Rev. Timothy Flint, some time editor of the " Cincinnati Monthly Review," author of a novel called " Francis Berrian," and of a work on the Mississippi Valley, had agreed to supply the required papers, but he having left New York for Louisiana Territory, and failed to come to time, Willis was invited to take his place. He wrote the articles hastily, though he asserted that he had " read the productions of two hundred poets and seventy-two prose writers whose works have been printed in America since the settlement of New England." He made no approach to an exhaustive treatment of the subject, but gave a number of graphic personal sketches of American authors, one in particular, of Channing as a pulpit orator, which excited Lady Byron's interest, as has been mentioned, and another of Cooper, whom he indignantly defended against the slanders of a portion of the

American press. The literary judgments are not always sound (Poe said that Willis had good taste, but was not a good critic), but they were the current opinions of the day rather than of Willis individually. They were in the air. Thus he pronounces Bryant's " Evening Wind " the best thing he had written, and prefers Percival to Bryant, saying that he is "the most interesting man in America. He has not written anything equal to the 'Evening Wind' of Bryant, but his birthright lies a thousand leagues higher up Parnassus." Timothy Flint afterwards supplemented these papers by a dozen of his own, which amply made up in heaviness for any want of ballast in Willis's, and were full of "general views," which, if not correct, were harmless because unreadable. Willis's "Athenæum" articles first introduced the English public to "The Culprit Fay," long passages of which he gave from a manuscript in his possession, the poem having not as yet appeared in print. Miss Mitford, who took a warm interest in American literature, wrote him a note of thanks on the publication of this series, praising it in the highest terms.

It appears by a letter to Willis from Carl August, Freiherr von Killinger, dated Carlsruhe, April 13, 1836, that some of the "Inklings" had already attained to the honors of translation.

The Freiherr, it seems, was engaged in translating " Pencillings " also, and wanted material for a biographical notice.

"To the author of the ' Slingsby Papers,' " he wrote, " It is, perhaps, flattering to hear that his ' Lunatic,' his ' Incidents on the Hudson,' ' Adventures on the Green Mountains,' [1] his ' Niagara and So Forth,' etc., etc., which I had translated into a little periodical of mine, or, rather, a choice collection of interesting articles from English periodicals and annuals, have been read with much interest, and repeatedly been reprinted in Germany. . . . I could wish to be favored by you with some biographical notices *of your own* in token, as it were, of your consentment to my translatory attempt."

[1] Not written by Willis.

CHAPTER VI.

1836–1845.

GLENMARY — THE CORSAIR — THE NEW MIRROR.

WILLIS was now fully committed to the profession of letters, but he wished to connect it with foreign residence, if possible. His sojourn abroad had been pleasant and successful, and when he sailed for home it was with a strong expectation of returning before long to the Old World in some diplomatic capacity. This hope he did not cease to entertain for several years. In a letter to Mrs. Skinner, written from Niagara October 12, 1836, he said that he had missed the secretaryship to France by a hand's-breadth, and that he wanted the next diplomatic mission that turned up; that the climate of the United States did not agree either with him or with Mrs. Willis; that he was constantly subject to the rheumatism, etc. During the winter of 1836–37, while in Washington, he made interest to secure the post of secretary of legation at St. Petersburg, with the view of writing a book on Russia, but Mr. Dallas, the newly-appointed minister to that country, had promised the place to a kinsman. Later, in a letter to Mrs. Willis at Glenmary, written from Boston, where he had just met Sumner and Longfellow and was about to dine with the latter, he speaks of a letter from a friend who says that the President had told him that " no young man in Washington had impressed him so favorably. It *looks* like going abroad," he adds, " and not for six or nine months merely." This letter is dated simply " February," but was written, probably, in 1842, during Tyler's administration. To the same year, doubtless, may be referred another, dated at New York, July 9th, in which he speaks of having made the rounds of the men-of-war in the harbor with John Tyler, the President's son, " who seems very much my friend," and of being invited to dinner by Dakin, to meet Tyler, Halleck, and Bryant. " A politician," he says, tells him that he will be appointed abroad soon. These hopes were all doomed to disappointment, and to the end of his career his pen was destined to be his best reliance.

The first few months after his return to America were spent in visiting his home and friends, and in presenting his young English bride to her new relatives. He stayed some time at the Astor House, in New York, then newly opened under the hosting of the genial Stetson, and regarded as the greatest wonder on the continent in the way of metropolitan caravansaries. On September 20th he signed an agreement with the agent óf George Virtue, the London publisher, to furnish the letterpress for a big illustrated work on American scenery, the drawings for which were to be supplied by Bartlett, the English artist, who was then in America for the purpose. The work was to come out in monthly numbers, each containing four plates and eight pages of letterpress, and Willis was to receive fifteen guineas a number. The first installment, containing descriptions of twenty drawings, was to be ready November 1st. It was in pursuance of this agreement that Willis went to Niagara in the autumn of 1836, retracing ground which he had visited eight years before. A part of the winter of 1836–37 and the early spring of 1837 he passed in Washington, whence he contributed to the " Mirror " the four letters afterwards included in "Sketches of Travel." He found Washington society agreeable, and Mrs. Willis was greatly admired and became an especial favorite with Henry Clay. But the national capital was then a raw, straggling town, built, said Willis, " to please nobody on earth but a hackney coachman." It had not begun to grow up to the ambitious plan on which it was projected, and there was a ludicrous contrast be tween the wide, radiating avenues, with their imposing public buildings scattered here and there, and the wastes between, dotted at intervals with naked brick houses or mean negro cabins. The large shifting population, which fled as soon as Congress rose, lodged uncomfortably in hotels and boarding-houses. In short, Washington was a dismal place to live in. Willis set his practiced observation at work to describe the picturesque and humorous social aspects of this unfinished city. He never took more than the most casual interest in politics, but he lounged about the rotunda and lobbies of the Capitol, climbed up into the stifling galleries of the old House and Senate chambers, whence the ladies' toilets could be observed, though the voices of speakers on the floor, owing to the acoustic defects in the building, reached the ear " as articulate as water from a narrow-necked bottle." He was present at Van Buren's inauguration, went to a levee at the White House, and to a dinner with Power the comedian, at which several Indian chiefs were present who behaved in an extraordinary manner. In the summer of 1837 he traveled about with Bartlett, who was making his sketches for "American Scenery." In the course of these peregrinations he found a lovely spot on the banks of Owego Creek near its junction with the Susquehanna, which so took his fancy that he decided to pitch his tent there. He bought from his college friend Pumpelly, who lived near by, a domain of some two hundred acres, which he named Glenmary, in honor of his wife, and there in the fall of 1837 he set up his household gods. In his paper on "The Four Rivers," contributed to one of the September "Mirrors" of that year, he thus announces his discovery : —

"Owego Creek should have a prettier name, for its small vale is the soul and essence of loveliness. A meadow of a mile in breadth, fertile, soft, and sprinkled with stately trees, furnishes a bed for its swift windings ; and from the edge of this new Tempé, on the southern side, rise three steppes or natural terraces, over the highest of which the forest rears its head, and looks in upon the meeting of the rivers ; while down the sides, terrace by terrace, leap the small streamlets from the mountain springs, forming each again its own smaller dimple in this loveliest face of Nature. . . . Here would I have a home ! Give me a cottage by one of these shining streamlets, upon one of these terraces that seem steps to Olympus, and let me ramble over these mountain sides, while my flowers are growing and my head silvering in tranquil happiness."

In this secluded Arcadia his Penates had rest for five years, and hence he wrote his "À l'Abri, or the Tent Pitched," contributed to the "Mir-

ror" as "Letters from under a Bridge," the
first one appearing July 7, 1838. This is Willis's happiest book, and reflects the happiest part
of his life. There was a side of him which
turned gladly to rural repose and simple household pleasures. He imagined it to be "the kind
of life best suited to his disposition as well as to
his better nature," and it had at the time the
zest of novelty. For the last five years he had
been a vagabond "in the gayest circles of the
gayest cities in the world."

"There is a curious fact," he writes, "I have
learned for the first time in this wild country; that,
as the forest is cleared, new springs rise to the surface of the ground, as if at the touch of the sunshine. . . . You have yourself been in your day, dear
doctor, 'a warped slip of wilderness,' and will see
at once that there lies in this ordinance of nature a
beautiful analogy to certain moral changes that come
in upon the heels of more cultivated and thoughtful
manhood. There is no divining-rod whose dip shall
tell us at twenty what we shall most relish at thirty.
. . . You can scarce understand with what pleasure
I find this new spring in my path, the content with
which I admit the conviction that, without effort or
self-denial, the mind will slake its thirst and the heart
be satisfied with but the waste of what lies so near
us."

The "dear doctor" to whom these letters were

addressed was Dr. T. O. Porter, with whom their
author afterwards formed a literary partnership.
The little bridge under which they were written,
with its stone seat, its "floor of running water,"
its nest of swallows, and its diminutive fresh-
water lobster — which reminded Willis of Tal-
leyrand — deserves remembering with Pope's
famous grotto at Twickenham. Like Cowley,
Willis acknowledged himself fond of little
things. He disliked the ocean and great rivers,
— though he finally came to live on the banks
of one. He loved small streams and narrow
valleys. The lawny, homelike scenery of. the
Owego was just suited to his taste. Above all
things in nature, he delighted in running water,
which had an affinity with his own lively and
sparkling temper. " À l'Abri " was, and remains,
a thoroughly enjoyable book, chatty, pleasantly
digressive, and filled with sunshine and the air
of out-doors. It must be confessed that Willis
was something of a cockney in the presence of
great Nature. He viewed her more as a landscape gardener than as a naturalist. He had not
the intense passion for her, the rapt communion
with her, of elect spirits like Wordsworth and
Thoreau. She furnished him rather with a hundred pretty and playful analogies, a hundred
texts for little sermons on cheerfulness and content, in which he rode his fancy sometimes too

far and let his sentiment answer too quickly to
trifling provocations. He must have been but an
amateurish farmer, too, ordering his breakfast
served under a balsam fir, and selling his crops
"for the oddity of the sensation." Naturally, except in literary harvests, his farm did not pay,
though he was always exclaiming with grateful
surprise at the bounty of nature in yielding him
actual buckwheat, in addition to the health,
amusement, and moral lessons derived in the
process of cultivating that interesting grain. One
suspects that he grew more flowers of speech
than any grosser product from his two hundred
acres. If the crows ate his corn in the blade, he
merely philosophized, "Think what times we live
in, when even the crows are obliged to anticipate
their income!" If the red heifer chewed up a
lace cape bleaching on the lawn, he humorously
excused the heifer on account of the drought.
If the boys reported that the deer were browsing
in troops on his buckwheat, by the light of the
moon, he answered, "Let them!" One is reminded by this last discouragement to agriculture
that Owego was still in the backwoods. Some
of the most interesting passages in the letters
describe the wild life of the lumbermen, whose
rafts glided past the Glenmary meadows "like a
singing and swearing phantom of an unfinished
barn," and whose fires by night lit up the bends

of the Susquehanna, where their huge flotillas lay moored. Willis once descended the river on the top of a freshet in a steamboat of light draught, but his usual way of coming and going was by stage over very rough roads, the Erie railway having not as yet penetrated those solitudes. Another picturesque feature of the neighborhood were the forest fires, the "blazing and innumerable pillars swept by the wind till they stood in still and naked redness, while the eye could see far into their depths." This phenomenon furnished a vivid description for his story, "The Picker and Piler," contributed to the "Corsair" of March 16, 1839, and to the April number of the "New Monthly" for the same year, the plot of which seems to have been furnished him by Rand, the portrait painter, to whom Willis sat in London in 1835, and who regaled him during the sittings with stories of wild adventure. Willis kept up communication with the great world by frequent trips to New York, and by frequent visits from his metropolitan friends to Glenmary. Neither was he by any means cut off from civilization at home. He explains to the doctor in one of his letters that Owego, two miles away, and even the village of Canewana, a mile nearer, are within the latitude of silver forks and their accompanying vanities, morning calls, cards, dinner giving, champagne, and French bonnets. R. H. Stoddard, the poet, who visited Glenmary in the fall of 1841, with Mr. Mackay, a congressman from New York, has given a pleasant reminiscence of his pilgrimage, from which I quote the following interior : —

"The cottage," he says, "had within it and about it the evidences of a subtle, nice, clear refinement ; of a thought that, even out of the solitude of a rural life, could frame the pleasant things that make the four and twenty hours turn to soft and kindly ways. . . . Mr. Willis opened the door, received us cordially; and we found, in his conversation and in such observation of all around us as a guest might in propriety make, the hours of the evening as brilliant in-doors as without. That thoroughly well-bred lady, so unpretending and gentle, was at the table ; at her feet, a large greyhound. On the side table stood a large tulip-shaped vase of stained glass, whose burden was, of course, bright flowers. There was everywhere copious evidence that it was a home for literature. The books were abundant and were gayly set. . . . And there was a miniature of lovely Mrs. Willis. It was painted by Saunders, who had been a pet of the King of Hanover. His exquisite work deserved the smile of royalty and, what is better, of beauty. Amidst such scenes and the conversation which came of such associations, our night went on. We left the lawn of Glenmary with the memories of a night of romance. . . . Mr. Willis belonged to a past school

of men. He had the ways and tastes of a more
isolated and restricted society than belongs to our
day, when fortunes are fusing men and manners
into one great glittering ball that rolls through the
year, before us and over us; but Mr. Willis — whether
in his early days, when the prince regent ruled, or
in our day, when we all rule, monarchs of ephemera
— was an author whose writings have added to what
Doctor Johnson calls 'the gayety of mankind.' He
believed them better and higher and more philosoph-
ical than this ; and I believe there was truth and
right in his thought."

The " Letters from Under a Bridge " are so
heartsome in feeling and so much mellower and
more leisurely in style than Willis's later work,
that one naturally speculates, in reading them,
as to what might have been the effect upon his
literary product had fortune granted his wish,
to be allowed to end his days at Glenmary.
Would study and the quiet of nature have ripened it to something deeper and richer than
anything that he has left? Or would he have
grown rusty with absence from the stir of cities
and the gay society that had hitherto seemed
his congenial element? It is impossible to answer this question with confidence. Undoubtedly
his later work would have been other and better
than it was if he had had the time to select
and condense. He would have written more

and scribbled less. But whether he would ever
have excelled the best parts of his earlier writings is doubtful. His talent was of the kind
which discipline does not always improve. It
was the expression of his temperament, fresh,
facile, spontaneous, but impatient of continu-
ance. He was best at a dash — a sketch, or a
short tale. His gift was of the sort that shows
more gracefully in youth than age. *Idem ma-
nebat neque idem decebat.* It is not improbable that, even under the most favoring conditions, he would have kept on writing Jottings,
Loiterings, Hurrygraphs, etc., lacking, as he
evidently did, the power of construction required for a large and serious work. But this
speculation is perhaps an idle one. Whether
or not it lay in his nature to sing or to say
that " something " of which Ben Jonson tells,
" that must and shall be sung high and aloof,"
fate denied him the proof. His necessities
drove him back to the city and the editor's
chair, to write hastily and incessantly for a
livelihood. Possibly the finer work might have
shaped itself in silence, but " not in these
noises." Meanwhile his present content found
utterance in his " Reverie at Glenmary," — a
single breath of gratitude to God, — the most
sincerely devout of all his religious poems, and
pathetic when one reflects how soon the shel-

tered happiness for which it gives thanks was to
pass away.

Not long after his return to America, he had
begun to try his hand at play writing. The
" Mirror " of August 19, 1837, gave passages
from a five act tragedy that he had lately completed, " Bianca Visconti, or the Heart Overtasked," with the announcement that it was to
be acted at the Park Theatre on the 24th
instant. It was founded upon the life of
Francesco Sforza, a soldier of fortune in the
fourteenth century, who obtained the hand of
Bianca, daughter to the Duke of Milan, and
thereby succeeded to the duchy. The play was
composed expressly for Josephine Clifton, a
popular actress of some talent, and of great
physical force and beauty of the large, queenly
type, who took the part of the heroine. The
rôle of Pasquali, " a whimsical poet," was written for Harry Placide, a favorite player in his
generation, whose " Grandfather Whitehead "
and other impersonations, humorous or pathetic,
are still affectionately remembered by old play-
goers. When this tragedy was published in the
spring of 1839, with some changes in the fifth
act, the " Mirror " declared that its success
upon the stage had been complete. This was
an overstatement, but whatever partial success
or qualified failure it may have met with on its

first representation, Willis felt sufficiently encouraged to persevere in his dramatic experiments. In a private letter from New York,
December 15, 1838, he said that Colman had
just given him $300 for an edition of " Bian-
ca," which he considered a good price, as Epes
Sargent had sold his " Velasco " for $60. Wal-
lack, he continues, who managed the National,
the rival theatre to the Park, was full of admiration of it, and was coming to see the whole
play rehearsed. Willis was going to charge
him $1,000 for the use of it, and a benefit
which, he calculated, would be equal to from
$500 to $700 more. On the 1st of September, 1837, just after the first representation of
" Bianca " at the Park, Willis entered into an
agreement with its manager, Turner Merritt, by
which the latter agreed to pay him $1,000, one
year from date, provided he should write a
comedy for Miss Clifton, pronounced successful
by her after three months' acting. In pursuance of this agreement, he had ready in two
months "The Betrothal," a comedy, which was
announced in the " Mirror " of November 25th
as to be acted at the Park on the Monday following. The notice added that the play would
probably take with the public, as it had pleased
the actors, — a good criterion. "The Betrothal," however, was unequivocally damned, much

to Willis's mortification, though not to his permanent discouragement. The text of this play
was never published, nor was that of another
comedy, "Imei, the Jew," with which he was
busy in January, 1839, and of which he seems
to have finished only a few scenes. Rumors
were in circulation that Willis had sued Miss
Clifton for failing to complete the engagement
in the matter of "The Betrothal," but these
were officially contradicted in the "Mirror."
He had better luck with another comedy, successively entitled "Dying for Him," "The
Usurer Matched," and "Tortesa the Usurer,"
based on the Florentine story of Genevra
d'Amori and written with more care than
his two previous attempts. He prepared the
way for its representation by printing four installments of it in the "Mirror;" and about a
year after the first of these appeared it was
put on at the National, April 8, 1839, with
Wallack cast for Tortesa, the principal character. It ran four times the first week, and
kept the stage to the 20th, "being received,"
said the "Mirror," "with acclamations by one
of the most crowded and fashionable audiences
ever assembled within the walls of a theatre."
In spite of this glowing language, "Tortesa"
seems to have had a *succès d'estime* merely.
Wallack had agreed to pay the author one half

the proceeds of the fourth, ninth, thirteenth, and eighteenth nights, after deducting $300 each night for expenses. If it was produced in England, Willis was to have one third of the proceeds of the fourth, eighth, and twelfth performances there. Wallack did bring it out at the Surrey Theatre in London, in August of this same year. Willis was in England at the time and wrote to Dr. Porter that it had had "a splendid run — crammed houses every night." It shared the honors of the "first night" with Willis's old adversary, Captain Marryat, whose "Phantom Ship" was the afterpiece. All this brought the author nothing but empty glory, as Wallack was distressed for money and could not afford to pay him his one third share of the profits. "So I gave it up," wrote Willis, "and he pocketed the whole. By the way," he adds, "I have two more nights at the National which I authorize you to look after and receive for me. The thirteenth and eighteenth representations remain for me. Will you see if you can get Kean or Vandenhoff in for Angelo on those nights? I have seen a great deal of Kean since I have been here, and he is truly a good fellow and a great actor. He breakfasted with us a day or two ago and Mary was very much interested that he should do well in America. I have given Vandenhoff ' Bianca ' for himself

and daughter to play in America. She is a fine,
handsome girl, but I have not seen her play."

These two plays of Willis did not add many
leaves to his laurels. His genius was undra-
matic; in his stories the dramatic element is
not the most pronounced. Both " Bianca " and
" Tortesa " have passages which are good as
poetry or declamation, and here and there occur bits of spirited dialogue; but in general the
characters are only half vitalized, the situations
are not firmly grasped and presented, and the
language is stilted. In short, they are book
plays merely, with nothing to distinguish them
from the numerous experiments of other American literary gentlemen who have essayed to
feed the stage with manuscripts from their
library tables. In " Bianca Visconti " the main
situation — the heroine's connivance at her
brother's murder, in order that her husband
might become Duke of Milan — is strongly
imagined but feebly carried out. One cannot
help thinking how Victor Hugo, for instance,
would have dealt with this motive. " Tortesa
the Usurer " seems to be made up of hints from
Shakespeare. The hero has some slight resem-
blance to Shylock; the heroine drinks a sleep-
ing potion, like Juliet, to escape an odious marriage; and in the last act, which is constructed
with some skill, she stands in the frame of a

picture, like Hermione in "Winter's Tale," though with a different purpose.

Willis's official connection with the "New York Mirror" had stopped with the termination of his " Pencillings," and after January 16, 1836, his name ceased to appear at the head of the editorial column. His contributions, however, as we have seen, went on, and included not only " Letters from Under a Bridge," but poems and miscellaneous correspondence, besides a half dozen of stories, afterwards collected in " Romance of Travel." The verse contributions were added to the American edition of " Melanie," 1837, which contained a number of things written since the appearance of the English edition two years previous. Notable among these were " Lines on Leaving Europe," "To a Face Beloved," — both of which have been mentioned, — " To Ermengarde," and a song-like little piece entitled " Spring," the opening lines of which are especially Willisy : —

> " The Spring is here, the delicate-footed May,
>   With its slight fingers full of leaves and flowers ;
> And with it comes a thirst to be away,
>   Wasting in wood-paths its voluptuous hours."

There are evidences in Willis's private correspondence, about this time, of some coolness between himself and General Morris, which appears to have originated, or perhaps to have found

expression in a series of three letters signed
" Veritas," written from London and printed in
the " Mirror," in the fall of 1838. These letters,
after taking the " Mirror " to task for misleading the American public by the false pictures of
London society given in the " Pencillings," proceeded to set its readers right, in a series of the
coarsest and most slanderous little biographies
of English men and women of letters, retailing
with unction all the gossip of the clubs about
Lady Blessington, Count d'Orsay, the Bulwers,
Disraeli, Mrs. Norton, Miss Landon, Fraser, and
many others. Some of these had been Willis's
friends; others he had never met; but he wrote
an indignant rejoinder to the " Mirror " of November 10th, denying, out and out, many of the
lies in " Veritas's " communication, and explain-
ing away some of the misrepresentations and exaggerations. This letter Morris prefaced with an
editorial note in which he said that he had been
much censured on account of the " Pencillings,"
and, therefore, " the object of these letters was to
disabuse the public mind in this country of what
seemed to the author a wrong and injurious impression with regard to the position in English
society of certain distinguished but unworthy
characters, whose example and many of whose
writings are of a pernicious tendency. With
one or two exceptions, we believe that our corre-

spondent has merely stated well attested facts."
One of these exceptions was the slander upon
Miss Landon, for printing which Morris apol-
ogized. This partial indorsement of " Veritas "
by the editor naturally displeased Willis ; and
naturally, too, he was pleased by an answer to
it by Dr. Porter, in the " Spirit of the Times,"
which was then edited by his brother, William
T. Porter, "the tall son of York," and with
which Dr. Porter himself was editorially connected. " The Skylight letter," Willis writes to
the latter, " was capitally done, and the ' Mirror ' was touched on all its sore places to a
charm. My brother was in New York just after
and called at the office, and the fury the General was in will amuse him for the next six
months. Morris called you a gallipot, said it
was a poor article, and will hurt your paper, and
all that ; but sits down and writes *me* a most
affectionate letter of four foolscap pages, denying all possible thought of me in the London
matter, and swearing he was my defender and
best friend." Elsewhere in his correspondence
with Dr. Porter, Willis expresses some doubts
as to the sincerity of Morris's friendship, and
seems to suspect that it was more than half policy and a desire to exploit him. It does not appear that this little misunderstanding ever came
to a breach. The " Mirror " continued most

courteous in its tone towards Willis, and its editor became and remained, till his death, one of
his closest friends. But for a time Willis felt
inclined to draw off, and to find some other avenue through which to address his public. This
feeling took shape in December, 1838, in his ac-
ceptance of a proposal from Dr. Porter to join
him in establishing a weekly paper. The "Corsair," which was the outcome of this arrangement, was, like "Brother Jonathan" and the
"New World," one of the crop of weeklies which
sprang up in the wake of the first transatlantic
steamers. On May 19, 1838, the Great Western, the first steam vessel that had crossed the
ocean, weighed anchor in New York harbor for
her return trip. A company of gentlemen,
among whom were Chevalier Wikoff and General Morris, were on board by invitation and accompanied the ship as far as Sandy Hook, where
they were taken off by a pilot. It may perhaps
have occurred to the general at the time, that
here was what would work a change in the conditions of American journalism. It was now
possible to get the freshest supply from the London literary market within a fortnight, and the
news of Europe before it was cold. Willis and
Porter proposed frankly to live on the plunder
of this foreign harvest; and since there was no
international copyright, to raise the black flag,

and take reprisals wherever they could find
them. In a letter to his intending partner, dated
at Owego, Christmas eve, 1838, he proposed to
call their venture the "Pirate," and sent the
following draft of a prospectus : —

THE PIRATE,

A GAZETTE OF LITERATURE, FASHION, AND NOVELTY.

T. O. Porter and N. P. Willis propose to issue
weekly, in the city of New York, a paper of the above
designation and character. It is their design, as editors, to present as amusing a paper as can be made
from the current wit, humor, and literature of the
world; to give dramatic criticisms without fear or favor; to hold up the age in its fashions, its eccentricities, and its amusements; to take advantage, in short,
of the privilege assured to us by our piratical law of
copyright; and in the name of American authors
(for our own benefit) "convey" to our columns, for
the amusement of our readers, the cream and spirit
of everything that ventures to light in France, England, and Germany. As to original American productions, we shall, as the publishers do, take what we
can get for nothing (that is good), holding, as the
publishers do, that while we can get Boz and Bulwer for a thank-ye or less, it is not pocket-wise to
pay much for Halleck and Irving.

"If anybody says the name is undignified," writes
Willis, "tell them there are very few dignified people
in the world, and still *fewer lovers* of dignity, and by

the Lord, we must live by the *many*. Then again we want a root, a reason, a rail, a runner to start upon, and this bloody copyright will answer the purpose. People will say, ' Why, damme, Willis can't get paid for his books because the law won't protect him, so he has hauled his wind, and joined the people that robbed him.' "

Willis felt very bitterly the absence of an international copyright. By the act of 1838, the English Parliament, acting in self-defense, had refused to protect any longer the literary property of American authors, until America should have the decency to reciprocate. This cut double upon the American author. It deprived him of any gain from the circulation of his writings in England, and it discouraged native literature by flooding this country with cheap reprints of English books, for the copy of which the American publisher paid nothing. The former loss would not have been serious to many American writers at that date, possibly not to so very many even now. But England had been Willis's best market, literary work in America was wretchedly paid, and he saw starvation staring him in the face.

The " Pirate " was finally toned down into the " Corsair," and a prospectus which was a modification of the one drafted by Willis in the above letter was printed and circulated in Jan-

16

uary, 1839. He sent one to Henry Clay, and
begged him to mention the " Corsair " in his
argument on the copyright, as a good comment
on the state of the law.   Mr. Clay replied in a
very polite letter, giving his views upon the copyright question, and inclosing his subscription.
The office of the " Corsair " was in the Astor
House, No. 8 Barclay Street.   The first number
was published March 15, 1839, and the last
(No. 52) March 7, 1840.   At the head of the
sheet was a rakish looking craft under full sail,
and Willis led off with a truculent editorial,
" The Quarter Deck " proclaiming the policy of
the new paper.   To the earlier numbers he contributed art notes and miscellaneous chat, " The
Pencil," " The Gallery," " The Divan," etc. ;
two papers on autographs ; a " Letter from Under a Bridge," a generic name that he gave to
much correspondence about this time, not comprised in the original " Letters " ; some reminiscences of Miss Landon as " The Departed Im-
provisatrice," and a very harsh review, " Paulding the Author Disinterred."   This last was
unlike Willis, who was almost always kind in
his notices of brother authors, and it provoked
much unfavorable comment, particularly a rejoinder in the " Courier and Enquirer," by Colonel James Watson Webb, a gentleman who afterwards fell foul of Willis in various ways.   In

this article he held him up to scorn as a writer
" who revels on the cut of a coat or the otto-
mans of a lady's boudoir, and delights in the
soft shades of a glen ; " and whose works were
only fit to " make the papillotes of ladies'
chambermaids." Willis had an unaffected dis-
relish for Paulding's writings, which he thought
coarse and pointless. But the Secretary of the
Navy was an old man, whose books belonged already to the past, and it was ungracious to disturb his age with taunts about their obsoleteness.
One suspects, in reading this review, that its
writer had some personal grudge against the author of " The Dutchman's Fireside."

Willis also contributed to the " Corsair " " A
Story Writ for the Beautiful," which he described as a " gay, off-hand tale," and never reprinted. It is a rather nonsensical yarn, but
has one pretty passage in it descriptive of the
end of a ball, — perhaps at Devonshire House ?
— where the servants raise the balcony awnings
to let in the dawn, and the ladies walk in the
garden, " sprinkling their gloves with picking
wet roses."

On May 20, 1839, Willis sailed for England
on the packet ship Gladiator. His wife accompanied him, and, on landing, they were met by
the news that her father, General Stace, had
died a week before their arrival. This made

their stay in England, which was protracted to
April, 1840, a sad one in many respects, and of
course a quiet one.   They passed most of the
time with relatives of Mrs. Willis at Old Charlton, Kent, after a short visit to her sister Anne,
who was married to the Rev. William Vincent,
son of the vicar of Bolney Priory, in Sussex.
Willis had his hands full of literary business
which required his presence frequently in London, Ireland, and elsewhere.   Among other
things, he had contracted with Virtue to furnish
the letterpress for an illustrated work on Can-
ada, and another on Ireland, uniform with the
" American Scenery."   He was to write 240
pages for each, and to be paid in all £950.   By
some five or six weeks of hard work he finished
the Canadian book in August, and then started
for a tour in Ireland preparatory to writing up
its scenery.   He left Mrs. Willis at Dublin,
while he recrossed to Scotland, and took in the
famous tournament at Eglintoun Castle, which
filled the land for months with its noise of preparation, and ended in fizzle and rain-water.   Of
this he gave a capital description in his letter to
the " Corsair," " My Adventures at the Tournament."   Mrs. Willis remained with some kinsfolk of her mother, at Borrmount Lodge, near
Enniscorthy, County Wexford, while her husband
spent a fortnight in doing the Lakes of Killar-

ney and other show places in the south of the island. He wrote to her there from Tarbert-on-the-Shannon, September 13th : —

" The poverty on this side Ireland makes me sick at the stomach. Such a God-and-man-abandoned collection of disease and misery I never believed possible. Death and disease seem clutching their victims away in your very sight, and you see them struggle and go through their last agony in the streets — unpitied. How people can ride in carriages and wear white gloves and smile and look happy, in this great lazar-house, is beyond my conception. I keep my great cloak pocket full of pence, and shut my eyes while I give them into their skinny hands, — poor devils ! "

Madden sings the wrath of Campbell over this literary undertaking of Willis : " What could he know of Ireland ? How could any American know anything about it ? Fourteen days ! All the knowledge he possesses of Ireland might have been acquired in fourteen hours." Willis might have retorted by asking what a Scotchman could know about the Valley of Wyoming. Or he might have pointed out that, even as early as 1839, Americans had fuller sources of information about Ireland than they found altogether comfortable. After three weeks more of touring in that ragged commonwealth, he returned with his wife to England.

Bolney was but twelve miles from Brighton, where the Wallacks were staying, and while visiting at the former place Willis had run across country and taken dinner with them. In November he spent a few days at Brighton, where he lodged at the Ship Hotel, found several old acquaintances, — Lady Stepney and Lady Georgiana Fane among them, — and made some new ones. At a dinner at Lady Macdonald's he met Charles Kemble, the actor, and Horace Smith, of the " Rejected Addresses," whose brother James he had known at Lady Blessington's four years ago. One of Willis's cherished plans had been to spend the winter in Spain, a country rich in matter for future pencillings, but this scheme he had to forego, Ireland proving a longer job than he had anticipated. The last day of 1839 found him still at Charlton, working four hours a day on the book, and in January and February he had to make another trip to Ireland, visiting the Giant's Causeway and other celebrated bits of scenery in the north. Lady Georgiana Fane had procured him a letter from her father, the old Earl of Westmoreland, to Lord Ebrington, the lord lieutenant of Ireland, in which Willis was described as " a gentleman of fortune, likely to attain to the presidency "! He dined with Lord Ebrington at Dublin, and, happening to be there at the time of the ball

given in honor of the queen's wedding, he made
a letter of it for the "Corsair," afterwards included in "Sketches of Travel."

The three books on American, Canadian, and
Irish scenery were hack work, and there is, of
course, little of personal or purely literary interest in them. They were written, however, with
more taste and animation than the run of subscription books of the kind. Willis was a natural traveler, with a good eye for landscape effects,
and the best chapters are those descriptive of
spots with which he was already familiar, Niagara, the Hudson, Trenton Falls, Saratoga, and
the like. Here he occasionally drew on his
"Inklings." For places that he had not visited
he trusted to the narratives of former travelers,
such as President Dwight, John Bartram, and
Peter Kalm. The description of the White
Mountains was taken mainly from a friend's
manuscript diary; and for statistics and local
legends he went to the authorities. The American book contained, among its two hundred
and forty-two engravings, a view from Glenmary lawn and another of Undercliff, General Morris's place on the Hudson. The last
gave Willis opportunity for a eulogy on his
former partner, and quotations from his songs.
"Canadian Scenery" was "lifted," almost entire, from the narratives of Charlevoix, Adair,

Heriot, Hodgson, Murray, Talbot, Cockburn, and other travelers and historians — of course with ample acknowledgments. It was not so purely descriptive as the American book, but contained chapters on the native Indians, the history of the settlement of the country, the present condition of the inhabitants, sporting, immigration, etc. In fact, there is very little of Willis in the book. In "The Scenery and Antiquities of Ireland" he had the assistance of Mr. J. Sterling Coyne, who prepared the whole of the second volume and a part of the first, Willis's share consisting only of descriptions of the North of Ireland, a portion of Connemara, the Shannon, Limerick, and Waterford.

Before leaving America he had arranged with Colman for the publication of "The Tent Pitched" ("À l'Abri"), "Tales of Five Lands" ("Romance of Travel"), and "The Usurer Matched." He was to have twenty per cent. on sales, and received $2,000 on account in advance. Meanwhile the Longmans offered him £200 for "Romance of Travel," if published in advance of the American edition. Willis wrote to Dr. Porter, July 26, 1839, to delay the Colman publication. "If it is printed in America before I get the sheets here, I lose exactly $1,000. I trust in Heaven you have not forgot-

ten my earnest injunctions on this subject. A
London publisher will buy it if a published
copy has not come over, else he may have it for
nothing." The book was accordingly published
first in London, in January, 1840, in three volumes, with the title " Loiterings of Travel," and,
later in the same year, in America, as " Romance
of Travel," in a single volume, very shabbily
printed. Virtue also paid him £50 for an English edition of " À l'Abri," with illustrations by
Bartlett. A fourth London edition of " Pencillings," with four illustrations, was coming out,
and, finally, Cunningham, Macrone's successor,
printed an English edition of " Bianca Visconti "
and " Tortesa " as " Two Ways of Dying for a
Husband." This was published on half profits,
and Willis expected to make about £50 from it.
Serjeant Talfourd, the author of " Ion," wrote
him a complimentary letter on its appearance.
" My literary receipts in England this year,"
wrote Willis to Dr. Porter, on the last day of
1839, "will amount to $7,500, all gone for ex-
penses, back debts, etc."

" Romance of Travel " was a collection of
seven stories contributed to the " Mirror," the
" New Monthly," and the " Corsair." They were
crowded with duels, intrigues, disguises, esca-
pades, assassinations, masked balls, lost heirs,
and all the stock properties of the romancer's

art. The view of life which they presented
was unreal to the verge of the fantastic, but
they abounded in descriptions of great elegance
and even beauty, and the narrative went trip-
pingly along. Willis had many of the gifts of
the born *raconteur.* He lacked a large con-
structiveness, but in the minor graces of the
story-teller he was always happy. He was skill-
ful in managing the *callida junctura*, good at
a start, a transition, or a finish. One must not
look in these artificial fictions for truthful de-
lineation of character, or expect to have his
emotions deeply stirred. The tragic incidents,
especially, fail in the time-honored Aristotelian
requirement. They are exciting enough, in a
way, but move neither pity nor terror. The high
spirits of the narrator carry his readers buoy-
antly along over the bloodiest passages with
scarcely an abatement of their cheerfulness.
Willis did not take room enough to develop
character and motive to the extent required in
order to give his thick-coming events an air of
vraisemblance. "This tale of many tails," he
said of "Violanta Cesarini," "should have been
a novel. You have in brief what should have
been well elaborated, embarrassed with difficulties, relieved by digressions, tipped with a moral,
and bound in two volumes, with a portrait of
the author." From this defect and from the

author's light way of telling his stories, it followed that the more serious of these carried no conviction of reality to the reader's mind. "Violanta Cesarini" is the history of a humpbacked artist, who turns out to be the heir to the estates of a Roman noble, thereby supplanting his sister, but enabling her to marry his chum, a poor artist, with whom she was secretly in love. The outlines of the plot were from a true story told him by Lady Blessington, but he added the love passages and, of course, all the particulars in the development of the tale. "Paletto's Bride" was the legend of a Venetian gondolier, who made — and as suddenly lost — a fortune in a single night's play, figured as a mysterious unknown in the high society of Florence, and carried off a titled beauty to share his home among the lagoons. "The Bandit of Austria" was a modification of a story related to Willis by D'Orsay. The heroine was a Hungarian countess, who had run off with a famous outlaw. The latter having been killed by the Austrian police, the lady, without wasting much time in unavailing regrets, falls in love with the narrator's handsome English page (a glorified William Michell?), and is wedded to him after a series of extraordinary adventures. Willis worked in here a striking description of the grotto of Adelsberg, in which the most effective scene of

the story takes place. "Lady Ravelgold" is a
tale of English high life. The hero is a young
London banker, who proves in the end to be a
count of the Russian Empire, and the inheritor
of vast possessions in that conveniently indefi-
nite country. Three high-born beauties are des-
perately enamored of him, among them a mother
and daughter, the latter of whom ultimately gets
him. As in "Ernest Clay," and, in fact, in
nearly all Willis's stories of high life, it is the
women who make love to the men. The scene
of the garden party at "Rose Eden" was suggested by a *fête-champêtre* at Gore House, and
the delicious picture of Lady Ravelgold's boudoir
was doubtless borrowed from the same mansion.
The high-piled luxuriance of the upholstery in
these "Romances of Travel," their *nonchalant*
young heroes, their jeweled and embroidered
heroines, with Aladdin-like resources in the way
of palaces, gardens, retainers, and stalactite cav-
erns, point to "Vivian Grey" and the other
expensive fictions of the youthful Disraeli as
Willis's nearest models. Upon the whole, the
best story in the book is "Pasquali, the Tailor
of Venice," which was more within the natural
compass of Willis's talent. It has a malicious
irony that reminds one of "Beppo" and the "De-
cameron," and it is not without an undercurrent
of pathos.

In spite of his other literary preoccupations
he found time to write a series of weekly or
fortnightly letters to the "Corsair," — "Jottings
down in London," — a portion of which stand in
his collected writings as "Passages from an
Epistolary Journal." They are naturally not as
fresh as the earlier "Pencillings," though very
good foreign correspondence of an ephemeral
sort. In search of matter for these letters,
Willis went about a good deal in London. He
visited the theatres and the House of Commons,
looked up his old acquaintances of 1835, was
present at a reception to the Persian ambassa-
dors at Lady Morgan's, — where he saw Mrs.
Norton again, — dined with the Nawaub of Oude,
went to a public dinner given to Macready at
the Freemasons' Tavern, — where he sat next
Samuel Lover, — to a ball at Almack's, and
a tournament in St. John's Wood. Disraeli
walked home with him from a ball and said
he was going to Niagara on his wedding trip.
Willis noted some changes in England since
his first visit. Among other things William IV.
was dead and Victoria on the throne, and the
London shops had increased greatly in splendor.

One of the most interesting results of this
second stay in England was his meeting with
Thackeray — then a young and comparatively
unknown writer — and his engaging him as a

contributor to the "Corsair," a stroke of journalistic enterprise which ought to have pro-
longed the life of that piratical journal, but
did not. In a private letter to Dr. Porter,
dated July 26th, Willis wrote : —

"I have engaged a contributor to the 'Corsair.'
Who do you think? The author of 'Yellowplush'
and 'Major Gahagan.' I have mentioned it in my
jottings, that our readers may know all about it. He
has gone to Paris, and will write letters from there,
and afterwards from London, for a guinea a *close
column* of the 'Corsair' — cheaper than I ever
did anything in my life. I will see that he is paid
for a while to see how you like him. For myself, I
think him the very best periodical writer alive. He
is a royal, daring, fine creature, too. I take the responsibility of it. You will hear from him soon."

The mention in the jottings here referred to
appeared in the "Corsair" of August 24th.

"One of my first inquiries in London was touching the authorship of 'The Yellowplush Papers'
and the 'Reminiscences of Major Gahagan,' — the
only things in periodical literature, except the 'Pick-
wick Papers,' for which I looked with any interest or eagerness. The author, Mr. Thackeray,
breakfasted with me yesterday, and the 'Corsair'
will be delighted, I am sure, to hear that I have engaged this cleverest and most gifted of the magazine-
writers of London to become *a regular correspond-*

ent of the ' Corsair.' He left London for Paris the day after, and having resided in that city for many years, his letters thence will be pictures of life in France, done with a bolder and more trenchant pen than has yet attempted the subject. He will present a long letter every week, and you will agree with me that he is no common acquisition. Thackeray is a tall, athletic man of about thirty-five, with a look of talent that could never be mistaken. He has taken to literature after having spent a very large inheritance ; but in throwing away the gifts of fortune, he has cultivated his natural talents very highly, and is one of the most accomplished draftsmen in England, as well as the cleverest and most brilliant of periodical writers. He has been the principal critic for the ' Times,' and writes for ' Fraser ' and ' Blackwood.' You will hear from him by the first steamer after his arrival in Paris, and thenceforward regularly."

The same number contained Thackeray's first letter, dated at Paris, Hôtel Mirabeau, July 25, 1839, and concluding with a characteristic little address to the editor, in which he speaks of his feelings " in finding good friends and listeners among strangers far, far away — in receiving from beyond seas kind crumbs of comfort for our hungry vanities." These letters were signed T. T. (Timothy Titcomb), and eight of them in all were published in the " Corsair." A few appear in Thackeray's collected works in a volume entitled " The Paris Sketch Book," and all

of them, with a few changes, in " The Student'
Quarter; or Paris Five and Thirty Years since,'
published by Hotten after Thackeray's death.
Thackeray humorously alludes to this episode
in his early literary struggles in his novel of
" Philip," the hero of which contributes a weekly letter, signed " Philalethes," to a fashionable
New York journal entitled " The Gazette of the
Upper Ten Thousand."   " Political treatises,"
writes the excellent Dr. Firmin to his son, " are
not so much wanted as personal news, regarding
the notabilities of London."   This description
of the " Mirror " pointed, of course, at Willis's
authorship of the phrase, " The Upper Ten
Thousand."

It may be not uninteresting to compare
Thackeray's opinion of Willis with Willis's
impressions of Thackeray.   The author of the
" Book of Snobs " paid his respects twice, at
least, in print to the author of " Pencillings by
the Way:" once in a review of " Dashes at
Life " in the " Edinburgh " for October, 1845,
and again in an article " On an American
Traveler," being the sixth number of " The
Proser," contributed to the nineteenth volume
of " Punch " (1850), and occasioned by Willis's
" People I have Met."   In both of these papers
he quizzes Willis, though not unkindly.   He
laughs especially at his fashion in " Ernest

Clay," of representing the aristocratic English
dames as all throwing themselves at the head of
the conquering young genius who writes for the
magazines.

" The great characteristic of high society in England, Mr. Willis assures us, is admiration of literary
talent. As some captain of free lancers of former
days elbowed his way through royal palaces with the
eyes of all womankind after him, so in the present
time, a man by being a famous *Free Pencil* may
achieve a similar distinction. This truly surprising
truth forms the text of almost every one of Mr. Willis's ' Dashes ' at English and Continental life."

" That famous and clever N. P. Willis of former
days, whose reminiscences have delighted so many of
us, and in whose company one is always sure to find
amusement of one sort or the other. Sometimes it
is amusement at the writer's wit and smartness, his
brilliant descriptions and wondrous flow and rattle of
spirits, and sometimes it is wicked amusement, and,
it must be confessed, at Willis's own expense. . . .
To know a duchess, for instance, is given to very
few of us. He sees things that are not given to us
to see. We see the duchess pass by in her carriage
and gaze with much reverence on the strawberry
leaves on the panels and her Grace within ; whereas
the odds are that the lovely duchess has had, at one
time or the other, a desperate flirtation with Willis
the conqueror. . . . He must have whole mattresses
stuffed with the blonde or raven or auburn memories

17

of England's fairest daughters. When the female English aristocracy reads this title of 'People I have Met,' I can fancy the whole female peerage of Willis's time in a shudder : and the melancholy marchioness, and the abandoned countess, and the heart-stricken baroness trembling, as each gets the volume, and asking of her guilty conscience, 'Gracious goodness ! Is the monster going to show up *me?*' "

Especially does he chaff Willis about his story of "Brown's Day with the Mimpsons," the hero of which adventure, an American who is hand in glove with noble dukes, etc., is asked home to dinner by Mimpson, a plain, blunt British merchant, whose wife snubs Mr. Brown, mistaking him for a plebeian person. The latter avenges himself by a somewhat cavalier deportment, and by obtaining, through his dear friend Lady X., a ticket to Almack's for Mrs. M.'s companion, the pretty Miss Bellamy; while the matron herself and her haughty daughter, who are dying for a ticket, are left out in the cold. Thackeray remonstrates as follows with Mr. Brown, under whose modest mask he fancies that he sees the "features of an N. P. W. himself : " —

"There 's a rascal for you ! He enters a house, is received coolly by the mistress, walks into chicken-fixings in a side room, and, not content with Mimpson's sherry, calls for a bottle of champagne — not for a glass of champagne, but for a bottle. He catches hold of it and pours out for himself, the rogue, and for Miss Bellamy, to whom Thomas (the butler) introduces him. Come, Brown, you are a stranger and on the dinner list of most of the patricians of May Fair, but is n't this *un peu fort*, my boy ? If Mrs. Mimpson, who is described as a haughty lady, fourth cousin of a Scotch earl, and marrying M. for his money merely, had suspicions regarding the conduct of her husband's friends, don't you see that this sort of behavior on your part, my dear Brown, was not likely to do away with Mrs. M.'s little prejudices ? "

In April, 1840, Mr. and Mrs. Willis sailed for America, taking with them Miss Bessie Stace, a younger sister of Mrs. Willis, who was to make them a visit at Owego. The "Corsair" had not been a success financially, and Dr. Porter had become discouraged and discontinued publication in March, transferring his subscription list to the "Albion." Since the establishment of the paper, a year before, Willis had ceased his contributions to the New York "Mirror," and he did not resume them until the end of 1842. But meanwhile he was not left without a market for his literary wares. Just before leaving England he had received a letter from Mr. J. Gregg Wilson, the publisher of "Brother Jonathan," a new weekly printed in New York, with a circulation of some twenty thousand, in-

forming him of the " Corsair's " suspension, expressing a warm admiration for his talents, and
inviting him to write the " Brother Jonathan " a
weekly letter, a column in length, for which he
promised to pay him at the highest current rates.
To this paper Willis contributed about a year
and a half, or up to September, 1841. His humorous poem, " Lady Jane," was published in
installments in the " Dollar," the monthly edition of " Brother Jonathan." With both of
these periodicals he had a *quasi* editorial connection, though the real editor was Mr. H. Has-
tings Weld. He received similar invitations from
the two monthlies, " Graham's Magazine " and
" Godey's Lady's Book," which were paying
their contributors — among whom were nearly
all the principal writers in the country — prices
hitherto unknown to American periodicals. Willis was paid at the rate of $50 for an article of
four printed pages of the " Lady's Book," —
less, no doubt, than a writer of equal reputation could command now, but regarded as wildly
munificent in 1841. Twelve dollars a page were
the regular rates of both these magazines. " The
burst on author-land of Graham's and Godey's
liberal prices," said Willis, " was like a sunrise
without a dawn." Mr. Charles T. Congdon, in
his interesting " Reminiscences of a Journalist,"
says that " Mr. Willis was the first magazine

writer who was tolerably well paid. At one time, about 1842, he was writing four articles monthly for four magazines, and receiving $100 each." This means an income of $4,800 a year, but the strain required to keep up such a rate of production must tax the powers of the readiest writer, and it was no wonder if the product was of very uneven excellence. The four magazines here referred to were undoubtedly the " Mirror," " Graham's," " Godey's," and " The Ladies' Companion," of which Mrs. Sigourney was for a time the editor, and to which Willis contributed in 1842 and 1843 a half dozen stories and a few " Passages from Correspondence " and " Leaves from a Table Book." Two of these stories are not found among his collected writings : " Poyntz's Aunt," a Saratoga tale, which has been mentioned before, and " Fitz Powys and the Nun, or Diplomacy in High Life," a very impossible fiction, and not worth describing. Such of the " Leaves " and " Scraps " as deserved preserving found their way into " Ephemera." His contributions to " Godey's " began with the January number for 1842, and continued, though with greatly diminished frequency, till January, 1850. During the first year he had an article in nearly every number, most of them stories. For " Graham's " he began to write in January, 1843, and contributed occasionally as late as 1851. " The Marquis in Petticoats " and " Broadway ; A Sketch " were published in 1843 in Epes Sargent's short-lived magazine; " The Power of an Injured Look " in the " Gift " for 1845, an annual issued in Philadelphia. He edited another annual, the " Opal " for 1844, and wrote articles of various kinds for other periodicals. During the two years and a half from January, 1842, to June, 1844, he published, all in all, some forty stories, collected, with two or three exceptions, in " Dashes at Life with a Free Pencil." Willis was at this time, beyond a doubt, the most popular, best paid, and in every way most successful magazinist that America had yet seen. He commanded the sympathy of his readers more than any other periodical writer of his day, and his reputation almost amounted to fame. Colonel Higginson tells a story, illustrating his vogue, about a solid commercial gentleman in Boston, who, finding himself by chance at some literary dinner or tea, is reported to have entered into the spirit of the occasion by saying that " he guessed Gō-ēthe was the N. P. Willis of Germany."

Willis lived at Owego till 1842, and continued to date his letters to " Brother Jonathan," " Graham's," etc., " from under a bridge." He had expected something like £1,000 from General Stace's estate, but it yielded him nothing.

His publisher failed about this time, and his arrangement with " Brother Jonathan " coming to an end, he engaged with a Washington paper, the " National Intelligencer," to send it fortnightly correspondence from New York. All these causes combined made it necessary for him to take up his residence in the city and to offer Glenmary for sale; which he did with a heavy heart, taking the public into his confidence, as usual, in his affecting " Letter to the Unknown Purchaser and Next Occupant of Glenmary," first printed in " Godey's " for December, 1842, and included in all subsequent editions of " Letters from under a Bridge."

" I thought to have shuffled off my mortal coil tranquilly here; flitting at last in some company of my autumn leaves, or some bevy of spring blossoms, or with snow in the thaw. . . . In the shady depths of the small glen above you, among the wild flowers and music, the music of the brook babbling over rocky steps, is a spot sacred to love and memory. Keep it inviolate, and as much of the happiness of Glenmary as we can leave behind stay with you for recompense ! "

This sacred nook — reserved from purchase — was the spot where his own hands had broken the snow and frozen earth to bury the little body of his first child, a daughter, born dead December 4, 1840. The father's grief and disappointment found a voice in one of the most naturally and simply written of his poems, " Thoughts while making the Grave of a New-Born Child." On June 20, 1842, a second daughter, Imogen, was born, his only surviving child by his first wife. Later in the same summer he broke up his home at Glenmary and removed to New York. For a while he " pitched his uprooted tent " in Brooklyn lodgings ; then he went to housekeeping for a time, and afterwards took rooms at the Astor. When in London in 1836, Willis had accompanied his publisher, Macrone, on a visit to Dickens, then " a young paragraphist for the ' Morning Chronicle,' " living in lodgings at Furnivall's Inn. This visit he afterwards described in his " Ephemera," and Forster says that he and Dickens " laughed heartily at the description, hardly a word of which is true." Be this as it may, when Mr. and Mrs. Dickens came to America in 1842, Willis ran down to New York to be present at the " Boz " ball. He wrote to his wife at Glenmary that he had spent an afternoon in showing Mrs. Dickens the splendors of Broadway, and had danced with her at the ball, where, encountering Halleck, the two poets " slipped down about midnight to the ' Cornucopia ' and had rum toddy and broiled oysters." Among Willis's private papers is a cordial letter from Dickens, dated at Niagara, April 30, 1842,

regretting that he should not have time to accept
his invitation to make him a visit at Owego.

A *rapprochement* now took place between
Willis and his former associate General Morris.
The " New York Mirror " of December 31, 1842,
announced that, expenditures having largely ex-
ceeded receipts, the paper would henceforth be
discontinued, but that a new series would begin
in a few weeks. The issue of the 17th of the
same month had contained two short sketches,
" Imogen and Cymbeline " and " A Charming
Widow of Sixty," which were afterwards joined
into one and worked up into " Poyntz's Aunt."
These were of no importance except as being his
first direct contributions to the " Mirror " since
the establishment of the " Corsair," over two
years and a half before. On Saturday, April 8,
1843, the first number of the " New Mirror "
was issued under the joint editorship of Morris
and Willis. The latter had now entered upon
an active career of journalism which lasted, with
a single brief interruption, for nearly a quarter
of a century, till his death in 1867. With the
" New Mirror " he resumed the duties of an editor, which he had laid down when he sold out the
" American Monthly " in 1831. He had been,
it is true, a nominal editor of the old " New York
Mirror " and of the " Corsair," but virtually he
was merely a contributor and foreign correspond-

ent of both these papers, and had felt no real
responsibility for their conduct. In the three
periodicals which Morris and Willis now edited
successively, the "New Mirror," the "Evening
Mirror," and the "Home Journal," the business
management remained in the hands of the former, but the literary policy was largely shaped
by Willis, and almost the entire time and ener-
gies of both partners were given to their enter-
prises. The office of the new journal was at No.
4 Ann Street, and its title in full ran as follows : —

"The New Mirror of Literature, Amusement, and
Instruction : Containing Original Papers, Tales of
Romance, Sketches of Society, Manners, and Every-
day Life ; Domestic and Foreign Correspondence ;
Wit and Humor ; Fashion and Gossip ; the Fine Arts
and Literary, Musical, and Dramatic Criticism; extracts from New Works ; Poetry, Original and Selected; the Spirit of the Public Journals, etc., etc.,
etc."

Willis could not afford to give up all the other
strings to his bow until he saw how the new venture was going to succeed. He retained his
position as New York correspondent to the "National Intelligencer," and his "Daguerreotype
Sketches of New York," published in that paper,
were regularly reprinted in the "New Mirror."
His stories in "Graham's" and "Godey's" went

on up to January, 1844, after which time he announced that he should write in future exclusively for his own paper. His contributions to
the " Mirror," while editor, included tales, poems,
sketches, reminiscences, letters, book notices,
besides editorial papers of a miscellaneous sort,
such as " Jottings," " Slipshoddities," " Diary of
Town Trifles," " More Particularly," " Just You
and I," " While We hold You by the Button,"
and what not, in which he set himself to catch
and reflect the passing humors and picturesque
surfaces of town life. He might have said of
his muse at this time, as the psalmist of his soul,
Adhæsit pavimento. He wrote a number of
" City Lyrics," signed " Down Town Bard,"
celebrating beauties in white chip hats, whom he
had helped into omnibuses : Broadway odes, inviting his sweetheart to a moonlight walk up to
Thompson's for an ice ; or mock heroic lamen-
tations in blank verse, that the lady in the
chemisette with black buttons, whose sixpence
he had passed up to the driver, might be doomed
to pass him forever without meeting, —

> " Thou in a Knickerbocker Line, and I
> Lone in the Waverley."

It might have been expected that Willis, with
his peculiarly dainty instinct, would excel in this
carving of cherry stones. But his society verses
in this kind were too hurriedly done and fell

short of that perfect workmanship and fineness
of taste which float many a trifle of Praed or
Dobson.   Willis's city poems are flimsy and
sometimes a little vulgar, and their place is mid-
way between really artistic society verse and
such metropolitan ballads as "Walking Down
Broadway" and "Tassels on the Boots," which
Lingard used to sing.   The best of them, perhaps, is "Love in a Cottage," a charmingly
frank expression of a preference for the artificial, a quatrain from which has got into common quotation : —

> "But give me a sly flirtation
>   By the light of a chandelier,
> With music to play in the pauses,
>   And nobody very near."

These "City Lyrics" were not all humorous,
however.   The bitter contrasts which forced
themselves upon Bryant walking "slowly through
the crowded street" appealed also to the "Down
Town Bard," who expressed them in "The Pity
of the Park Fountain," and more successfully
in "Unseen Spirits," first printed in the "New
Mirror" of July 29, 1843.   This little poem —
suggested, perhaps, in some mood of abstrac-
tion when the poet was strolling listlessly up
Broadway, his spirits low and his eternal watch-
fulness for effects asleep — has, for that very
reason doubtless, the sudden touch of genius, the

unconsciousness and careless felicity which seem
likely to keep it alive and to make it, possibly,
the only work of Willis destined to reach posterity. It was a favorite with Edgar Poe, who
used to recite it at reading clubs and the like,
and who said that, in his opinion and that of
nearly all his friends, it was "the truest poem
ever written by Mr. Willis. There is about this
little poem," he continues, "(evidently written
in haste and through impulse) a true imagination. Its grace, dignity, and pathos are impressive, and there is more in it of earnestness of
soul than in anything I have seen from the pen
of its author." [1]

Willis took advantage of his new facilities to
become his own publisher, issuing successively,
as shilling extras in the "Mirror Library," his
"Sacred Poems," "Poems of Passion," and
"Lady Jane and Humorous Poems;" following
these up with the first complete editions, from
the "Mirror" press, of "Letters from Under
a Bridge," and "Pencillings by the Way." The

---

[1] In a late anthology, this poem of Willis is included under
the melodramatic title *Two Women.* An author's choice of
a title is almost as much to be respected as his text. In
this instance, Willis's own selection was not only much the
better, but it is interesting as probably suggested to him by
lines that were favorites of his in Longfellow's translation
from Uhland : —

> "For, invisibly to thee,
>   Spirits twain have crossed with me."

poems contained few notable additions to " Melanie " and earlier volumes, except those just
mentioned as printed in the " New Mirror," and
the lines on the death of President Harrison,
which were much admired at the time. They
were in anapestics, an unusual metre with him,
but one which he handled not without fire in
this excellent elegy. " Lady Jane " was a society
poem in some two hundred " Don Juan " stanzas and was by no means the worst of the many
imitations of Byron's inimitable masterpiece —
if the bull may be pardoned. The hero was
the inevitable dandy poet, — this time he was
twenty-two, — and the heroine who doted on him
with a half motherly affection was a well preserved English countess of forty, wedded to a
decrepit but accommodating earl. The noble
pair go traveling, with the boyish poet in their
train, and coming to Rome, the latter becomes
enamored of an Italian marchioness and cuts
loose from Lady Jane, who, " having loved too
late to dream of love again," grows old as best
she may. This is all, but the poet has caught,
as successfully as was possible for him, the alternate irony and sentiment, the rattling digres-
siveness, and the eccentric rhyming and audacious punning of his original. There is a delicate
suggestion of Lady Blessington in the heroine;
but Willis's English acquaintances could hardly

have felt pleased at being served up by name in
the picture of a London *soirée*, as " Savage
Landor, wanting soap and sand," as " frisky
Bowring, London's wisest bore," or even as
" calm, old, lily-white Joanna Baillie." Willis
was now in considerable request for lectures
and occasional poems. On August 17, 1841,
he delivered a poem before the Linonian Society of Yale College, extracts from which appear in his collected poems as " The Elms of
New Haven." This address was not without
touches of fancy and tender reminders to the
assembled scholars of

" The green tent where your harness was put on,"

and of summer nights in Academus, when the
bird

" Sang a half carol as the moon wore on
And looked into his nest."

But the blank verse carried him along into that
smooth diffuseness which was his besetting sin,
and the poem, as a whole, did not rise above
commonplace. It compares but poorly with
Dr. Holmes's noble " Astræa," delivered in 1850
before the Phi Beta Kappa society at New
Haven by a poet who, though the son of another
Alma Mater, gracefully acknowledged himself
the grandson of Yale. At another time, in response to an invitation from James T. Fields to
recite a poem in Boston, Willis wrote : " I took

the time to consider whether there *could be*
such a thing as an effective *spoken* poem. I
am satisfied now, that my style depends so much
on those light shades which would be lost on
more ears than two at a time, that I should
make an utter failure." In 1843 he lectured
on the formation of character before the Mer-
cantile Library Association of Baltimore, and
the audience — a large one — was disappointed
by the serious nature of the address. A " Lecture on Fashion " given before the New York
Lyceum and published in 1844 was more characteristic, at least in subject. He lectured also
in Boston and Albany, perhaps in other places,
but without marked success, being an indifferent
orator and not at home on the platform. " The
calling on a hen for an egg, while she stands on
the fence, would seem to me reasonable," said
he, " in comparison with asking for my sentiments, to be delivered on my legs."

In the issue of the " New Mirror " for September 28, 1844, the editors announced that
they had been driven out of the field of weekly
journalism by the United States Post Office.
The " Mirror," being stitched, could not go at
newspaper rates, but was taxed, at the caprice
of postmasters, from two to fifteen cents a copy.
This more than doubled the price to country
readers and killed the mail subscription. Re-

monstrances addressed to the authorities at
Washington only brought, in reply, a letter of
" sesquipedalian flummery." Accordingly the
editors decided to change the shape of the paper
and publish it as a daily. The first number of
the " Evening Mirror " came out October 7,
1844. It was published every day in the week
but Sunday, and ran till the close of the following year, under the joint conduct of Morris,
Willis, and Hiram Fuller. The last was a
young man, and a far-away cousin of Margaret
Fuller. He continued the paper, under the
same name, for years after his partners had left
him. It was of Fuller that Bennett said, " We
saw the editor of the ' Evening Mirror,' the
other day, treating his subscribers to an excur-
sion ; he drove them all down Broadway to the
Battery in an omnibus." Edgar Poe was engaged upon the " Evening Mirror" as critic and
sub-editor in the autumn of 1844, and remained
upon it about six months. His relations with
Willis were of the pleasantest. The latter tried
to befriend him in various ways and lent him
the hearty support of his paper. His recollections of his former associate were given in the
" Home Journal " for October 13, 1849, shortly
after Poe's death, in an article bearing generous
testimony to his perfect regularity, reasonable-
ness, and courtesy, while engaged upon the

18

"Mirror." Poe's own estimate of Willis is given at some length in his series of papers on "The Literati of New York." [1] It is friendly in tone, but quite impartial and discriminating. Its literary criticism need not be here repeated, but Poe's personal impressions of Willis are worth giving : —

"Mr. Willis's career," he writes, "has naturally made him enemies among the envious host of dunces whom he has outstripped in the race for fame ; and these his personal manner (a little tinctured with reserve, *brusquerie*, or even haughtiness) is by no means adapted to conciliate. He has innumerable warm friends, however, and is himself a warm friend. He is impulsive, generous, bold, impetuous, vacillating, irregularly energetic, apt to be hurried into error, but incapable of deliberate wrong. He is yet young and, without being handsome in the ordinary sense, is a remarkably well-looking man. In height he is perhaps five feet eleven and justly proportioned. His figure is put in the best light by the ease and assured grace of his carriage. His whole person and personal demeanor bear about them the traces of 'good society.' His face is somewhat too full or rather heavy in its lower proportions. Neither his nose nor his forehead can be defended. The latter would puzzle phrenology. His eyes are a dull bluish

---

[1] See also his paper on *The American Drama*, for an elaborate review of *Tortesa*, which, with all its defects, he thought the best American play.

gray and small. His hair is of a rich brown, curling naturally and luxuriantly. His mouth is well cut, the teeth fine, the expression of the smile intellectual and winning. He converses little, *well* rather than fluently, and in a subdued tone."

It was after Morris and Willis had dissolved their connection with the " Evening Mirror " that that journal published the article, by Thomas Dunn English, reflecting severely on Poe's character, for which he sued Fuller and recovered $225 damages. His " Raven " was written while he was on the paper, and first published anonymously in the " American Review." Willis reprinted it in the " Mirror " over Poe's name, with a send-off, in which he said, " We regard it as the most effective single example of fugitive poetry ever published in this country." [1]

The year 1844–45 was a sad one for Willis. In the preface to " Poems of Passion," 1843, he had written, " We are accused daily of writing nothing that is not frivolous. These poems are from the undercurrent of our frivolity ; and they run as deep, we are inclined to think, as a man ever sees into his heart till it is rent open with a calamity — and calamity as yet, we never knew." But in March, 1844, he lost that admirable mother whose love had been to him both

[1] See Gill's *Life of Poe* for a fac-simile letter of Willis to Poe.

a stay and an inspiration. His youngest sister,
Ellen, had died the month before. And a year
later, March 25, 1845, at the Astor House,
his wife died in childbirth. "An angel without
fault or foible" is the comment which the
broken-hearted husband wrote against the record of her death in his note-book. The child,
a girl, for whom he had chosen the name
of Blanche, was born dead. The labor of editing a daily paper had proved unexpectedly bur-
densome and, added to the grief of his bereavement, left him greatly exhausted and under the
need of breaking away from work for a time.
In the early summer of 1845 he sailed on the
Britannic for Liverpool, taking with him his
little daughter Imogen, and the faithful colored
woman, Harriet Jacobs, who had been the child's
nurse during Mrs. Willis's lifetime. Before
starting for England he had gathered up his
recent story contributions to the magazines and
published them, together with " Inklings of Adventure," and " Romance of Travel," in a single
large volume, " Dashes at Life with a Free Pencil." This was divided into three parts: "High
Life in Europe and American Life," " Inklings
of Adventure," and " Loiterings of Travel."
A fourth part, " Ephemera," was added in
1854. The tales which he had written since
1840, and which now appeared for the first time

in book form, exhibited more range and variety
of subject than his two previous collections, but
a decided falling off in literary quality. Those
who had seen promise in some of the earlier
stories — such as " Edith Linsey," " The Picker
and Piler," and " The Lunatic's Skate " — of a
capacity for stronger and graver work were disappointed by these later " Dashes." None of
them was without clever strokes, but they were,
as a whole, very light. The " High Life "
stories were mostly repetitions of Willis's favorite plot. Sometimes the hero is a spoiled child
of genius, as in " Countess Nyschriem and the
Handsome Artist," and "Leaves from the Heart
Book of Ernest Clay." Sometimes, as in " The
Revenge of the Signor Basil," he is a designing
villain. Again, as in "Love and Diplomacy,"
he turns out to be a very great person in dis-
guise, who flings off his cloak in the *dénoue-
ment* and confounds his adversaries. In " Getting to Windward," he is a French adventurer,
for whom three English peeresses contend — like
the Goddesses on Ida. In " Flirtation and Fox
Chasing," he is a Kentucky lady-killer, sojourn-
ing at an English country house. In " Lady
Rachel," he is nobody in particular. But in
each and all of these protean shapes, he is
equally fascinating and invincible. In " Beware
of Dogs and Waltzing," the author entered the

confessional with even less precaution than usual. It is quite plain to one reading between the lines, that the hero, Mr. Lindsay Maud, with his *retroussé* nose, sanguineous tint, curly hair, and dimpled chin, is no other than Willis himself; that the Surrey manor where the scene is laid is Shirley Park; that its hospitable occupants, the Becktons, are in truth the Skinner family; that Mabel Brown, the heroine, is identical with Miss Mary Stace; and, lastly, that Miss Blakeney, the dazzling but heartless heiress, whose hand Mr. Maud's hostess kindly destines for her young *protégé*, but whom, yielding to his better angel, he flings overboard in favor of the gentler and sweeter Mabel, is a certain belle of fortune, who figures in Willis's private correspondence as "trotted out" by Mrs. Skinner for his inspection with a view to his making a rich marriage.

In "A Revelation of a Previous Life" and "The Phantom Head upon the Table," the supernatural is introduced, but not with success. Willis had not the weird, haunting imagination of Hawthorne or Poe. He does not prepare the reader's belief by creating the atmosphere of mystery required for illusion. In the midst of the fashionable, real life where they are set, his supernatural incidents lose their effect, and have no *vraisemblance*. Nor was he more at home in

broad comedy. His humor — and he had humor
— was delicate rather than robust; was made out
of irony, pleasantry, and gay spirits, and depended more upon situation than character. If
the situation was droll, the humor was good;
otherwise not. " Miss Jones's Son," " The Spirit
Love of Ione S——," " Nora Mehidy," " Meena
Dimity," and " Born to love Pigs and Chickens "
were all *manqué.* The best of the humorous tales
is " The Female Ward," which tells of the em-
barrassments of a rather fast young gentleman in
Boston, who receives an unexpected consignment,
in the shape of a raw heiress, from a Southern
plantation; her confiding parents intrusting her
to his guardianship, with a request that he place
her at school in some high-toned seminary. His
difficulties in trying to perform this commission,
ending with his lodging her temporarily in a private lunatic asylum, are very happily imagined.
" The Female Ward " would lend itself nicely to
the dramatizer, and make up into a most amusing little farce. " Those Ungrateful Blidg-
imses " was funny, but wicked. It was Willis's
way of avenging himself upon two maiden ladies
with whom he had fallen in, and subsequently
fallen out, during his travels in Italy, and who,
on returning to America, had circulated reports
not to his credit. He had another hit at them
in " Ernest Clay," as " two abominable old

maids by the name of Buggins or Blidgins, representing the *scan. mag.* of Florence." The
story caused a good deal of scandal. The victims
(whose names were thinly disguised) were high
in Knickerbocker social circles, and the doors
of many of the best houses in Albany and New
York were closed forever against Willis, as a
consequence of this indiscretion. There was
even some rumor in the Albany newspapers to
the effect that he had been challenged by a friend
of the injured ladies, and had declined the challenge, but this he denied. "Kate Crediford"
is a clever specimen of anti-climax. The writer
sees an old love at the theatre and, fancying
that she looks unhappy, his flame revives, and
he goes home and writes her an impassioned dec-
laration. His letter is answered by the lady's
husband, who informs him of her recent marriage, and explains her pensiveness by the fact
that she had eaten too heartily of unripe fruit
before going to the play. In "The Poet and
the Mandarin" and "The Inlet of Peach Blossoms," the descriptions are richly fanciful. But
the most truly imaginative of all these tales is
"The Ghost Ball at Congress Hall." The
theme is one that would have delighted Hawthorne, and though he might have treated it
more meaningly, he could not have improved
upon its wild, half-eerie gayety, with its under-

current of regret — the old Horatian regret for
the shortness of life and vanished youth. A su-
perannuated beau, lingering in the empty col-
onnade of Congress Hall after the close of the
Saratoga season, sees a spectral procession of
coaches drive up to the door and deposit, one
after another, their loads of ladies with escorts
and baggage. Later in the evening, peering in
through the ball-room windows, his brain reels
as he beholds the well-remembered belles and
dandies — apparently grown no older — of the
golden age of the springs, the days of " the
Albany regency." They dance to the same old
waltz music, played by the same old negro fid-
dlers, by the light of spermaceti tapers that floods
the dusty evergreens " with a weird mysterious-
ness, an atmosphere of magic, even in the burning
of the candles," and drink champagne of " the
exploded color, rosy wine suited to the bright
days when all things were tinted rose."

It is needless to say that there is an abundance of pretty and clever things scattered
through these tales of Willis. " Flirtation" —
as an instance of his epigrams — " is a circulat-
ing library in which we seldom ask twice for the
same volume." " His politeness," he says of one
of his characters, " had superseded his character altogether." He tells of " a person of excellent family, after the fashion of a hill of pota-

toes, the best part of it under ground ; " and of
the Frenchman who could trace his lineage back
to " the man who spoke French in the confusion
of Babel." " Mr. Potts's income was a net answer to his morning prayer : it provided his
daily bread." " Wigwam *vs.* Almacks," which
follows out the suggestions of a true story told
in " À l'Abri," is not very satisfactory as a fiction, but is worth noticing for the lovely description, with which it opens, of a wayside spring in
the valley of the Chemung.

CHAPTER VII.

1845-1852.

THIRD VISIT TO ENGLAND — THE HOME
JOURNAL.

On his arrival in London, Willis was attacked
with a brain fever, which confined him to his
bed for a fortnight. As soon as he could get
about he brought his little daughter to see Lady
Blessington, and then took her and her nurse to
Steventon Vicarage, near Abingdon, in Berk-
shire, to stay with her aunt, the wife of Rev.
William Vincent, formerly of Bolney Priory.
He took lodgings for himself in the village near
by, and, after a short trip to Bath, returned to
London and spent some time in visiting, dining
out, sight-seeing, and making new acquaintances.
He met a Mr. Stiles of Georgia, an old schoolmate, who was passing through England on his
way to Vienna, where he had lately been appointed *chargé d'affaires*, and who gave him a
complimentary appointment as *attaché* to his legation, an addition to his passport of the kind
that had proved so serviceable in the days of his

" Pencillings." This determined him to shape his course for the capital of Austria, taking in Germany, which was new to him, on the way. Leaving his daughter at Steventon, he crossed the Channel, went up the Rhine, and joined his brother Richard, who was studying music at Leipsic. Here he passed a month, and then, accompanied by his brother, went on to Dresden. There the two parted, and Willis traveled alone to Berlin, where he was again seriously ill, and was kindly ministered to by his old friend and associate on the " New York Mirror," T. S. Fay, at that time secretary of legation at Berlin. Mr. Henry Wheaton, the American minister, attached Willis also to the Prussian mission. But of these appointments and the opportunities they promised he was unable to avail himself. Continued ill health forced him to abandon his journey to Vienna, and to make his way back to England, whence he sailed for home in the spring of 1846. He had meant to leave Imogen with her mother's family for a time, to be put to school in England. But his heart failed him at the last, and he brought her back with him to America, sending her, still in charge of her nurse, to live with his sister, Mrs. Louis Dwight, in Boston. He himself took rooms in New York until other arrangements could be made. His child's nurse, Harriet Jacobs, who

was in his employ from 1842 to 1861, was a
remarkable woman, whose career, if fully told,
would form an interesting chapter in the history
of American slavery. She was an escaped slave
from a plantation near Edenton, North Carolina. She had run away from her master when
a young woman, and taken refuge with a family
of free negroes, her kinsfolk. They kept her hidden for five years in a cubby under the roof, during which time she supported herself by fine
needle-work which her friends sold for her in
town. At last she escaped to the North, and was
engaged by Willis as a house servant when he
went to Glenmary. Her attachment to the interests of the family during the whole period of
her service was a beautiful instance of the fidelity and affection which sometimes, but not often,
distinguish the relation of master and servant
even in this land of change. Mrs. Jacobs's
former owners, having got wind in some way of
her whereabouts, came North in quest of her, and
spared no pains to reclaim the runaway. Several times she had to leave the Willises and go
into hiding at Boston and elsewhere. At last,
tired of these alarms, Willis sacrificed whatever
scruples he might have had against such a step,
and bought her freedom out and out. When
the civil war began she went to Washington, and
employed her practical abilities, which were of

a high order, in the post of matron to a soldiers' hospital. In that city she is still living, at an advanced age.

Though ill nearly all the time of this his third trip abroad, Willis managed to write a number of "Invalid Letters" to the "Evening Mirror," which were collected in "Famous Persons and Places" and in "Rural Letters." They were scarcely worth preserving. England was now a twice-told tale, and in Germany, which was a pasture new, he was too tired and sick and borne down by his recent bereavement to take much interest in anything. His articles about the great fair at Leipsic — "What I saw at the Fair," in "Godey's" for October, 1847; and "On Dress," in "The Opal" for 1848, and "Godey's" for June, 1849 — were the most considerable literary results of the journey. He also superintended the publication of an English edition of "Dashes at Life," in three volumes, and came home under engagement to write for the London "Morning Chronicle."

Meanwhile the editorial corps of the "Evening Mirror" had tapered down to Hiram Fuller. Willis had practically retired from any active share in its management when he left the country in the spring of 1845. He was still abroad when Morris withdrew from it and started a new paper, the "National Press," to-

ward the close of the same year. Willis joined
him in this enterprise as soon as he got back
from England. During the spring and summer
of 1846 he was often in Washington, as correspondent of the "National Press" and the
"Morning Chronicle," and while there he met
Miss Cornelia Grinnell, the niece and adopted
daughter of the Hon. Joseph Grinnell, who was
then representative in Congress from New Bedford, Massachusetts. To this lady he was married on October 1, 1846, the eleventh anniver-
sary of his first marriage. She was his junior
by nearly twenty years, but she united to her
graces of person and character a penetrating
mind and an uncommon energy and firmness of
will, which made her an invaluable helpmate
through the years of trial that were in store for
both. On the 21st of November following, the
name of the "National Press" was changed to
the "Home Journal," under which title the paper
has ever since been published. This was Morris's and Willis's final and most prosperous experiment in journalism. They both remained
connected with it till death: in Willis's case a
service of twenty-one years, during which his literary toil was devoted almost exclusively to building up the paper. "For the cultivation of the
memorable, the progressive, and the beautiful,"
ran the legend upon its title-page, followed by a

sentence from Goethe, which still stands as the
motto of the paper, and would have served well
enough as the motto of Willis's own career :
" We should do our utmost to encourage the
beautiful, for the useful encourages itself." It
was not a very solid type of literature which was
fostered by the " Home Journal," but it made
for itself a peculiar constituency, and a place in
the world of letters which it still successfully occupies, under the editorship of Morris Phillips,
General Morris's adopted son, who has carried
out the traditions of the paper as established by
his predecessors. It was and is the organ of
" japonicadom," the journal of society and gazette of fashionable news and fashionable literature, addressing itself with assiduous gallantry
to " the ladies."

Willis set himself more especially in both the
" New Mirror " and the " Home Journal " to
portray the town. He became a sort of Knickerbocker Spectator, and his " Ephemera," published in 1854, is a running record of the notabilities of New York for a dozen years. He chron-
icled the operas and theatres : Ole Bull, Jenny
Lind, and Macready ; the shops, the omnibuses,
the endless procession of Broadway, the museum,
the art galleries, the·Tombs, the Alhambra, the
Five Points, the Croton water, the cafés, the
hotels, the balls and receptions, the changes in

equipages, customs, dress. He grew to be a
recognized *arbiter elegantiarum*, and his correspondence columns were crowded with appeals
on knotty points of etiquette or costume. His
decisions of these social problems were always
marked by good sense and good taste. There
are many nice bits in " Ephemera," and some
little wholes, — like the letter from Saratoga,
" To the Julia of Some Years Ago," — which
deserve to be rescued from the oblivion of a
book of scraps and trifles. He was a skillful
paragrapher ; he had unfailing tact and knew
when to stop. Above all, he was eminently human ; his gregariousness and his cheerful philosophy cast a gleam of their own on this look-
ing-glass of urban life. He imported a rural
air into the city ; watched how April greened
the grass in the public squares, and June spread
the leaves in Trinity Churchyard ; stopped to
pick " a clovertop or an aggravating dandelion
'twixt post office and city hall ; " and discovered
even in the stream that washed the curbstone,
" a clear brook — a brook with a song, tripping
as musically (when the carts are not going by)
as the beloved brook " in Glenmary. Pan, we
know, has been found in Wall Street ; and Willis contrived to find something like a nymph in
the waste of the Park fountain. When his
work kept him at the desk all through the hot

summer, he borrowed a breeze from "the outer-
most bastion of Castle Garden," and made the
Jersey ferryboat his "substitute for a private
yacht."

When he came to New York to live, in 1842,
and during his continued residence there for
more than ten years from that date, Manhattan
was by no means the metropolis that it is to-
day, though it had begun to assume already that
cosmopolitan and intensely commercial character which distinguishes it from all other American cities. It had a considerable and swiftly
growing foreign population, and its society was
marked by a liveliness and extravagance which
contrasted with the plainer and more earnest
tone prevailing in Boston, and with the somewhat provincial cast of Philadelphia life. The
Battery was still the fashionable promenade,
Canal Street was "up town," Hoboken, a rural
suburb, Pine, Ann, and William Streets, and
the Bowling Green were genteel residence quarters. The old Park Theatre was — after the
burning of the National — the only respectable
playhouse, until Niblo's was opened in what was
then the outskirt of the town. New York prided
itself, moreover, on being a literary centre. The
term "Knickerbocker School," which has been
invented to describe a group of metropolitan
writers who owed their inspiration, in some sort,

to Washington Irving, is of uncertain application; and there was no such cohesion among the members of the group as to warrant the name of a school. But if the term be extended to cover all the authors whose birth or long residence identified them with New York city, it may include Bryant and Halleck, who were the most prominent literary figures when Willis went there to live, though both of them, like him, were of New England birth and breeding. Bryant had been since 1826 editor of the "Evening Post" and Halleck, who had almost ceased to write and was devoting himself exclusively to his duties as secretary to Mr. John Jacob Astor, left the city in 1849, and retired to his old home in Guilford, Connecticut. With both of these Willis was more or less intimate, meeting them frequently at dinners and in general society. Irving himself, the starting-point of the Knickerbocker writers, was out of the country when Willis settled in New York, having gone as minister to Spain in 1842. He came back in 1846 and took up his residence at Sunnyside. Cooper was living at Cooperstown, where Willis made him a flying visit and renewed the acquaintance so pleasantly begun at Paris in 1832. This was in the summer of 1848, which Willis spent at Sharon Springs, recovering from an attack of rheumatism. Theodore Fay too

was abroad, filling diplomatic posts in Germany
and Switzerland. Years after, on his return to
America, he visited Willis at Idlewild, and the
latter found him greatly aged and saddened
since the days when he wrote mild town satires
and humorous sketches for the " New York
Mirror." Eastburn, Sands, and Drake were
all dead, and Paulding had signalized the close
of his literary career by publishing a collection
of his works in numerous volumes. He too had
been a contributor to the old " Mirror," and so
had another of the Knickerbockers, Charles
Fenno Hoffman, who had once edited the paper
for a month, before Willis had any connection
with it. Hoffman, who died just the other day,
is known to this generation almost solely by his
still popular song, " Sparkling and Bright," and
his hardly less popular "Monterey." The former
is sung by collegians and the latter declaimed
by school-boys. He was the first editor of the
" Knickerbocker Magazine." His " Winter in
the West " and his novel, " Greyslaer," founded
on the famous Beauchamp tragedy in North Carolina, had wide currency in their time, and his
amusing story, " The Man in the Reservoir,"
may still be read with enjoyment. He was a
man of many friends, greatly beloved for his
frank and cordial nature. By 1846 he had already begun to show symptoms of the mental

disease which issued in his chronic insanity. He kept on writing up to 1850, when it was found necessary to send him to an asylum, in which confinement he lived for over thirty years. Hoffman once said of Willis's eyes that they "always seemed to have nothing but cold speculation in them, — to be two holes, looking out through a stone wall." Then there were Verplanck, the editor of Shakespeare, and Duyckinck the compiler of the " Cyclopædia of American Literature," and many forgotten worthies, whose names may be read in such limbos of departed fame as Poe's " Literati of New York." Many of these literati used to meet each other informally at the weekly receptions given by Miss Anne Lynch (now Mrs. Botta) the poetess, and author of the " Handbook of Universal Literature," whose hospitable parlors have been for forty years a rallying place for interesting and distinguished people. With this lady Mr. and Mrs. Willis formed a close and lasting friendship. Willis used to go often to Horace Greeley's, where he got interested for a time in spirit rappings, and wrote some papers on the subject in the "Home Journal." Greeley once urged him in a letter (November 18, 1854) to publish a volume of selections from his lifelong writings. " I want such a one," he wrote, " for my boy, so that, should I live to see him sixteen,

I may try ' Unwritten Music ' on him and see if it impresses him as it did me at about that age, when it appeared."

During the first winter and spring after their marriage, Willis and his wife lived in lodgings. In the autumn of 1847 they went to housekeeping at No. 19 Ludlow Place, where their eldest son, Grinnell, was born, April 28, 1848. In the fall of that year they bought the house No. 198 Fourth Street, where they remained till the fall of 1852. A daughter, Lilian, was born April 27, 1850.

For ten years Willis's tall and elegantly dressed figure was a familiar sight on Broadway, and was often pointed out to strangers at public assemblages, or in private society, where his agreeable manners made him a general favorite. He was never what is called a brilliant conversationalist, but he was an easy talker and quick at an impromptu, many of his "good things " in which kind are remembered and quoted by his contemporaries. Thus, on one occasion, at a dinner party in Washington, a young lady who sat between Willis and a gentleman named Campbell was rather too partial in her attention to the former. Her mother sitting opposite, and considering Mr. Campbell a desirable *parti*, slipped her a note across the table, " Pay more attention to your other neighbor." This being shown to Willis, he wrote on the back of it, —

"Dear Mamma don't essay my flirtation to trammel :
I but strain at a Nat while you swallow a Campbell."

When in Germany, he went with some gentlemen to visit a deaf and dumb asylum which had an inscription over the gate, *Stiftung*, etc. "Stifftongue," said Willis, looking up; "very appropriate."

Like most men who overwork their pens, he was impatient of private correspondence. When in England, he excused his brevity on the plea that he was paid a guinea a page for everything he wrote, and could not afford to waste manuscript. "Private Letters," he declared in a note to Edgar Poe, "are the 'last ounce that breaks the camel's back' of a literary man." And he once answered a friend who proposed a correspondence, that to ask him to write a letter after his day's work was like asking a penny postman to take a walk in the evening for the pleasure of it. His letters to his family and friends have seldom any literary quality, though they contain, now and then, characteristically quaint or playful touches. "Kiss mother on her sad expression" is a message in one of them; and in another he refers to one of his little nieces as the most charming "copy of Willis" extant. Having been invited to sit on the stage, at the Commencement of Rutgers Female College, as " the author of ' Absalom ' and ' Hagar,' " he wrote, " I shall try to have the air of the Old Testament, but have my doubts as to success."

The easy *dégagé* air of his writing was, as is usually the case with seemingly ready writers, the result of laborious care. It appears from the testimony of Poe, Parton, Phillips, and others who were his associates on the " Mirror " or " Home Journal " and knew his habits of composition, that his manuscript was full of erasures and interlineations. He blotted, on an average, one line out of every three, but his copy was so neatly and legibly prepared that the compositors preferred it to " reprint," even his erasures having " a certain wavy elegance." He was likewise very particular about having his articles printed just as he wrote them. " My copy *must* be followed," he wrote to an offending foreman. " If I insert a comma in the middle of a word, do you place it there and ask no questions." Once a slight alteration by Morris in the wording of a paragraph in Willis's manuscript came near causing a quarrel between the two old friends, " probably the only misunderstanding or disagreement," says Mr. Phillips, " which occurred during the whole of their literary life and business association." " I would not stay one week a partner with a man who ventured to alter a word of my copy and send it to press without my knowledge," wrote Willis in his angry note to Morris on this occasion. Mr. Phillips adds that "General Morris proved his love for Mr. Willis by not replying to this letter, but simply wrote on the back of it, 'I would have received this from no other man living.'" From similar testimony it appears that Willis took no share in the business management of the paper, never examined the books, nor asked any questions as to the circulation. He felt or affected a horror of figures, and confided the matter of receipts and expenditures entirely to General Morris, between whom and himself, during the entire period of their partnership, no statement of account was ever rendered. In money matters Willis was liberal, — not to say reckless, — and his hospitality knew no limit. Nor was it only his roof and his table that were at his friends' service; his literary latch-string was always out to every new-comer in the field of letters. It was an honorable trait in his character, and should never be forgotten in casting his account, that, whatever may have been his foibles, the jealousy which is the besetting sin of authors and artists was not among them. He was perpetually on the lookout for young writers of promise, and was the first to praise them, and

to give circulation to their good things by copy-
ing them into his columns.   He was the intro-
ducer and literary sponsor of many reputations
now fallen silent, and of some which have survived.   Among the last were Mr. T. B. Aldrich
— who succeeded James Parton as assistant editor
of the "Home Journal " — and Bayard Taylor.
The latter was greatly in Willis's debt.   His
desire for travel was first awakened by reading
the "Pencillings by the Way" when he was a
lad of sixteen.   And afterwards when he came
to New York to seek the means for foreign
travel he applied at once to the author whose
brilliant pictures of European life had roused
his young enthusiasm.   Willis befriended him
in every way; gave him letters to wealthy gentlemen in New York, and bestirred himself to
interest people in his adventure and raise the
sum necessary to start him on his journey.   On
his departure he gave him a letter to his brother
Richard, in Frankfort, with whom the young
handwerksbursch tarried for a time, while he was
picking up the German language.   His "Views
Afoot" — the fruits of this venture — were dedicated to Willis, who contributed the preface.
This patronage was unkindly referred to in Du-
ganne's "Parnassus in Pillory," a little Dunciad
of the old downright "English Bards and Scotch
Reviewers" variety, which made some noise in
New York in the year 1851 : —

"What time Nat Willis, in the daily papers,
Published receipts of shoemakers and drapers;
What time, in sooth, his 'Mirror' flashed its rays,
Like Barnum's 'drummond' on the Broadway gaze,
When lisping misses, fresh from seminaries,
Worshiped 'mi-boy' and 'brigadier'[1] as *lares;*
Then Bayard Taylor — *protégé* of Natty,
Dixon-like walked into the 'literati;'
And first to proper use his genius put,
Like ballet-girls, by showing 'Views Afoot.'"

In another part of his squib the lampooner returns to the charge against Willis as follows: —

"I almost passed by Willis — 'ah, *miboy!*
Foine morning! da-da!' Faith I wish him joy —
He's forty-three years old — in good condition —
And, positively, he has gained 'position.'
Gad! what a polish 'upper-ten-dom' gives
This executioner of adjectives;
This man who strangles English worse than Thuggists,
And turns 'the trade' to trunk-makers or druggists;
Labors on tragic plays that draw no tiers —
Writes under bridges, and tells tales of peers;
His subjects whey — his language sugared curds;
Gods! What a dose! — had he to 'eat his words!'
His 'Sacred Poems,' like a rogue's confessions,
Gain him indulgence for his worst transgressions:
His 'Fugitive Attempts' will doubtless live —
Oh! that more works of his were fugitive!
Fate to his fame a ticklish place has given,
Like Mahomet's coffin, 'twixt the earth and heaven;
But be it as it will — let come what may —
Nat is a star, his works — the Milky Way!"

[1] An allusion to the interlocutors in Willis's *Cloister* and *Cabinet,* dialogues between the editors of the *Mirror* in not very successful imitation of the *Noctes Ambrosianæ.*

> " ' Why so severe on Willis ? ' Julia cries
> (Who reads *De Trobriand* in an English guise),
> Why so severe ?   Because my muse must make
> Example stern for injured Poesy's sake.
> Not that Nat Willis curls his yellow hair —
> Not that his sense can breathe but perfumed air —
> Not that he plays the ape or ass I mourn,
> For ape and ass are worth not even my scorn.
> But that, with mind, and soul, and haply heart,
> He yet hath stooped to act the fopling's part;
> Trifled with all he might have been to be
> The *blasé* editor — at forty-three ;
> Flung off the chaplet which his boyhood won,
> To wear the fool's cap of a ' man of ton.'
> I lash not Willis even for this his crime —
> Through him I strike the bastard tribe of rhyme ;
> The race o'er whom, in his own native power,
> Jove-like mid satyrs might this Willis tower ! "

Another young poet whose career Willis watched with interest was J. R. Lowell.   There was a friendly correspondence between the two in 1843–44, the younger writer thanking the older for his encouragement, sending him his new volume of verse, and promising to contribute to the " Mirror," but remonstrating with him upon his declared intention — in a very appreciative review of Lowell's poems in the " Mirror " — to omit the *James* from his " musical surname " and call him simply Russell Lowell : —

" Suppose I, dropping the ' N.,' should call you by that mysterious middle letter — whose signification, without reference to the Parish Register (or perhaps

Griswold's equally entertaining bead-roll) no man can fathom — and call you ' P. Willis.' Under such painful circumstances you could imagine how I feel, when you amputate one sound limb of my name.

" However, it is too cold to say any more about it. What I have left unsaid shall be frozen up in me like the tune in Munchausen's bugle, and thaw out eloquently and startlingly when I meet you in the warmer atmosphere of New York — as I shall before long." [1]

In point of fact — if the item is not below the dignity of biography — this threat of Lowell's to mind Willis's P's for him was without terror for the latter, who favored his middle initial at the expense of his scriptural and baptismal *prænomen*, and used to figure on the title-pages of his later books as N. Parker Willis. He disliked to be called Nathaniel; respecting which prejudice, his wife and brothers and sisters, as well as his intimate friends, were accustomed to address him simply as Willis. "Truly one's sponsors," said he, " have much to answer for." In Lowell's smart pasquinade, " A Fable for Critics," published in 1848, which contains not only headlong fun, but good poetry and just criticism, there is a passage on Willis, from which I venture to quote a few lines, — in spite of its familiarity to many readers, — because its

----

[1] Cambridge, January 13, 1844.

spirit is kindly and it is one of the best estimates
of Willis ever written : —

"There's Willis so *natty* and jaunty and gay,
  Who says his best things in so foppish a way,
  With conceits and pet phrases so thickly o'erlaying 'em,
  That one hardly knows whether to thank him for saying
    'em. . . .
  His prose had a natural grace of its own,
  And enough of it, too, if he'd let it alone,
  But he twitches and jerks so one fairly gets tired,
  And is forced to forgive where he might have admired.
  Yet whenever it slips away free and unlaced
  It runs like a stream with a musical waste,
  And gurgles along with the liquidest sweep.
  'T is not deep as a river, but who'd have it deep? . . .
  No volume I know to read under a tree
  More truly delicious than his À l'Abri,
  With the shadows of leaves flowing over your book,
  Like ripple-shades netting the bed of a brook ;
  With June coming softly your shoulder to look over,
  Breezes waiting to turn every leaf of your book over,
  And Nature to criticise still as you read —
  The page that bears that is a rare one indeed. . . .
  His nature's a glass of champagne with the foam on 't,
  As tender as Fletcher, as witty as Beaumont ;
  So his best things are done in the flush of the moment :
  If he wait, all is spoiled : he may stir it and shake it,
  But, the fixed air once gone, he can never remake it. . . .
  He'd have been just the fellow to sup at the Mermaid,
  Cracking jokes at rare Ben, with an eye to the bar-maid,
  His wit running up as canary ran down, —
  The topmost bright bubble on the wave of The Town."

One proof of popularity is parody. Until a
statesman's face is so familiar to the public that
its caricature in the comic papers needs no

label, and until an author's style is so easily recognized that a travesty of it hits the sense of the reader, neither statesman nor author may consider himself as really popular. " Excelsior," and " The Raven," and " Abou ben Adhem " are by no means the best poems in the English tongue, but their currency is attested and doubtless kept up by the innumerable burlesque imitations of them that swarm the press. Willis had a share of these left-hand honors: his epistolary style in particular was often caricatured in the newspapers. In " Godey's Lady's Book " for December, 1849, he was selected together with Poe, Morris, Whittier, and John Neal for humorous imitation.

" My dear Sir : " he is made to write in response to an imaginary request for a contribution, " to be obliged to penetrate with the pump-buckets of necessity, prompted by the piston of a fifty-dollar compensation, with a publisher as the pump-handle, in search of a poem, is, of itself, annoying enough. To draw one up with the rope and bucket of gratuity, is a labor which qualifies one for a long residence in fatiguedom. Your letter found me fagging away over my work-desk — chasing a brilliant idea in and out of the myriads of convolutions of my brain. All the while that I was aping Prometheus (the window being half-opened), I could sniff the delightful odors of a rose which a fair neighbor will insist on keeping," etc., etc.

The requested poem is annexed — a scriptural poem, "The Fishwoman's Son : " —

> "Night on the market. Through the colonnade
> Of red-brick pillars not a sound was heard,
> Save of some whistling urchin as he strode
> With stamping footfalls, listening to the noise
> Which wore his shoe-soles and the hearer's patience ;
> Or the low mutter of the drunken man,
> As his wild song, proclaiming fix'd resolve
> Not to go home till morning, sank to low
> And nearly inarticulate murmurs."

The fishwoman's son sings a song, whose first stanza runs : —

> "I will not go,
> Like a whipt dog, unto the public school,
> To wear the cap and tokens of a fool,
> While Mexico
> Invites me on to glory and to fame, —
> Or a cracked crown, which after all 's the same."

Willis was forty when the " Home Journal " was begun — an age at which writers who have thought and studied deeply are often no more than ripe, and have their most productive years before them. But his best work was already done. After 1846 he wrote hardly any more stories or poems — none at all of any value. His pen was devoted more and more steadily to editorial duties, to ephèmeræ and paragraphs and fragments of all kinds, and his well-wishers lamented that wit and fancy which, if properly directed, might have produced something that

would live and delight future generations, were
wasted in dissertations upon the cut of a beard
or the fashion of a coat. To all remonstrances of
his friends over his literary trifling and their
exhortations to write for posterity, his invariable
answer, in and out of print, was that the public
liked trifles, and that posterity would not pay his
bills — that he must go on " buttering curiosity
with the ooze of his brains." That this answer
satisfied himself, or that he was without those
aspirations after a more enduring fame which
are natural to all, cannot be believed. It is
probable that he sadly acknowledged in his in-
ner consciousness that the best part of his career was over. His talent, as has been said
before, was the result of, or was closely dependent upon, his physical temperament. When
health began to decay, and youth was over, and
his animal spirits had effervesced, life commenced to have a flat taste. The bloom was off.
His writing, too, as we have seen, was always
closely related to his personal experiences ; and
as these grew tamer, he had less and less to
report, and his writing grew tame in proportion.
With some, mere study and contemplation supply, to a degree, the ravages which time makes
upon the freshness of young impressions. But
it had been Willis's misfortune in youth that a
premature success had deprived him of the dis-

20

cipline of early rebuffs, and had made a painful self-culture needless. He never drew much
inspiration from books, and in later life he read
very little. He said that he could not afford
to read, partly for want of time, partly from a
notion that much reading would be fatal to
originality. Neither was it his privilege to command, at this or at any time, the stimulating
and bracing association with men of high serious intellects and strenuous aims, such as he
might, perhaps, have had if he had remained in
Boston. The occasional hasty meetings with
men of brains and literary tastes in general society did not at all take the place of that intimate communion with a circle of gifted spirits
which has been so stimulating to others. Moreover it should be borne in mind, as accounting
largely for the mediocrity of his later work,
that for the last fifteen years of his life Willis
was a chronic invalid.   Indeed, he was never
really a well man after his illness of 1845.

Next to Cooper, Willis was the best abused
man of letters in America. It is easy to understand how the former, who was pugnacious and
struck hard, should have been always in hot
water. But why a man of Willis's urbanity
should have been a target for the newspaper
critics is more difficult of explanation. "Colonel" William L. Stone of the "Commercial

Advertiser," and " Colonel " James Watson
Webb of the "Courier and Enquirer," distinguished themselves especially by their stern con-
demnation of Willis's literary affectations, and
of what they were pleased to consider the weak-
nesses of his private character and life. It is
suggestive, by the way, of the militant disposition of the New York press at that time, that so
many editors were generals and colonels — or
at least were breveted such by public consent,
and graced with titular embellishments of a
warlike character. Henry J. Raymond, who
joined the "Courier and Enquirer" in 1842,
proved his zealous adhesion to the traditions of
the paper by an onslaught upon Willis, in which
he asserted that the latter had snobbishly represented himself as received in the best circles
abroad, "when in truth 't was no such matter."
Willis replied to this in an editorial which Poe
mentions as a clever specimen of skill at fence.
An effort was afterwards made by friends of both
to bring them together, at a time when Willis
was living at Idlewild and Raymond was visiting in the neighborhood. The plan miscarried
for some reason or other, though Willis, who
seldom cherished a resentment, was quite ready
for a reconciliation.

In 1850 Willis became unpleasantly involved
in the famous divorce suit between Edwin For-

rest and his wife. He had known Forrest as
early as 1836, admired his acting, and praised it
constantly in the " Mirror " and " Home Journal," preferring it to the more studied performances of his English rival, Macready. He had
seen little of Forrest for a number of years; but
after his return to New York, in 1846, the
two families grew quite intimate, exchanging
visits and dinners. Mrs. Willis and Mrs. Forrest especially became fast friends, and on one
occasion, when the former was seriously ill, she
sent for Mrs. Forrest to come and stay with her.
Mrs. Forrest was the daughter of Sinclair, the
great English singer. She was a lady of refinement, beauty, and social accomplishments.
Her sister Mrs. Voorhies, who lived with her
for a time, had inherited her father's musical
talents, and Mrs. Forrest soon got about her a
pleasant circle of friends, which included many
persons of literary and artistic tastes, editors,
authors, professors, clergymen, and their wives.
The Bryants, the Godwins, Dr. Dewey, Henry
Wikoff, and Samuel Raymond, the actor, were
among the frequenters of the house. When
Richard Willis returned from his musical studies
in Germany in 1848, his brother introduced
him there, and he found so much enthusiasm for
his art, that he called repeatedly, to practice his
compositions with Mrs. Voorhies.

Edwin Forrest was a tragedian of great natural force and genius, endowed with a wonderful voice and a magnificent physique. But he
was a man of passionate and overbearing temper; his education was defective, his language
and manners sometimes offensively coarse, and
he had little relish for intellectual society. He
does not appear, however, to have felt any objection to his wife's hospitalities, or to have suspected any impropriety in her receiving her
friends, during his frequent absences from home
on professional engagements, until long after
other causes of estrangement had arisen between
them. At Cincinnati, in the spring of 1848, he
thought that he had discovered evidence of a
guilty intimacy between Mrs. Forrest and an actor named Jamieson; and although she solemnly
protested her innocence and her husband agreed
to accept her oath, his jealousy smouldered and
occasionally broke out in scenes of violence. At
length, in April, 1849, they agreed to separate.
Mrs. Forrest made her home for a time with
Mr. and Mrs. Parke Godwin, and Forrest took
up his residence in Philadelphia, where in February, 1850, he made an application for divorce
to the Pennsylvania legislature, based upon affi-
davits, charging his wife with adultery. This
application was ultimately denied, but meanwhile the lady's friends in New York had taken

the matter up.   She had the sympathy and moral support of such men as William C. Bryant and his son-in-law, Mr. Parke Godwin, and Dr. Orville Dewey, the eminent Unitarian divine.   Up to this time Forrest had not implicated Willis in his charges, but hearing that he was among those who were taking sides with Mrs. Forrest, he had stopped him in the street one day in January, 1850, and warned him against intermeddling between him and his wife, denouncing her unfaithfulness in the strongest terms.   Willis replied that he did not believe a word of the slanders against her.   The next day Mrs. Willis received an anonymous letter, accusing her husband of criminal relations with Mrs. Forrest.   On March 28th the "Herald" published extracts from the evidence on which Forrest had based his application to the Pennsylvania legislature, which compromised, among others, Mr. Richard Willis.   This drew from his brother a letter of explanation, printed in the "Herald" of the following day.

"It was not my intention," wrote Willis, "to say a word in this letter upon the merits of the case to which this evidence belongs.   To rescue the good name of an absent brother, who, in moral conduct is irreproachably correct, was my only object.   A court of justice will soon sift the testimony, and better inform the public as to its credibility on other points.

But the mention of my wife's name, as a friend and visitor of Mrs. Forrest, makes it incumbent on me to add that the description of Mrs. Forrest's manners and style of hospitality which is given in that evidence is totally at variance with all we have ever seen and known of that dignified, well-bred, and delicate mannered lady."

And in the " Home Journal " for April 6th he published a severe review of the " Forrest testimony," warmly defending Mrs. Forrest, expressing the belief that her husband's chief motive in the late proceedings had been to rid himself of the expense of her support; that the real cause of their separation had been his jealousy of her intellectual superiority; and condemning indignantly his attempt to " enlist kitchen and brothel against her, and so sully her fair name by cheap and easy falsehood that he can throw her off like a mistress paid up to parting." The article concluded as follows: —

" We have written the above under the editorial plural, but the facts being mostly of personal knowledge, and wishing to evade no manner of responsibility, we close with the writer's individual signature,

" N. P. WILLIS."

These two articles, coupled with testimony elicited from Forrest's household servants, decided him to drag Willis into the case. His bill filed in Philadelphia contained the names of nine co-respondents, among them a clergyman, Mrs. Forrest's family doctor, and Forrest's old friend and traveling companion, Chevalier Wikoff. The last three were afterwards dropped from the case. Mrs. Forrest, having been served with a copy of the application and the process issued by the Pennsylvania legislature, filed a bill in the New York Supreme Court in September, 1850, and obtained an injunction to restrain her husband from proceeding with his suit in Philadelphia. She then began suit against him in New York for a divorce on the ground of adultery, which he defended with cross-accusations; and in New York the case was finally tried and decided. Meanwhile Forrest was prowling about his wife's lodgings in New York, threatening people who went in or out, and stopping others in the street to warn them against interference.

On the 17th of June, while Willis was walking in Washington Square, near his own residence in Fourth Street, Forrest came up to him quickly and knocked him down with a blow from his fist. He then stood over him, and, holding him down by the coat collar with one hand, beat him with a gutta-percha whip till the police came up and interfered. To the group of spectators which had rapidly assembled, he said, " That is the seducer of my wife." Willis would at no time have been physically the equal of his antagonist, who was a man of powerful frame; but when this assault was made it was doubly safe from the fact that the victim of it had been ill for months with a rheumatic fever, and was in an unusually feeble condition of body. Two days after this heroic action, Forrest met Bryant and Godwin walking down Broadway and furiously demanded who had put the account of it into the " Evening Post," in which he was represented as having struck Willis from behind.

" I told him," said Mr. Godwin, in his testimony, "I was responsible for the article. He then turned round to me in a very ferocious way, and said there were several things that he was going to hold me responsible for; he said the article was a damned lie from beginning to end ; he said he meant to attack Mr. Willis, and he believed that he had told me so formerly. I replied that these were not just the terms that he used, and that he told me formerly that he meant to cut his damned heart out; to which Mr. Forrest muttered something in reply — I don't know what it was distinctly ; I think he said something about what he would have done if they had not taken him off."

Willis brought an action against Forrest for this assault, in the superior court of the city of New York, and secured a verdict in March, 1852, for $2,500 and costs. The case was appealed on exceptions, and, upon the new trial which was ordered, the damages were reduced to one dollar. Forrest sued Willis for libel in the " Home Journal " article, and got $500 damages. But in the mean time the suit for divorce had come to trial, in December, 1851, and had been decided in Mrs. Forrest's favor. The jury found the defendant guilty of adultery, found the plaintiff innocent, and granted her the decree prayed for with $3,000 a year alimony. This was one of the *causes célèbres* of the last generation. The trial occupied the then extraordinarily long period of six weeks, and the printed testimony fills two large volumes. Charles O'Conor, who was Mrs. Forrest's counsel, dated his great reputation as an advocate from his conduct of this case. For eighteen years he fought the battle for his fair client relentlessly and triumphantly. The case was appealed five times, and judgment affirmed every time with an increase of alimony. It was not till 1868 that the defendant tired of resistance, and paid over to the plaintiff the sum of $64,000. His costs and expenses of litigation, additional to this, were of course enormous. It is unnecessary to review the evidence given at the trial, by which it was sought to incriminate Willis in this affair, further than to say that it consisted almost solely of the testimony of servants, who

were thoroughly discredited in their cross-exami-
nation. One of these witnesses was a man who
had been discharged from Willis's employ. Another was an ex-chambermaid in the Forrest
household, who was brought all the way from
Texas to testify, and who was shown to be a
thief, and the mother of an illegitimate child by
a friend of the defendant. Public opinion, it is
needless to say, was divided about the verdict.
Forrest was the idol of the Bowery, and the as-
serter of the American stage against the "dudes"
and "Anglo-maniacs" of that day. "The boys,"
who had stuck by him in his quarrel with Macready till its upshot in the bloody Astor Place
riot of May 10, 1849, stuck by him now in his
domestic tribulations, and gave him a rousing
ovation on his first appearance at the Broadway Theatre, following the close of the trial.
A number of people in society, too, of those
who "demen gladly to the badder end," made
up their minds to Mrs. Forrest's guilt. But it
is not unfair to say that the great majority of
the decent people and respectable newspapers
greeted the verdict with acclamation. A large
party maintained that Forrest was a selfish and
licentious brute, who was tired of his wife and
wanted to be rid of her; that, knowing he had
no valid cause of action against her, he trumped
up charges and suborned witnesses. It is not

necessary to go so far as this in order to assert the innocence of Mrs. Forrest and of those who were made parties to the accusations against her. Alger, in his big " Life of Edwin Forrest," after acknowledging that " the innocence of Mrs. Forrest is publicly accredited, and is not here impugned;" that she " was believed by her intimate and most honored friends to be innocent, was vindicated by a jury after a most searching trial, and is now living in modest and blameless retirement," simply urges in Forrest's behalf that he honestly believed himself a wronged man, and acted with his usual fury and unforgivingness upon that conviction. Willis and his brother were both among the witnesses for the plaintiff on the trial, and both, of course, denied peremptorily the charges against them. But the one circumstance which more than all else influenced the decision of the jury was the constant presence in court of Mrs. N. P. Willis, side by side with Mrs. Forrest, and the brave, clear, and simple way in which she testified in her friend's behalf. No one could believe that a spirited and refined lady, like Mrs. Willis, would have consented, for an instant, to put herself into such a position, without a full assurance of her husband's innocence; and no one who listened to her testimony could have thought her a woman likely to be deceived. John Van Buren, who was Forrest's lawyer in all these cases, was quite generally censured for the needlessly abusive way in which he handled the witnesses for the other side. In the trial of the assault and battery case, " Willis *v.* Forrest," his personalities went so far beyond the limits usually set to the licensed insolence of the bar, that on the termination of the suit Willis, who was about starting on a trip to the South, and had learned from an item in the " Herald " that Van Buren was going South too, sent him a letter demanding an apology. In case he should decline to make such apology, the letter proposed a hostile meeting at Charleston or any other convenient point in the Southern States. This note the recipient returned (after carefully making a copy of it) with a short reply, describing it as a " silly and scurrilous communication." This it certainly was not, but, on the other hand, a very dignified and gentlemanly letter ; rather too long, it must be owned, for on these occasions Willis's pen generally ran away with him. However, on the receipt of this answer to it, which was forwarded to him at the South, he replied with sufficient brevity : " I now pronounce you a coward, as well as a proper companion for the blackguards whose attorneyship constitutes your career."

This challenge was something of a flourish on

Willis's part, and his experience with Marryat might have taught him the folly of such attempts to get " the satisfaction of a gentleman " from railing editors and attorneys. He took little by his motion, which simply gave Van Buren an opportunity to publish the correspondence in a New York morning paper with comments of his own, characteristically ugly and characteristically smart. The fact remained, however, that Van Buren had been challenged to fight and had declined, and the general note made upon the affair by a venal press was to the effect that " Prince John had shown the white feather." Of the many letters of sympathy and congratulation received by Mr. and Mrs. Willis after the Forrest verdict, the following, from Mr. J. P. Kennedy, the author of " Swallow Barn," will serve as an example : —

BALTIMORE, *February* 2, 1852.

MY DEAR WILLIS, — I have often resolved during the war — the *late* war, I hope I may call it — to assume the privilege of a friend and send you the only succor I could supply, a word of comfort and a cheer or two, to let you see that there was some sympathy abroad for your sufferings, which I know were pungent enough to make a very respectable saint, if your ambition lay in that way. Now that you have got through certainly the worst part of your Iliad in the termination of that horrible trial, I think it a good time to redeem my promise to myself, and to say to you that I have felt a friend's part in the whole progress of your troubles, and the confidence of a friend that the end would bring you a bright sky and a pleasant outlook for the future. I particularly congratulate Mrs. Willis on this result, as I know, or can imagine, the full measure of her griefs. We *all here* — I mean our household, with whom Mrs. Willis is associated in so many affectionate remembrances — unite very sincerely in this message to her. Your defense in the " Home Journal " of an injured woman, which I noted and applauded from the first, was, at its least, a manly and generous act, and it became the more worthy of your manhood as it grew to be perilous. I use this word much more in reference to the social clamor than to the ruffian assault it brought you. I trust you are now to triumph very signally over both. Present Mrs. Kennedy and her sister very kindly to your wife, as also Dr. Gray, and believe me

Very truly yours,

J. P. KENNEDY.

The result of the Forrest trial was, in a sense, a triumph for Willis. Yet in all affairs of the kind, although the charges are disproved, the very fact that they have been made leaves, illogically and unfairly, perhaps, but still inevitably, a sediment of prejudice in the public mind. It is in the nature of such cases that the inmost truth about them can seldom be known to more than two persons. To all others there remains nothing beyond inference and suspicion. Hence the uncertainty which survives the judicial decision of the cause and works injustice to the innocent who have been unlucky enough to be drawn into compromising situations. An impression has always obtained in many quarters that Willis was profligate in his relations with women. Rumors to this effect were industriously circulated by his ill-wishers, and, in one instance, they got into print in the shape of an accusation publicly brought against him by his ancient foe, Colonel James Watson Webb of the "Courier and Enquirer." It is needless to revive this venerable scandal or any of the less tangible, miscellaneous gossip once afloat on the current of New York society. It is no part of a biographer's duty to "vindicate" his subject from any and all charges of the kind. I have read the published documents in the Webb-Willis affair with a sincere effort to be impartial, and they left upon my mind no impression of anything worse on Willis's part than vanity and indiscretion in permitting himself to be drawn into a half literary, half sentimental correspondence with a very romantic young woman, without her parents' knowledge. He was easily flattered by attentions from female worshipers of genius. He maintained in print and in person a constant attitude of gallantry toward the sex, which doubtless stimulated the rumor of his immoralities, and led the reader to identify him with the Lotharios of his tales. Moreover, it is not to be denied that when a young man in Italy, and in the fast set of his London acquaintances, he was exposed to temptations which he did not always resist, and probably had his share of those adventures which the French indulgently call *bonnes fortunes*, but less liberal shepherds of Anglo-Saxon race give a grosser name; and which always turn out the reverse of good fortunes for everybody concerned. As to his later life, one who knew him well but had quarreled with him and had small cause to like him, writes : " My belief is that N. P. Willis was, as he said, perfectly free from fault in that business [the Forrest affair], and had *no* intrigues with women after his marriage."

The spring of 1852 found him much broken in health. He had a wearing cough, and it was thought that his lungs were diseased. He waited only the termination of his assault and battery case in March, to start on a journey to the South with his father-in-law, Mr. Grinnell. The trip included a cruise to Bermuda and the West Indies, a short stay in Charleston, Savannah, and New Orleans, a visit to the Mammoth Cave, and a sojourn at the neighboring watering-place of Harrodsburg Springs. His letters to the

"Home Journal" from these and other points in the South were reissued in book form as "A Health Trip to the Tropics." During the years covered by this chapter he published a number of volumes similarly made up of periodical correspondence and miscellaneous contributions to his paper. "Rural Letters" contained his "Invalid Letters from Germany;" a reprint of "Letters from under a Bridge," with two additional to those in the earlier editions; "Open Air Musings in the City;" letters from Sharon Springs and Trenton Falls in the summer of 1848; and one story, "A Plain Man's Love." "Hurrygraphs" comprised a series of letters from Plymouth, New Bedford, Cape Cod, and places on the Delaware and Hudson rivers; besides sketches — often very acute pieces of mental portraiture — of public men, authors, and other celebrities, and a good deal of chit-chat about society, the opera, etc., from the columns of the "Home Journal."

All that can be said of these traveler's letters is that they are fairly good reporting. They hardly attain the rank of literature, and were as a whole not worth putting between covers. But Willis sold well and, therefore, found his account in continued book-making, bringing out, usually, simultaneous editions in London and New York. It is instructive to compare his letters

from Cape Cod — a journey on which Mr. Grinnell was again his companion — with Thoreau's
book on the same piece of geography. Both
men had quick eyes, and had taught themselves
the art of observation. But Willis's letters were
the notes of an "amateur casual," or "here-and-
thereian," on a flying trip over a sand-spit inhab-
ited by queer people, who was always on the
lookout for points which would interest the lady
readers of a metropolitan journal. Thoreau, on
the contrary, was like a palmer on a solemn pilgrimage to one of nature's peculiar shrines, with
loins girt up and staff in hand, tramping along
the heavy sands, with the eternal thunder of
" The Reverend Poluphloisboio Thalasses " in
his ear; in serious and vigilant mood, watching
every least token of the ways of the sea, but
careless of men and reading publics.

Now and then there is a quaint or poetic
fancy in these itineraries of Willis which recalls
his youthful manner ; as where, speaking of the
absence of an atmosphere in the tropic seas, he
says : " As to the horizon, it seems so near that,
if you were washing your hands on deck, you
might try to throw the slops over it, as you
would over the ship's side. The sun goes down,
as it were, next door." In the letters from Trenton Falls — which he had visited twenty years
before and described in " Edith Linsey " — oc-

curs a startling anticipation of the most admired
figure in Tennyson's " Queen Mary : " —

" As we stood gazing at this, last night, a little after midnight, the moon threw the shadow of the rock
slantwise across the face of the fall. I found myself
insensibly watching to see whether the delicate outline of the shadow would not vary. There it lay, still
as the shade of a church window across a marble slab
on the wall, drawing its fine line over the most fren-
zied tumult of the lashed and agonized waters, and
dividing whatever leapt across it, foam, spray, or driving mist, with invariable truthfulness to the rock that
lay behind. Now, my song-maker, if you ever have
a great man to make famous — a hero who unflinch-
ingly represents a great principle amid the raging opposition, hatred, and malice of mankind — there is
your similitude : *Calm as the shadow of a rock across
the foam of a cataract.*"

Willis was induced by Mr. Moore, the proprietor and landlord, to edit a small illustrated
guide-book to Trenton Falls ; his own contributions to which consisted of descriptions reproduced from these letters and from " Edith Linsey," and a short biography of the Rev. John
Sherman, the first settler and a grandson of
Roger Sherman. In the same way and in the
same year (1851) he put together a little " Life
of Jenny Lind," for whom he had an ardent admiration, and whom he had been privileged to meet

often and familiarly during her first visit to America. This was, of course, not a formal biography, but was made up from articles that he had written about her from time to time for the "Home Journal," and extracts from the English papers. He also issued selections from his former volumes under new names. Such were "People I have Met," and "Life Here and There," which were stories from "Dashes at Life," and contained little or nothing new, and "A Summer Cruise in the Mediterranean," which was a mere reprint of a part of "Pencillings by the Way."

CHAPTER VIII.

1853–1867.

MR. and Mrs. Willis, with their children, had passed the summer of 1850 at Cornwall, in the highlands of the Hudson, boarding at the farm-house of a Mrs. Sutherland. They grew so attached to the beautiful neighborhood that they resolved to make it their home some day, and with this in view, in the fall of the same year, they had bought the fifty acres of land which afterwards became widely known as Idlewild. This little domain lay upon a shelf or terrace on the western bank of the Hudson, lifted some two hundred feet above the level of the river, at the point where its waters received the slender tribute of Moodna Creek. Behind the site chosen for the house was a wild ravine, shaded by hemlocks, at the bottom of which a brook, swollen to sizable rapids and cascades by the spring freshets, but a mere trickle in midsummer, ran down to join the creek. The location seemed destined by nature for a gentleman's

country seat, from its variety of surface, its con-
trasting prospects, and its noble timber. The
outlook in front was upon a wide bend of the
river and the opposite heights and distant mountain perspectives of the eastern shore. Behind
the house was a private landscape of glen and
forest, sunk away quite out of sight of the sails
and steamers that passed continually up and
down the watery highway before the front door.
To the south, a mile away, was the imposing
shape of Storm King, a mountain which owes
its baptism to Willis, having previously figured
in geography as Butter Hill. Four miles below
this were West Point and the gate of the highlands, and on the other bank General Morris's
summer home of Undercliff. Four miles above
Idlewild was the considerable town of Newburg,
for a market; and only a mile from his door,
the post office village of Moodna.

Willis's trip to the tropics had been of small
benefit to his health, and, on his return in the
summer of 1852, he joined his family at their
boarding place at Cornwall. His doctor warned
him that a return to New York would be at the
risk of his life. He had grown tired, himself,
of the city and of gay society, and longed for
the repose of the hills. *Levavit oculos ad arces.*
In the hope that rural quiet and the drier air of
the highlands might restore his health, he de-

cided that autumn to begin building at once, and
to take up his permanent abode in the country.
During the winter and spring he remained with
his family at the Sutherlands', and busied himself in superintending the erection of his house,
laying out roads and paths, cutting vistas through
his trees, building stone walls, constructing a
dam for his brook, and reporting progress in
gossipy letters to the " Home Journal." In the
spring of 1853 the New York house was sold,
and on the 26th of July Idlewild received its
tenants,

Willis had a happy knack at inventing names,
and if everything that he wrote should become
obsolete, he will still have left his sign manual
on the American landscape and the English
tongue. " Idlewild " was an apt and beautiful
name, and like Sunnyside, the place became and
remains one of the historic points of the scenery
of the Hudson. The story that Willis tells of
the origin of the word is this : The old farmer
and fisherman who owned the land — uncle of
the " Ward boys," of aquatic fame — was showing him over the property, and Willis, inquiring
the price of this particular piece, was answered
that it had little value, being " an idle wild of
which nothing could ever be made." I fancy
that this little anecdote is in part a myth, invented after the fact to give the name a history

and a justification. Willis was particular, not to say fussy, in such matters, and the title finally chosen was obtained by a process of elimination from a list that I have seen, of several hundred " pretty, fond, adoptious christendoms," such as Everwild, Mieux-ici, Lodore, Loudwater, Idlebrook, Wanderwild, Up-the-brook, Shadywild, Loiterwild, Demijour-brook, etc.

Thus ten years after the break-up of his home at Glenmary, he had again pitched his pavilion — this time for good — by green pastures and running waters. Henceforth he abjured fashionable life and devoted himself to the domesticities ; to the care of his health and his grounds, the entertainment of his guests, and the preparation of his weekly letter to the " Home Journal." There was little left in him of that dandyism which had distressed his critics. But the old coats and hats which he loved to wear were worn with a certain grace peculiar to the man. He could not put on the seediest garment without straightway imparting to it an air of jauntiness. He was fond of pets and was a most playful and affectionate companion to his children, the number of whom gradually increased to five by the birth of a third daughter, Edith, on September 28, 1853, and a second son, Bailey, on May 31, 1857. All of these survive, but his last child, a daughter, born October 31, 1860. lived only a few minutes.

From early spring till after Christmas the
family at Idlewild kept open house, having almost always company staying with them, and in
summer constantly receiving transient guests.
The place had become celebrated through Willis's descriptions in the "Home Journal." Cornwall was growing to be a summer resort, and
there were daily visits to the glen and to the
house from all manner of people. Willis's
habit was to breakfast in his own room and
write till noon. Sometimes he would take a
stroll to the post office or the glen before dinner.
After dinner he would write letters or do " scis-
sors work " before the afternoon drive or ride.
The evening was spent with his guests, or, if the
family were alone, he would write again and
come down to a nine o'clock supper.

From the trivial incidents of this daily life he
wove his correspondence; enough of it, at last,
to fill two volumes, " Out Doors at Idlewild "
and " The Convalescent; " the former dedicated
to Mr. Grinnell, the latter to Doctors William
Beattie and John F. Gray, his physicians, and
both books addressed more particularly to the
author's " parish of invalids." These letters
have by no means the literary merit of the " Letters from under a Bridge," and it was, perhaps,
presuming too far on their claim to even contemporary respect to bind them up at all after

they had once done duty in the newspaper column. They were eagerly read, nevertheless, as
they appeared from week to week, and a sympathetic public was interested in Willis's kindly
prattle about his landscape gardening, his tree
planting, the deluges in his brook, his children,
his horses and dogs, the eccentricities of his
country neighbors, the humors of his poultry,
the daily voyage of the family wagon to Newburg, the sleighing on the frozen Hudson, and
the occasional picnics and excursions to Storm
King, West Point, Poughkeepsie, or remoter
points. Willis found himself not without amusement, becoming something of a country gentleman and public-spirited bulwark of society,
taking part in local interests. There was a picturesque little Episcopal church a mile from
Idlewild, in which he became a vestryman and
used to pass the plate. Once he even made a
speech at a public meeting, in favor of dividing
the county. Letters xxxix. and xl. in "Out
Doors at Idlewild," giving a graphic description
of the ascent of Storm King, are perhaps the
best thing in the volume.

Among the many guests attracted to Idlewild
by the hospitalities of its owner and his inviting
'pictures of his highland retreat were numbers
of literary men and artists.[1] Bayard Taylor,

[1] J. Addison Richards visited Idlewild to make sketches

Charles A. Dana, De Trobriand, of the " Cour-
rier des États-Unis ; " Hicks and Kensett, the
painters, came up from New York at various
times, and rambled, bathed, or otherwise dis-
ported themselves in the glen.   Whipple and
Fields ran across from Boston and made a pleasant visit of two or three days, of which both afterwards gave reminiscences.   Fields loved to
recall an anecdote that Willis told him, " of his
watching a little ragged girl, one day in London,
who was peering through an area railing.   A
window of a comfortable eating-house gave upon
this area, and a man sat at the window taking
a good dinner.   The child watched his every
movement, saw him take a beefsteak and get all
things in readiness to begin ; then he stopped and
looked round.   ' Now a pertaty,' murmured the
child."

In the summer of 1854, Willis had a call
from his down-river neighbor, Washington Irving, and repaid it at Sunnyside in 1859, in company with J. P. Kennedy and Lieutenant Wise,
the author of " Los Gringos," who had both
been passing a day or two with him at Idlewild.
Irving drove them through Sleepy Hollow, as
recounted in " The Convalescent," in which this
visit fills an agreeable chapter ; and Willis char-

for his illustrated article in *Harper's Magazine* for January,
1858, *q. v.* for a full description of the place.

acteristically begged his host to give him his blotting-sheet for memorabilia, as being " the door-mat on which the thoughts of Irving's last book had wiped their sandals as they went in." " The Convalescent " (1859) was the last book which Willis published, if we except some late editions of his poems, but there are gleams in it, here and there, of the wit and fancy that never quite forsook him. There was, for instance, a long and very dark covered bridge over Moodna Creek, which he always entered with dread, when on horseback, and which he described as giving " a promise of emergence to light on the other side, which required the faith of a gimlet." Upon the whole, it would be a very difficult reader who should refuse to admit the plea which the author urges in behalf of books of " The Convalescent " kind. " I learned also, to my comfort, that Nature publishes some volumes with many leaves, which are not intended to be of any posthumous value — the white poplar not lasting three moonlight nights after it is cut down. Even with such speedy decay, however, it throws a pleasant shade while it flourishes ; and so, white poplar literature, recognized as a class in literature, should have its brief summer of indulgence."

Willis found that his best medicine was horse-back riding, and spent as many hours as he could

in the saddle. His horses and dogs were a great
source of amusement to him. One of his spe-
cial pets was Cæsar, a superb Newfoundland,
that had been with Dr. Kane on one of his Arctic voyages, and was afterwards presented to
Willis. When it died its grave at Idlewild was
marked by a marble slab, the gift of Brown, the
famous Grace Church sexton, with an epitaph of
his own composition. The slab was on exhibi-
tion for a time, in July, 1862, at Barnum's museum, and the inscription on it ran as follows:—

CÆSAR,

WHO MADE THE VOYAGE TO THE ARCTIC
REGIONS WITH DR. KANE,
AND WAS AFTERWARDS THE FAVORITE DOG OF THE CHIL-
DREN OF IDLEWILD,
LIES BURIED BENEATH THIS STONE.

Died December 7, 1861, aged thirteen years.

Thy master's record of thy worth made thee of great renown,
And caused this tribute to thy memory from Sexton Brown.

In 1854 a book was published which became
the occasion of many heart-burnings, and of accusations against Willis that have not yet ceased
to go the rounds of the newspapers. This was
" Ruth Hall, a Domestic Tale of the Present
Time," by Fanny Fern. The lady who wrote
under this pen name was his younger sister, Sarah, the author of much cleverish literature —
" Fern Leaves," and the like — which once en-

joyed a prodigious circulation. She was the *en-
fant terrible* of the family, a warm-hearted, impulsive woman, but not always discreet. By the
death of her husband, Charles Eldridge of Boston, she had been suddenly reduced from comfort to poverty. She afterwards contracted an
unfortunate marriage with a Mr. Farrington,
from whom she was finally divorced. To support herself and her children, she turned instinc-
tively to literature, in which she at last made a
decided hit. Among other things she offered
some contributions to the " Home Journal; "
but Willis, whose literary taste, though certainly
not severe, was fastidious in its way, could not
see merit enough in his sister's writing, and disliked what he regarded as its noisy, rattling
style. He felt obliged to decline her articles,
but that there was any literary jealousy in this,
as is intimated in " Ruth Hall," will hardly be
believed, when his eagerness to welcome and
patronize young writers is remembered. It
seems to have sprung from an original opposition
in character and taste between the two. But it
naturally made hard feeling and led to recrimi-
nations. Mr. James Parton, who was then sub-
editor of the " Home Journal," took Fanny
Fern's part, and the acquaintance thus begun
soon ripened into an engagement of marriage.
There was a scene, in consequence, in the office

of the " Home Journal," and Mr. Parton retired from the paper, his place being supplied by Mr. T. B. Aldrich. Smarting under a sense of neglect by her kinsfolk, Fanny Fern wrote and printed this novel of " Ruth Hall," in which, under a very thin mask of fiction, she washed a deal of family linen in public. Willis figures therein as Hyacinth, a " heartless puppy," who worships social position, has married an heiress, inhabits a villa on the Hudson, and is the prosperous editor of the " Irving Magazine." When Ruth asks him to help her by printing her pieces in this periodical, he coldly assures her that she has no talent, and advises her to seek " some unobtrusive employment." But when she becomes famous and begins to get letters from college presidents, begging her for her autograph, and from grateful readers, saying, " I am a better son, a better brother, a better husband, and a better father than I was before I commenced reading your articles. God bless you ! " then, under these triumphant circumstances, Hyacinth, who had given $100 for a vase when Ruth was starving, is proud to point out to a friend, as they sit together in the porch of his country seat, a beautiful schooner tacking up stream with " Floy," his sister's *nom-de-plume*, painted on the bows.

Against this caricature of himself Willis made

no public protest. When a man is wounded in the house of his friends, his only refuge is silence. But in private and to his intimates he asserted that the attack upon him in "Ruth Hall" was most unfair; that he *had* helped his sister in the early days of her widowhood, but that after her second marriage and divorce he had ceased to have any communication with her, and felt justified in letting her alone. Willis was doubtless a man who took his responsibilities lightly. But had he felt called upon to do his utmost for Fanny Fern, even to the end, it is easy to see how his hands were tied in various ways. He had an expensive family of his own, whose support depended upon his pen. His home on the Hudson had been purchased with his wife's inheritance. As to paying his sister for articles in the " Home Journal," supposing them to have been otherwise acceptable, the editors were constantly reiterating that the paper did not, as a rule, pay its contributors anything, and could not afford to do so. It paid its own editorial staff, and that was all. Contributors were glad to write for it for the pleasure of seeing themselves in print.

Willis continued to put forth permutations and combinations of old matter under new titles, as long as his books would sell. "Fun Jottings," " Ephemera," " Famous Persons and Places,"

22

and "The Rag-Bag" were all made up from the contents of previous volumes, or the teeming sheets of the "Mirror" and "Home Journal." But in 1857 he published something new, "Paul Fane," his only novel, and the only book which he wrote *as* a book, and not as one or more contributions to periodicals. So exclusively a *feuilletoniste* had he made himself, that any talent for construction on a larger scale which he may once have had was quite frittered away.

"It has been with difficult submission to marketableness," he had written in his preface to "Dashes at Life," "that the author has broken up his statues at the joints and furnished each fragment with head and legs to walk alone. Continually accumulating material, with the desire to produce a work of fiction, he was as continually tempted by extravagant prices to shape these separate forms of society and character into tales for periodicals; and between two persuaders — the law of copyright, on the one hand, providing that American books at fair prices should compete with books to be had for nothing; and necessity, on the other hand, pleading much more potently than the ambition for an adult stature in literary fame — he has gone on acquiring a habit of dashing off for a magazine any chance view of life that turned up to him, and selling in fragmentary chapters what should have been kept together, and moulded into a proportionate work of imagination."

If " Paul Fane, or Parts of a Life Else Untold " was a response to this artistic craving for unity in a sustained work, its author had waited too late. It was, in effect, a poor novel; and — what was unusual with Willis, even at his thinnest — it was dull. The story is told in the first person, and the hero is a young American artist, who, feeling his social equality challenged by a look in the eyes of a cold English girl of high birth, is driven abroad by a restless determination to put himself on a level with any nobility that hereditary rank can bestow. He brings the haughtiest daughters of Albion to his feet. Three or four women fall in love with him, including the original offender and her aunt, but he will none of them. It is Willis's old theme of nature's nobleman versus caste. The novel was an experiment, before the times were ripe, in that field of international manners which has since been so cleverly occupied by Henry James. It tries to deal with the perplexities and real miseries, which arise not so much from the deeper conflicts of character as from the attempt to adjust hostile social standards. Mr. James has made a very interesting story out of the simple episode of a young English lady marrying an American, coming to America to live, and then, not finding American ways to her taste, taking her husband back to England with her. But Willis was not well equipped for success in this field. He could not keep his fancy in check; there must be a dash of romance, of exaggeration in his tale. And he was a quick observer rather than a patient student of manners, as of other things. He lacked the sober, truthful vigilance of James and Howells. Miss Firkin, in this book, an overdone Daisy Miller, and Blivins, an American type once rumored to have existed, but inconceivable at this distance of time, show how far his execution fell below the fine and solid work of our contemporary realists. There are passages of vulgarity in " Paul Fane " which are a surprise in any book of Willis's, but which came rather from the weakness and failure of his hand in its attempt to execute scenes of broad humor, than from any crudity of feeling. This kind of violent and assumed indelicacy on the part of naturally refined writers, when they are trying to put on the healthy coarseness of a Hogarth or Teniers, is a not uncommon phenomenon; daintiness mistaking coarseness for the strength of which it is often a sign or an accompaniment.

In " The Convalescent " were included narratives of a trip to the Rappahannock, to Nantucket, and to the horse fair at Springfield, Massachusetts. In July, 1860, Willis accompanied Mr. Grinnell on a journey to the West, — reported for the "Home Journal" as a "Three

Weeks' Trip to the West," — going to Yellow Springs, Ohio, and Chicago, and as far as Madison, Wisconsin; then descending the Mississippi in a steamboat to St. Louis, and returning East by way of Cincinnati and Pittsburgh.

In Willis's later writings his verbal affectations gained upon him to an intolerable extent. " Mr. N. P. Willis," says Bartlett in his " Dictionary of Americanisms," " has the reputation of inventing many new words, some of which, though not yet embodied in our dictionaries, are much used in familiar language." One of the phrases which Bartlett accredits to him is, " the upper ten," — originally and in full, " the upper ten thousand of New York city." This seems likely to keep its place in the language. " Japonicadom " took at the time, but has now gone out. He had a fondness for agglutinations. " Come-at-able " is a convenient word which is traced to his mint; and Professor George P. Marsh, in his " Origin and History of the English Language," lends the weight of his authority to Willis's " Stay-at-home-itiveness," as a synonym for the Greek οἰκουρία, and the early English *studestapelvestnesse*. But such philological monsters as re-June-venescence, worthwhile - ativeness, fifty - per - centity, with which some of his books are strewn, have a painfully forced effect, and the trick became, from repetition, a tedious mannerism. Punning, likewise, was a habit which grew upon him, though both of these offenses are commoner in his private correspondence than in his published work.

At the outbreak of the civil war in the spring of 1861, there was a rush of newspaper men to Washington. It was decided that the "Home Journal," too, should have its war correspondent, and accordingly Willis, bidding good-by to Idlewild, flung himself into the tide of journalists, soldiers, politicians, office-seekers, contractors, and speculators of all sorts, setting toward the seat of government. At Baltimore he stayed over a day with his friend Kennedy, who was prominently mentioned for the secretaryship of the navy, and who went on to Washington with Willis, where the latter introduced him and Reverdy Johnson to Mrs. Lincoln. The feeding of the "Home Journal" press with "Lookings-on at the War" proved a longer job than Willis had anticipated. It kept him in Washington for over a year, with occasional furloughs for a hurried visit home. He had always been curiously indifferent to politics. His opinions had been Whiggish, and he was, of course, a Union man. But he retained a secret sympathy with the South, and a liking for "those chivalrous, polysyllabic Southerners, incapable of a short word or a mean action," whom he had known at Saratoga years before. Nevertheless, he dropped his light plummet of observation into the boiling sea of the civil war, where it was tossed about at no great depth below the surface. It is interesting to compare his letters from the capital with the patriotic fervor and swing of such martial sketches as Theodore Winthrop's "Washington as a Camp." The war, indeed, may be said to have made Willis and the kind of literature which he cultivated obsolete for a time. A more earnest generation of writers had come to the fore, who struck their roots deeper down into the life of the nation. Mr. Derby, the publisher, proposed in 1863 to make a book out of Willis's "Lookings-on at the War," but the project hung fire for some reason, and "The Convalescent" remained, as has been said, his last publication in book form.

Willis found all the world at Washington; among the rest, Lady Georgiana Fane, whom he presented to Mrs. Lincoln. "Fancy anticipating this at Almack's twenty-five years ago!" he wrote of this conjunction, in a letter to Mrs. Willis. He met Charles Sumner, whom he had known in Boston, and had a long talk with him about the political situation; found Pierpont, the poet, employed as a clerk in one of the departments, and got rooms for him and Mrs. Pierpont in the house where he lodged himself;

was introduced to General McClellan and to the cabinet officers, and the numerous congressmen and brigadiers who swarmed Pennsylvania Avenue and crowded the lobbies at Willard's. He went out to all manner of receptions and dinner parties, and became quite a favorite with Mrs. Lincoln, who drove him out frequently in her barouche, had him to dine *en famille* at the White House, sent him flowers, and promised him a vase presented to the President by the Emperor of China. In one of his letters to the " Home Journal," he had described her as having a " motherly expression," whereupon she addressed him the following note : —

EXECUTIVE MANSION, *July* 24*th.*

MR. N. P. WILLIS :

Dear Sir, — It will afford me much pleasure to receive yourself and ladies [1] this evening. Of course anything Mr. Willis writes is interesting, yet, pardon my weakness, I object to the " motherly expression." If you value my friendship, hasten to have it corrected before the public is assured that I am an old lady with *spectacles.* When I am *forty,* four years hence, I will willingly yield to the decrees of *time* and fate.

Rather an indication, is it not, that years have not passed *us* lightly by ? I rely on you for changing that expression before my age is *publicly* proclaimed.

[1] Lady G. Fane and Mrs. Clifford.

Quite a morning lecture, yet you certainly deserve it.
Be kind enough to accept this modest bouquet from
Your sincere friend,

MARY LINCOLN.

A sudden fit of sickness had hindered Willis's
plan to follow the army to Bull Run — fortunately, no doubt, as the correspondent who took
his place was made prisoner. He afterwards
took horseback rides into the enemy's country,
once narrowly escaping capture near Mount
Vernon, and made excursions to Fortress Mon-
roe, Manassas, Old Point Comfort, etc. On
March 15, 1862, he was of the party which visited Harper's Ferry at the invitation of the
president of the Baltimore and Ohio Railroad.
Hawthorne, too, was of the party and reported
the occasion in his article, " Chiefly about War
Matters," in the July " Atlantic " of that year.
" Hawthorne is shy and reserved," wrote Willis
in one of his letters to his wife, " but I found
he was a lover of mine, and we enjoyed our acquaintance very much." Emerson and Curtis
lectured in Washington while Willis was there,
and Greeley dined with him in January, 1862.
The novelty and excitement of life at the capital were agreeable at first, but he soon grew
homesick and pined for his beloved Idlewild.

In consequence of the war, the circulation of

the " Home Journal," a large proportion of whose subscribers were in the South, had fallen off seriously. Willis found himself greatly straitened, and was obliged to close his country house for a time. Mrs. Willis and the children had spent the winter and spring of 1861–62 at New Bedford, with her father. In April she rented Idlewild and went with her family to pass the summer at Campton, near Plymouth, New Hampshire. In June Willis left Washington and joined her at Campton for a few days, and then returned to New York and took lodgings for himself. Morris's health had grown so feeble that it became necessary for his partner to apply himself more closely to the management of the paper and do double work. He had been much opposed to the renting of Idlewild, and it troubled him to think of the place in the hands of strangers. He paid it a visit in August, by invitation of his tenant, a Mr. Dennis, and was very hospitably treated. In the autumn of the following year (1863) Mrs. Willis opened at Idlewild a little school for girls, in the hope of persuading her husband to leave New York and come home for life. He appreciated her energy and devotion, — shown through long years of failing health and fortune, — but he doomed himself to homeless exile, and refused to abandon his post. He was opposed to the school

project, as he had been to the renting of Idlewild, unreasonably, no doubt, since something
of the kind had to be done.   But it touched
his pride, and with increasing illness there grew
upon him a morbid horror of dependence on
any one.   He fancied that he could work better in his New York lodgings.   By 1864, moreover, Morris had become quite imbecile, and
the responsibilities of editorship weighed more
and more heavily on Willis.   He remained at
New York, therefore, running up to Idlewild
for an occasional visit of a day or two, over
Sunday, or sometimes for a week at a time.
In July, 1864, General Morris died.   Willis
was deeply moved as he stood by his coffin.
" My beloved old friend," he wrote, " looked
wonderfully tranquil, and so sweetly noble that I
could not forbear giving him a parting kiss,
though William sobbed as he looked on.   So
passes from earth one who loved me devotedly."
After Morris's death Willis took into partnership a young man named Hollister, who had
capital and enthusiasm ; but the business management of the " Home Journal " began to fall
more and more upon the shoulders of its present
editor, Mr. Morris Phillips.

The story of the last few years of Willis's
life is a melancholy chronicle of failing powers,
and of persistent struggle with disease and nar-

rowing fates.   He had long borne up against ill
health with the gay courage of a cavalier.   His
pen faltered, but nothing that it wrote gave
signs of bitterness or discouragement.   Toward
the last his temper, which had been uniformly
sweet, sometimes grew irritable and morbid,
though nothing of this appeared in his writing.
As early as 1852 he had fancied that he had
consumption, but his cough turned out to be
merely " sympathetic," and his lungs were pronounced sound.   His disease finally declared itself as epilepsy, and resulted at the last in pa-
ralysis and softening of the brain.   He was
subject for years to epileptic fits, occurring pe-
riodically, usually on the tenth day.   During
these attacks, so long as his strength lasted, he
was extremely violent, but as he grew weaker,
they simply made him unconscious, leaving him
greatly prostrated when the fit was over.   The
true nature of his malady was, for some years,
known only to his wife and his physician, Dr.
Gray, who feared that it might injure Willis's
business and literary interests if it were publicly
understood that his brain was affected, or in
danger of being affected.   Willis was himself
very sensitive on this point, and begged that no
stranger might see him during his attacks.   Accordingly, the matter was kept secret as long as
possible.   After Willis's death, one of his phy-

sicians, Dr. J. B. F. Walker, printed some
" Medical Reminiscences of N. P. Willis," in
the course of which he said : " Not only was he a
martyr to the agonies of sharp and sudden attacks, but he suffered all the languors of chronic
disease. With the exception of Henry Heine,
there has hardly been a man of letters doomed
to such protracted torments from bodily disease."

Under these trying circumstances he exhibited
a persistence in his work which astonished his
friends. They had not thought that such endur-
ance was in the man. But from some underly-
ing stratum of character, some strain of tough-
ness inherent in his Puritan stock, he brought
up resources of will and stubbornness which re-
sisted all appeals. Though complaining sometimes in his letters that he was " pitilessly over-
worked," he declared his intention of dying in
harness, and clung to his desk and his lonely
lodgings till the doctors pronounced him a dying
man. A part of the summers of 1865 and 1866
he spent at Idlewild, but the autumn of the latter year found him still at work in the city. He
was now so weak that he often fainted in the
street and had to be carried to his rooms. His
partner, Morris Phillips, was untiring in his attentions ; and finally, early in November, he
brought him home to Idlewild, Willis yielding

at last to the united entreaties of his wife, his father, and his sisters, and the imperative command of his doctor, to stop work. But he had come home only to die. He kept his room and seldom went down-stairs. During the first month he had some enjoyment of the home associations, taking pleasure in the daily visit of his children, and listening to the reading of poetry, more for its soothing effect than for any intellectual apprehension of it. He soon became helpless and slept much of the time, and when waking lived in continual visions and hallucinations. His recognition of his family was fitful during the last six or eight weeks of his life. He was watched and cared for by his wife and faithful Harriet, and no strange hand ministered to him or marked his failing consciousness. He died on the afternoon of the 20th of January, 1867, — his sixty-first birthday, — so quietly that the single watcher could not say when. He was taken to Boston, and buried in Mount Auburn. The funeral service of the Episcopal Church was read over his body in St. Paul's Church, by the Rev. F. D. Huntington, the bookstores of the city being closed, in token of respect, while the service lasted. His pall was borne by Longfellow, Dana, Holmes, Lowell, Fields, Whipple, Edmund Quincy, Dr. Howe, Merritt Trimble, and Aldrich. " I took the flower which lies be-

fore me at this moment, as I write," says Dr.
Holmes, in a recent number of the " Atlantic,"
" from his coffin, as it lay just outside the door
of Saint Paul's Church, on a sad, overclouded
winter's day, in the year 1867."

The obituary notices which were published after Willis's death made it evident that he had,
in a sense, survived his own fame. They were
reminiscent in tone, as though addressed to a
generation that knew not Joseph. It was forty
years since he had come before the public with
his maiden book. It was twenty since he had
put forth anything entitled to live ; and meanwhile a new literature had grown up in America.
The bells of morning tinkled faintly and far off,
lost in the noise of fife and drum, and the war
opened its chasm between the present and the
past. For a time even Irving seemed sentimental and Cooper melodramatic. Yet these survive, but whether Willis, whose name has so
often been joined with theirs, is destined to find
still a hearing, it is for the future alone to say.
" He will be remembered," wrote his kinsman,
Dr. Richard S. Storrs, " as a man eminently human, with almost unique endowments, devoting
rare powers to insignificant purposes, and curiously illustrating the ' fine irony of Nature,' with
which she often lavishes one of her choice productions on comparatively inferior ends."

But, laying aside all question of appeal to that formidable tribunal, posterity, the many contemporaries who have owed hours of refined enjoyment to his graceful talent will join heartily with Thackeray in his assertion : " It is comfortable that there should have been a Willis."

APPENDIX.

BIBLIOGRAPHY.

THE following is a list of the first editions of Willis's books. In a few instances these were published first in England. In such cases the London edition only is given. Most of his later works were published simultaneously, or nearly so, in England and America. In such cases only the first American edition is given. Of the various collective editions of his verse, published since 1844, only the final and most complete is mentioned, viz., the Clark & Maynard edition of 1868 (No. 29). No really complete edition of Willis's writings has ever been printed. The first collective edition which laid claim to being complete was entitled: The Complete Works of N. P. Willis. 1 vol., 895 pp. New York: J. S. Redfield, 1846. The thirteen volumes in uniform style, issued by Charles Scribner from 1849 to 1859, form as nearly a complete edition of Willis's prose since 1846 as is ever likely to be made.

1. Sketches. 96 pp. Boston: S. G. Goodrich, 1827.
2. Fugitive Poetry. 91 pp. Boston: Peirce & Williams, 1829.

3. Poem delivered before the Society of United Brothers, at Brown University, on the Day preceding Commencement, September 6, 1831, with other poems. 76 pp. New York : J. & J. Harper, 1831.

4. Melanie and Other Poems. Edited by Barry Cornwall. 231 pp. London : Saunders & Otley, 1835. The first American edition was published by Saunders & Otley, at New York, in 1837, and contained some additional pieces. 242 pp.

5. Pencillings by the Way. 3 vols. London : Macrone, 1835.

   This was an imperfect edition. The first complete edition was published by Morris & Willis, in the " Mirror Library," New York, 1844.

6. Inklings of Adventure. 3 vols. London : Saunders & Otley, 1836.

7. Bianca Visconti ; or, The Heart Overtasked. A Tragedy in Five Acts. New York : Samuel Colman, 1839.

8. Tortesa ; or, The Usurer Matched. A Play by N. P. Willis. New York : Samuel Colman, 1839.

   Nos. 7 and 8 were published in one volume in England. Two Ways of Dying for a Husband. 1. Dying to keep Him ; or, Tortesa the Usurer. 2. Dying to lose Him ; or, Bianca Visconti. 245 pp. London : Hugh Cunningham, 1839.

9. À l' Abri ; or, The Tent Pitched. New York : Samuel Colman, 1839.

   This was published as Letters from under a Bridge, together with poems, by George Virtue, in London, 1840 ; and under the same title, with the addition of the " Letter to the Purchaser of Glenmary," by Morris & Willis in the " Mirror Library," New York, 1844.

10. Loiterings of Travel. 3 vols. London : Longman, 1840.

Published in America as Romance of Travel ;
comprising Tales of Five Lands. 1 vol. New
York : S. Colman, 1840.

11. The Sacred Poems of N. P. Willis [Mirror Library].
New York, 1843.

12. Poems of Passion, by N. P. Willis [Mirror Library].
New York, 1843.

13. Lady Jane and Humorous Poems [Mirror Library].
New York, 1844.

14. Lecture on Fashion before the New York Lyceum.
New York, 1844.

15. Dashes at Life with a Free Pencil. New York :
Burgess, Stringer & Co., 1845.

16. Rural Letters and Other Records of Thought at Leisure. New York : Baker & Scribner, 1849.

17. People I Have Met. New York : Baker & Scribner,
1850.

18. Life Here and There. New York : Baker & Scribner, 1850.

19. Hurrygraphs. New York : Charles Scribner, 1851.

20. Summer Cruise in the Mediterranean. New York :
Charles Scribner, 1853.

21. Fun Jottings ; or, Laughs I have taken a Pen to.
New York : Charles Scribner, 1853.

22. Health Trip to the Tropics. New York : Charles
Scribner, 1854.

23. Ephemera. New York : G. W. Simmons, 1854.

24. Famous Persons and Places. New York : Charles
Scribner, 1854.

25. Out Doors at Idlewild ; or, The Shaping of a Home on
the Banks of the Hudson. New York : Charles
Scribner, 1855.

26. The Rag Bag. A Collection of Ephemera. New
York : Charles Scribner, 1855.

27. Paul Fane ; or, Parts of a Life Else Untold. A Novel.
New York : Charles Scribner, 1857.

28. The Convalescent. New York : Charles Scribner, 1859.
29. The Poems, Sacred, Passionate, and Humorous of N. P. Willis. Complete edition. 380 pp. New York : Clark & Maynard, 1868.

The following list includes the works, edited, compiled, and partly written by Willis, but not the various journals and magazines of which he was editor.

1. The Legendary. Edited by N. P. Willis. 2 vols. Boston : Samuel G. Goodrich, 1828.
2. The Token. A Christmas and New Year's Present. Edited by N. P. Willis. Boston : S. G. Goodrich, 1829.
3. American Scenery. From Drawings by W. H. Bartlett. The Literary Department by N. P. Willis, Esq. 2 vols. London : George Virtue, 1840.
4. Canadian Scenery. From Drawings by W. H. Bartlett. The Literary Department by N. P. Willis, Esq. 2 vols. London : George Virtue, 1842.
5. The Scenery and Antiquities of Ireland. Illustrated by Drawings from W. H. Bartlett. The Literary Portion of the Work by N. P. Willis and J. Sterling Coyne, Esqs. London : George Virtue, 1842.
6. The Opal. New York : J. C. Riker, 1844.
7. Trenton Falls. Edited by N. Parker Willis. 90 pp. New York : George P. Putnam, 1851.
8. Memoranda of the Life of Jenny Lind. By N. Parker Willis. 238 pp. Philadelphia : Robert E. Peterson, 1851.
9. The Thought Blossom. A Memento. New York : Leavitt & Allen, 1854.

INDEX.